Advance Praise

Combining motifs that are familiar with those that are utterly bizarre, the Apocalypse of John challenges even the most ardent reader. In this inviting commentary, Jamie Davies attends to the bewildering landscape of Revelation while never losing sight of the book's opening claim to convey a revelation from and about Jesus Christ. Highly recommended for students at all levels.

—Beverly Roberts Gaventa
Helen H.P. Manson Professor Emerita of
New Testament Literature and Exegesis
Princeton Theological Seminary

Jamie Davies's commentary on Revelation is eloquent as a literary work and wonderfully perceptive as a piece of theological writing. His delight in the multivalent, intertextual images of the canon's conclusion comes through on every page. The result is a significant contribution to the interpretation of the Apocalypse as a provocative, imagination-bending instrument of God's self-revelation and a call to faithful Christian witness.

—Michael J. Gorman
Raymond E. Brown Chair in Biblical and Theological Studies
St. Mary's Seminary & University
Baltimore, Maryland, USA

READING REVELATION

Smyth & Helwys Publishing, Inc.
6316 Peake Road
Macon, Georgia 31210-3960
1-800-747-3016
© 2023 by Jamie Davies
All rights reserved.

Library of Congress Cataloging-in-Publication Data

Names: Davies, J. P., author.
Title: Reading Revelation : a literary and theological commentary / by
  Jamie Davies.
Description: Macon, GA: Smyth & Helwys Publishing, 2023. | Series: Reading
  the New Testament ; ser. 2 | Includes bibliographical references.
Identifiers: LCCN 2023018465 | ISBN 9781641734530 (paperback)
Subjects: LCSH: Bible. Revelation--Commentaries. | Bible.
  Revelation--Chronology.
Classification: LCC BS2825.53 .D36 2023 | DDC 228/.07--dc23/eng/20230703
LC record available at https://lccn.loc.gov/2023018465

Disclaimer of Liability: With respect to statements of opinion or fact available in this work of nonfiction, Smyth & Helwys Publishing Inc. nor any of its employees, makes any warranty, express or implied, or assumes any legal liability or responsibility for the accuracy or completeness of any information disclosed, or represents that its use would not infringe privately-owned rights.

Reading Revelation

A Literary and Theological Commentary

Jamie Davies

Also by Jamie Davies

Paul Among the Apocalypses?

The Apocalyptic Paul: Retrospect and Prospect

For Dad, who taught me to love the Scriptures;

and

for Mum, who encouraged me to do what I love.

Faithful witnesses, both.

Contents

Editor's Foreword xiii
Author's Preface xv

Introduction 1
   What Kind of Commentary Is This? 1
   Reading Revelation as Literature 1
   Genre 2
   Author and Date 6
   Narrative Structure and Setting 10
   Use of Imagery and Liturgical Setting 15
   Revelation's Use of the Old Testament 19
   Reading Revelation Theologically 23
      'Revelation of Jesus Christ': Reading Revelation as
         Divine Self-disclosure 23
      'What Must Soon Take Place': Divine Sovereignty and
         Eschatology 25
      'Keep What Is Written . . . for the Time Is Near': The Church as
         Witness in the Time that Remains 28

Prologue and Opening Vision, 1.1–20 31
   Prologue, 1.1–3 31
   Epistolary Greeting, 1.4–8 35
   Vision of Christ, 1.9–20 39
      Instruction to Write, vv. 9–11 39
      Christ among the Lampstands, vv. 12–16 42
      Instruction to Write, vv. 17–20 46

Prophetic Oracles to the Seven Churches, 2.1–3.22 53
   The Seven Oracles Taken Together 53

The Message to Ephesus, 2.1–7	56
Message to Smyrna, 2.8–11	60
Message to Pergamum, 2.12–17	63
Message to Thyatira, 2.18–29	67
Message to Sardis, 3.1–6	71
Message to Philadelphia, 3.7–13	74
Message to Laodicea, 3.14–22	77

The Throne and the Lamb, 4.1–5.14	83
The Throne Vision, 4.1–11	83
John's Ascent to the Throne Room, vv. 1–6a	83
The Four Creatures, the Twenty-four Elders, and Their Songs of Praise, vv. 6b–11	89
The Scroll and the Lamb, 5.1–14	92
The Sealed Scroll, vv. 1–5	92
The Lamb, vv. 6–14	94

The Seven Seals, 6.1–8.5	99
Introduction to the Seven Seals	99
The First Six Seals, 6.1–17	100
Seals 1–4: The Horsemen	100
Seal 5: The Subaltern Saints	103
Seal 6: The Stars Fall from Heaven	105
Interlude, 7.1–17	107
The 144,000 Sealed	107
The Multitude, vv. 9–17	109
The Seventh Seal and Storm Theophany, 8.1–5	112

Seven Trumpets, 8.6–11.19	115
Introduction to the Seven Trumpets	115
The First Six Trumpets, 8.6–9.21	118
Trumpets 1–4: 'Cosmic' Disasters	118
Trumpet 5 (and First Woe): The Army of Locusts	122
Trumpet 6 (and Second Woe): The Cavalry	127
Interlude, 10.1–11.14	131
The Angel with a Little Scroll, 10.1–11	131
The Two Witnesses, 11.1–14	135
The Seventh Trumpet and Storm Theophany, 11.15–19	140

Contents   xi

Cosmic War, 12.1–13.18 145
    Introduction to 12:12–20 145
    The Woman and the Dragon, 12.1–6 147
    War in Heaven, 12.7–12 150
    The Dragon on Earth, 12.13–18 153
    The Sea Beast, 13.1–10 155
    The Earth Beast, 13.11–18 160

Final Battle and Harvest, 14.1–15.4 169
    The Lamb and the 144,000, 14.1–5 169
    Three Angels, 14.6–13 172
    Two Harvests, 14.14–20 175
    The Song of Moses and the Song of the Lamb, 15.1–4 178

Seven Bowls, 15.5–16.21 183
    Seven Angels Emerge, 15.5–8 183
    Seven Bowls, 16.1–21 184

Babylon, 17.1–19.10 189
    Babylon the Great, 17.1–18 189
        Vision of the Whore, 17.1–6a 189
        Interpretation of the Vision, 17.6b–18 193
    The Judgement of Babylon, 18.1–19:10 198
        Babylon Is Fallen! 18.1–8 198
        The Lament of Kings and Merchants, 18.9–20 202
        The Mighty Angel's Proclamation, 18.21–24 204
        The Multitude's Song of Praise, 19.1–10 205

Seven Final Visions, 19.11–20.15 209
    Vision 1: The Rider on the White Horse, 19.11–16 209
    Vision 2: The 'Supper of God,' 19.17–18 213
    Vision 3: The Beast Defeated, 19.19–21 215
    Vision 4: The Binding of Satan, 20.1–3 216
    Vision 5: The Millennial Reign and Satan's Defeat, 20.4–10 217
    Vision 6: The Great White Throne, 20.11 221
    Vision 7: The Dead Judged, 20.12–15 223

The New Jerusalem, 21.1–22.21 227
    The New Jerusalem: Prologue, 21.1–8 228
    The New Jerusalem: Vision, 21.9–22.5 232

    Description of the City, 21.9–21 232
    The Temple and the Nations, 21.22–27 236
    The River of Life, 22.1–5 239
The Angel's Closing Words, 22.6–7 241
Final Warnings and Benedictions, 22.8–21 242

Works Cited 249

Editor's Foreword

Like its predecessor (Reading the New Testament) and its companion series (Reading the Old Testament), Reading the New Testament: Second Series seeks to help readers—whether students or scholars, ministers or laypeople—gain a greater understanding of and appreciation for biblical texts in their original contexts. To this good end, commentaries in this series attend not only to lexical, historical, and critical concerns but are also attuned to and interested in, as the subtitle of each volume signals, literary matters and theological meaning.

Whereas some commentaries are committed to the necessary and salutary task of commenting on every jot and tittle (see Matthew 5:18), works in this series seek to trace the thought and observe the craft of biblical authors in a less atomistic manner. While attending to various trees, they are also intent on not missing the forest. Relatedly, while technically undergirded and academically informed, the commentaries within this series are intended for and are meant to be accessible and valuable to a broad readership. The seventeen volumes that will make up Reading the New Testament: Second Series, then, are written by scholars but are not exclusively, or even primarily, for scholars.

Contributors to this commentary series are accomplished academics, experienced teachers, capable communicators, and professing Christians who are committed to explicating Scripture thoughtfully, clearly, and sympathetically. To the extent that this series results in people reading the twenty-seven New Testament documents with greater skill, care, insight, devotion, and joy, the contributors and editor of Reading the New Testament: Second Series will be grateful and gratified.

Todd D. Still
Baylor University
George W. Truett Theological Seminary
Waco, Texas

Author's Preface

I doubt many biblical scholars plan to make the book of Revelation the subject of their first commentary, but that is what I seem to have done. I want to thank Todd Still for trusting me, when still a relatively junior scholar, with the task of writing on this challenging and profound New Testament book. Todd's invitation arrived in my inbox on New Year's Eve, 2016, and I set to work reading, thinking, and shaping my thoughts in the classroom, aiming for a 2020 completion. A challenging task was then made more challenging by the Covid-19 pandemic, and my original deadline soon flew by. Todd was characteristically gracious in granting a substantial extension, allowing me to give the writing and re-writing the attention it deserved. The first draft was written under quarantine conditions, and for a while my world shrank to the size of a home office-cum-laundry room. Our house was suddenly not only a home but also a school and two offices. I'm incredibly grateful to my wife, Becky, and our children, Pippa and Sam, for their patient endurance through it all as we all juggled various commitments. It was a strange time in which to write on Revelation, to put it mildly.

Along the way I've been greatly helped in my reading of Revelation by many fine students, scholars, and friends. My fascination with the book was first sparked fourteen years ago in a course taught by Grant Macaskill at the University of St Andrews, focussed on reading Revelation in relation to our contemporary world. Grant would go on to supervise my master's dissertation, and then my doctorate, and I remain grateful for his scholarly companionship. More recently, I'm indebted to colleagues at Trinity College, Bristol, not least for picking up my slack while I was on research leave. I'm particularly thankful for Stephen Finamore, my New Testament counterpart for the last eight years at our partner institution, Bristol Baptist College. As he retires this summer, I am grateful not only for his expertise on Revelation but also for his gracious stepping aside so that I could teach it for a few years. I share his conviction that this book has much to teach us about the shape of earliest Christian thought. Some of the material on Revelation 12–13 repeats (with permission) ideas I worked out in an essay for a volume in Steve's honour (Davies, J. 'Revelation 12–13 and "Systemic Evil"' in Paynter, H. and P. Hatton [eds]. Attending to the Margins: Essays in Honour of Stephen Finamore [Oxford: Regents Park College Press, 2022], 193–206). In navigating some of the more challenging theological territory of this commentary, I was greatly helped by my systematic theology colleagues, Justin Stratis and Taido Chino, who offered their expertise when I was way beyond my comfort zone. Of course, neither of them should be held responsible for my stumbling attempts at theological coherence.

Further afield, there are many from whom I have learned much, especially those who are regulars at the British New Testament Society Revelation seminar. Though I have been a less-than-regular attender (Paul has often drawn me away), I have enjoyed what I have gleaned from them. In particular, I'm grateful for the scholarship of Garrick Allen, Michelle Fletcher, Meredith Warren, and Simon Woodman. Meredith's work on sensory readings of Revelation has been particularly stimulating to read and incorporate into my thinking, and some of it also ended up in my classroom, much to my students' delight (another Mini ScRoll, anyone?). She also encouraged me to submit some of my ideas to the Journal for Interdisciplinary Biblical Studies, of which she is editor in chief. The section of the introduction on 'narrative structure and setting' repeats parts of that article ('Reading the Apocalypse with Christopher Nolan: Story and Narrative, Time and Space' JIBS 42, Vol 4.3 [2022]), generously made available through a Creative Commons license. Further afield, I am grateful to Joe Mangina for a couple of good conversations, to Garrett Best for sharing the fruit of his PhD research with me, and to Mary Farag and to Daniel Girgis for educating me on the details of the use of John's Apocalypse in the Alexandrian Paschal Rite.

I particularly want to thank my students at Trinity College, who demonstrated great hypomonē ('patient endurance') in suffering through my classes on Revelation from 2017–2022 as I worked my thoughts out with them. They will probably recognise much of what I have to say here from their notes, and perhaps even hear the echoes of their own perceptive questions and comments. I tried to note these down as they happened, but in the hurly-burly of a vibrant classroom I am sure I have forgotten many. I do remember the contributions of Elliot Grove and Kizzy Penfold (especially her ecclesial reflections on the words of the elder in Revelation 5.5). Perhaps these 'two witnesses' may stand as a symbol for all the students who have shaped me, and my reading of Revelation, over the years. I lost count of how many of them asked me 'when is the commentary coming out?' and

Author's Preface

so after all this delay I hope they are still interested. As well as undergraduates, my doctoral students have also played an important role in shaping my thinking on Revelation, and in particular, I want to thank Steve Whitacre, whose research on the book's genre and its use of the wisdom tradition has taught me much. Steve has had to demonstrate more than his fair share of patient endurance in the last few years (and not only due to his supervisor!) and I'm always inspired by his faithful dedication.

I grew up as the son of a pastor and have vivid memories of my father's shelves in the home office where he would write his weekly sermons. It was a very small space (probably about the same size as my quarantine study!) but filled floor to ceiling with books, especially commentaries. Some of those volumes now sit on my own shelves, and it is almost certainly because of him that I became a Bible scholar and a theologian, and now find myself adding my own commentary to his shelves (and perhaps to the shelves of a few other pastors). Together with that visual memory of written testimony, however, I also have the auditory memory of the sound of my mother's voice, saying 'find what you love, then find someone to pay you to do it!' It took me a while, but I think I've managed to follow her advice. I am immeasurably grateful to them both for everything they have passed on to me, and so it's with deep gratitude that I dedicate this book, my first commentary, to them.

—*Jamie Davies*
Bristol, June 2023

Introduction

What Kind of Commentary Is This?

As the subtitle of this book says, this is a 'literary and theological commentary.' It is not, then, the kind of commentary that attempts a thorough critical study of every historical detail or linguistic feature. I have not tried to say something about everything (let alone everything about everything!); a project like that would certainly take me beyond my abilities, and in any case far better attempts at that kind of commentary are already available. Though I follow the 'run of the text,' reading continuously through every line, I have mostly taken on several sentences or whole paragraphs at a time rather than going clause by clause or verse by verse. Too often the word, the clause, or the sentence are considered the basic unit of meaning, where that honour arguably belongs to the paragraph. Here and there, where I consider it valuable, I have commented on matters of lexicography, Greek grammar, or history, but for the most part the focus of this commentary lies elsewhere. It is a commentary with two parallel goals: to read Revelation as *literature* and to read Revelation *theologically*. This double interpretative focus has a number of entailments, which I will outline in this introduction. Those who would rather skip these introductory matters and get straight to the commentary may do so with my blessing, however, and you will find that some of these literary and theological discussions reappear where relevant in discussing the text itself.

Reading Revelation as Literature

Reading the book of Revelation responsibly requires that we attend to what it is as a work of literature. This raises a host of questions, among them the following: What kind of literature is it, that is, what is its literary *genre*? Who were its author and original intended audience? What are its structure, plot, narrative, and principal characters? What are its main narrative themes or stylistic features? What is its relationship to other literature? In answering some of these questions, we can usually find guidance in a text's opening lines, which often signal to the reader what it is they are reading. In this respect Revelation is no different, though, as we shall see, the situation rapidly becomes complex. Let us begin, then, with John's opening paragraph:

> The revelation of Jesus Christ, which God gave him to show his servants what must soon take place; he made it known by sending his angel to his servant John, who testified to the word of God and to the testimony of Jesus Christ, even to all that he saw. Blessed is the one who reads aloud the words of the prophecy, and blessed are those who hear and who keep what is written in it; for the time is near. (Rev 1.1–3)

Genre

One of the most important aspects of any literary reading is a proper understanding of the genre of the text being studied. Usually, we make such judgements instinctively. We do not read a recipe the same way we read a poem, or a newspaper article the same way as a letter. A competent reader of any text will quickly recognise its genre, following cues and conventions in the text itself, and (often unconsciously) adopt an appropriate reading strategy. When it comes to the book of Revelation, however, things are a little more challenging. Many mistaken readings of the book begin with a failure to account for its genre, leading to inappropriate interpretations and some theological confusion. It is common to think of genres as 'containers' for texts, the task of generic classification being one of assigning a given piece of writing to its appropriate generic category based on various motifs and textual features. In recent years, however, such approaches to genre have been challenged, with many scholars preferring to speak of genres as 'constellations' of features, and of texts *functionally participating* in genres rather than *formally belonging* to them. This more 'dynamic' approach to genre classification allows for a healthy fluidity, corresponding to the manifold vibrancy of the way any given text might share features with a galaxy of other texts, as well as the important ways in which that text does not fit in any one genre 'container.' As Alastair Fowler memorably put it, 'genre is much less of a pigeonhole than a pigeon' (Fowler 1982, 37).

When it comes to the book of Revelation, an attentive reader will quickly discern a complex constellation, since there is evidence that the book participates in several genres simultaneously. Notably, there are connections to the genres of *apocalypse*, *prophecy*, and *epistle*, as well as elements of the wisdom tradition. Whatever their approach to genre theory, most scholars recognise that Revelation is a work of significant generic complexity, deploying stylistic features and motifs common to a range of literary genres. As such, various 'hybrid' proposals for Revelation's genre have been offered. Probably the most well known and most cited is that of Richard Bauckham, who describes Revelation succinctly as 'an apocalyptic prophecy in the form of a circular letter' (Bauckham 1993, 2). With this short definition, Bauckham signals that Revelation participates in at least three genres.

First, it is an *apocalypse* (1.1). We have noted how the opening paragraph of a text will often provide vital clues to its genre. In this case, the generic label itself owes its existence to Revelation's first word, since *apokalypsis*, 'revelation' or 'unveiling,' has lent itself to what later became known as a genre of second temple Jewish and Christian literature: the 'apocalypse.' John did not use this word in our modern technical sense, but whether or not he was conscious of it, Revelation belongs within the family of texts to which we have since given the label 'apocalypses.' A sensitive literary reading of the book, then, must be conducted with awareness of these family resemblances. Perhaps the most-cited definition of the genre 'apocalypse' is the one given by John Collins:

> 'Apocalypse' is a genre of revelatory literature with a narrative framework, in which a revelation is mediated by an otherworldly being to a human recipient, disclosing a transcendent reality which is both temporal, insofar as it envisages eschatological salvation, and spatial insofar as it involves another, supernatural world. (Collins 1979, 9)

Apocalypses, as the name suggests, are *revelatory* literature, fuelled by the conviction that, as the oldest canonical apocalypse puts it, 'there is a God in heaven who reveals mysteries' (Dan 2.28). When John opened his book with the words 'revelation of Jesus Christ,' he signalled the central importance of a revelatory epistemology for what follows. The question of revelation of mysteries is at the heart of the genre. As Collins's definition observes, in the apocalypses, these revealed mysteries usually concern the nature of space and time, exploring the commerce between heaven and earth and revealing secrets of the primordial past and eschatological future. These revelations are placed in narrative frameworks, often structured around a seer's narrated experience of a mystical tour of heaven, or a series of visions on earth, under the guidance of an angelic interlocutor. Clearly, the book of Revelation shares many if not all of these classic apocalyptic features and so deserves its other title, the 'Apocalypse of John.'

Something is missing from Collins's famous definition, however, and that is the question of an apocalypse's *function*, a line of enquiry that has received lots of attention since (see especially the excellent study by Portier-Young). Much attention has been given to how the disclosures of 'transcendent reality' described in such writings have powerful theological and sociopolitical effects. Though the apocalypses regularly (though not always) contain eschatological visions concerning the future, their primary purpose is not to predict but to speak in symbolic terms about the theological importance of events contemporary with the author, or at least in their imminent future. They offer a 'heaven's-eye-view' on the political and social situation of the first readers, who are often caught up in situations of oppression or imperial domination of various kinds; think of Daniel's four beasts (Dan 7), which are usually understood as four contemporary empires. It is not for nothing that one commonly hears apocalypses described as 'the literature of the oppressed' or a 'literature of resistance.' However, these catchphrases, though signalling an important truth, can too easily mask how some of the original audiences might themselves be complicit with the oppressor (as Revelation's seven messages to the churches illustrate), and we do well to note that the nature and extent of any systematic persecution of Christians in first-century Asia Minor is much debated. Nevertheless, a faithful reading of any apocalypse, Revelation included, will attend to its complex orientation to political hegemony and domination, both in its original context and in that of the contemporary reader. This presents a particular challenge to those of us (myself included) who read Revelation from positions of power and comfort in modern Western society; as Amos Yong has observed, any reading of Revelation from a position of sociopolitical domination that fails to attend to such apocalyptic dynamics runs the risk of being blinded to its meaning. Sadly, the history of interpretation of this book has too often borne this out.

Second, Revelation is a *prophecy*. It names itself as such in the prologue (1.3) and repeats the label in the epilogue (22.18–19). It is also strongly implied that John himself is a prophet (22.6, 9), known to the churches in Asia Minor, to whom he delivers the seven oracles of chapters 2–3. The book was to be read aloud (1.3) in the churches so that this living word of prophecy might be heard in the communities. Even without such clear indications, however, we would likely reach the conclusion that Revelation is a work of 'Christian prophecy' on the basis of the huge number of allusions and echoes John makes to the Old Testament canonical prophets (on which see below). Among his many sources, Ezekiel, Daniel, and Zechariah are particularly prevalent, and it is no coincidence that these are also the prophets who are most fond of the kind of visionary imagery one finds in Revelation and in the other apocalypses. John's prophecy stands quite clearly in this tradition. Here, we must note that the boundary (if such a thing even exists) between the genres of 'prophecy' and 'apocalypse' is a fuzzy one and says much more about modern scholarly instincts concerning classification than it does about ancient literary practices.

Like the apocalypses, prophecy is not so much about prediction as it is about addressing the people of its time with a divine message (more 'forth-telling' than 'foretelling,' as I like to tell my students). It does this, however, in such a way as to leave open subsequent readings in the future. Prophetic imagery has, as Richard Bauckham so nicely puts it, a 'surplus of meaning' (Bauckham 1993, 10). As such, it is not accurate to say that prophecy is not concerned with the future. Daniel, for example, is told that the mysteries revealed to him concern 'what will happen at the end of days' (Dan 2.28) and is instructed to 'keep the words secret and the book sealed until the time of the end' (Dan 12.4). However, it is interesting to note that John is given the opposite command: 'do not seal up the words of the prophecy of this book, for the time is near' (Rev 22.10). This perhaps indicates a greater concern with the present and imminent future compared to his prophetic predecessors. John, arguably, understands his book as not only a part of the prophetic tradition but as the 'climax of prophecy' (Bauckham 1993).

Third, Revelation is a *letter*. Although the standard epistolary greeting is deferred until 1.4, it is unmistakable: 'John, to the seven churches that are in Asia. Grace to you and peace . . . .' John also signs off the book with an epistolary benediction (22.21). That Revelation is a letter is perhaps one of the most underappreciated aspects of its genre, and this neglect is, I think, the source of much confusion. In discussing every other letter of the New Testament, we expect to place a large amount of emphasis on the author's intent, on the first readers' context, and so on. Letters are sent in order to make the author 'present' to his or her recipients, that they might influence their lives and imaginations (a purpose, we might note with significance, that letters share with apocalypses and prophecies). And yet some interpretations of Revelation quickly allegorise the historical recipients of this letter, turning the seven churches of Asia Minor into ciphers for some other theological scheme. Much mischief can be avoided by taking seriously the simple truth that letters are usually intended for specific named recipients and that a proper understanding of the historical situation of those recipients is an indispensable guide for interpretation of its message.

The seven churches are listed in the order a messenger would encounter them in their journey around the region. This is not, however, simply giving us John's distribution list. As we will see in the commentary on chapters 2–3, that they are seven (a number achieved by excluding some obvious other candidates) is also a symbolic way of directing this letter to all the churches, as something of an encyclical, a letter to the Church in its completeness. Here, too, there is a 'surplus of meaning' in John's symbolism. While they are certainly useful, then, discussions of the historical setting of author and audience do not exhaust Revelation's scope of meaning. With this in mind, then, we turn briefly to some of these historical matters.

Author and Date

Unlike most apocalypses, which tend to be written under the pseudonym of an exalted figure from history (such as Enoch or Baruch), Revelation's prologue provides what appears to be the author's real name: John. Presumably he was known to his original audience (and so felt no need to identify himself more fully) and was accepted as a prophet among the churches to whom he writes. For us who do not know him, however, his name presents us with an enigma. Which John is this? Some consider the John of Revelation to be the same apostle John who wrote the fourth Gospel and the Johannine epistles, and this was the majority view in the writings of the Church Fathers. Others are not convinced, arguing on the basis of various stylistic and theological features that this must be a different John, often called 'John the Seer' or 'John of Patmos' to distinguish him from John the evangelist. This view, too, has some pedigree. Or perhaps there were more than two Johns (it was a common name then, as it is now). In the end we are simply not told and so must work by inference and deduction. This is a tricky business. Stylistic and theological differences, cited as evidence of a distinction between John of Patmos and John the evangelist, are often in the eye of the beholder and tend to rely on a questionable assumption: that the same author, working on various projects in various genres across a span of decades, is compelled to write with consistent vocabulary, style, and theological emphases. I for one see no reason why this should be so, and as such I do not find such arguments as compelling as others do. In any case, though I have a preference for the view that it is the same John, as someone who reads Revelation canonically I am content to draw contrasts and connections with John's Gospel without the need to insist on common authorship, and so I can safely remain somewhat agnostic on the authorship issue. That said, there may be other reasons to think there is another John or even that the book as we have it in its final form was the product of more than one hand, perhaps with John's original manuscript later developed into the form in which we have it now. For convenience, throughout this commentary, I will refer to the author simply as 'John,' the author with whom the text presents us, while remaining aware of such complex historical possibilities for the book's authorship.

Among the reasons to suggest another John, or a second editorial hand, is the matter of dating the book's composition. It is largely agreed that we are dealing with a work of the first century AD, but there are usually two options given: the late 60s and the mid- to late 90s. Arguments for the later date, placing Revelation's composition toward the end of the reign of Roman emperor Domitian (81–96), go back as far as Irenaeus (*Adv Haer* 5.50.3), second century bishop of Lyon and a native of Smyrna, and so should not be too quickly dismissed. Scholars attempting to nail down the book's date sometimes focus on the counting of the seven heads of the beast, interpreted to John by the angel as 'seven kings, of whom five have fallen, one is living, and the other has not yet come' (17.9-10, cf. 13.1). These seven heads, which are seven mountains (a reference to Rome), are also seven kings, suggesting Roman emperors are in view, and thus the passage promises some verifiable historical anchors. The seven 'heads' can be lined up with the list of Roman emperors of the first century, giving us a reliable date based on the sixth and reigning 'head.' This apparently simple task, however, quickly proves more complicated. In some versions of this approach, the seven are counted from Nero to Domitian, suggesting a later date for Revelation. But one might just as easily start the count with Julius (where many other ancient lists begin) or Augustus (considered by some to be the first true Roman emperor) and work forward in order to arrive at the earlier date, the sixth living 'head' being, perhaps, Galba (AD 68–69). As such, what promised to be a surefire way of establishing the date of Revelation proves to be nothing of the sort, for these are only two of the myriad ways of doing the count (Aune 2017, 947, lists no fewer than nine different versions of this approach). There are too many problems here for us to put much stock in such schemes. Not only do they require a certain amount of creativity in where one begins counting and who is included in the count (often becoming rather circular in argument), but they also treat John's symbolism too literally (a perennial problem in interpretation of Revelation, to be discussed shortly). Perhaps the seven kings were not intended as an encoded historical timeline at all, and we should avoid using the list to identify who was reigning when Revelation was written, for, as Richard Bauckham has argued, 'Revelation's first readers knew perfectly well who the sixth head, the reigning emperor, was, and did not need to work it out' (Bauckham 1998, 406). More important for them, and for John, was the political and eschatological point being made by the imminent completion of the seven 'heads' of the Roman beast: the end of its dominion was close at hand.

A more helpful line of enquiry for the later date is in examining socio-historical evidence concerning the state of the seven cities/churches of Asia Minor in the late first century and the nature of any contemporary persecution of Christians under Domitian's rule. It is suggested that his reign saw a particularly intense period of persecution, along with an increase in fervour in respect of the *imperial cult*, the Roman 'civic religion' of emperor worship (on which see the excellent book-length studies by Friesen and Price). This was especially true in the eastern provinces, where it was one of the most important aspects of civic identity, as well as being crucial to how time and space—eschatology and cosmology—were imagined. Some of the cities mentioned in the first few chapters of Revelation were certainly important centres for the imperial cult in Asia Minor. Ephesus, for example, was the site of several temples to Julius, Augustus, and Domitian (Aune 2017, 154). In the late first century, it competed with other cities of Asia Minor (especially Smyrna and Pergamum) for the coveted title of *neōkoros*, 'temple keeper,' which it won twice over (cf. Acts 19.35). Such a context has a number of suggestive resonances with the oracles to those churches in Revelation 2–3, the imaginative exposure of false worship in chapter 13, and critiques of idolatry in various other places, as well as its imaginative countering of imperial cosmology and eschatology. It also reminds us that our modern distinction between 'politics' and 'religion' is really not at all helpful when talking about the ancient world. However, the idea of an intense 'persecution' of Christians under Domitian has been subject to serious challenge and is considered lacking in credible external evidence. As such, we should hold lightly any arguments that assume a systematic persecution of Christians under Domitian in support of a late date for Revelation. In any case, we do well to note that not all of Revelation's first recipients are treated as victims of persecution; if anything, 'the chief dangers were complacency and compromise' (Sweet 1979, 26), as we shall see in our discussion of chapters 2–3.

There is a range of evidence in favour of an earlier date, and again, the bestial political imagery from chapter 13 is often the focus of attention. The 'mark of the beast' in 13.18 is almost universally understood as a coded reference to the emperor Nero (54–68), whose reign can more reliably be characterised by persecution of Jews and Christians and who was also infamous for the murder of his own mother (on all of which see the comments on 13.18). Many scholars detect another historical allusion to Nero in 13.3, where John sees that one of the beast's heads 'seemed to have received a death-blow, but its mortal wound had been healed.' A popular legend had it that Nero, who committed suicide by a sword to the throat in June 68, had not died but had fled across the Euphrates to Parthia and was gathering his strength before a triumphant return to Rome. This legend persisted in various forms for centuries, however, and so can't be relied upon to give us a precise date. Book 8 of the *Sibylline Oracles*, for example, weaves this *Nero Redivivus* legend together with apocalyptic imagery when it speaks of a 'matricidal fugitive' (88) who will come again and bring low the arrogance of Rome before the arrival of a fire-breathing dragon, a final judgement, and the end of the world (see also *Sib Or* 4.137–39). The year that followed Nero's death was one of the most chaotic ever seen in the Roman empire, with four emperors coming to power between June 68 and the summer of 69 (Galba, Otho, Vitellius, and Vespasian), marking the transition between the Julio-Claudian and the Flavian dynasties. That certainly sounds like the sort of 'earth-shattering' sociopolitical environment in which the apocalyptic imagery of Revelation might make sense (by some accounts, described above, this aligns well with Rev 17.10's note that the seventh king 'must remain only a little while' and that the eighth is 'the beast that was and is not' which 'belongs to the seven' [17.11]). To those living through this *Year of the Four Emperors*, it may well have felt like 'the end of the world,' aptly expressed in images of cosmic upheaval. As we have already seen, this is entirely in keeping with the rhetorical strategy of the contemporary Jewish apocalyptic literature, which flourished at such times of sociopolitical upheaval.

Other evidence points toward a late 60s date, in particular that which relates to the destruction of the Jerusalem temple in AD 70, the most useful fixed historical point in dating the books of the New Testament. Particularly noteworthy in the case of Revelation is the striking absence of any clear mention of the events of AD 70, and John's account of the temple measurement in chapter 11, which seems to imply that it was still standing when he wrote. When John does speak of the temple's destruction, he describes how only a 'tenth of the city' falls, and that because of an earthquake (11.13). This description seems quite tame when compared to the actual 'trampling of the holy city' by the Romans, which is described by Josephus as the demolition of 'the entire city and temple,' leaving only some towers and one wall to posterity (Josephus, *War*, 7.1.1). This suggests a date, for this section of Revelation at least, before 70. Again, though, our confidence must be tempered as we remember that John's temple imagery is symbolic, not literal, and so we mustn't rely too heavily on any of these arguments.

There are, then, strong arguments in favour of both dates, but at every turn these must be held lightly—John's apocalyptic imagery simply does not permit confidence when it comes to precise historiography. On balance, I am broadly convinced by the earlier date (at least for the bulk of the material; it may well be that the final form came together in the 90s), but since this is a narrative/theological commentary, and not primarily a historical-critical one, I am content to remain somewhat agnostic on matters of dating and authorship, since here we are far less interested in Revelation's origins than its final literary form.

Narrative Structure and Setting

Reading the book of Revelation can be a bewildering experience, especially when it comes to tracing its plot and structure. There seem to be as many proposals as there are commentators, and little sign of consensus any time soon. This is hardly surprising, since Revelation does not present the interpreter with clear guidance as to its structure. Several features are usually highlighted in structural proposals. Some proposals discern a fourfold structure based around the four places where John tells us he was 'in the spirit' (1.10; 4.2; 17.3; 21.10) as indicators of major sections of his developing ecstatic experience. Then there is the often-repeated refrain *kai eidon*, 'and I saw' (5.1, 6; 6.1; 7.2; 8.2; 9.1; 10.1; 13.1, 11; 15.1; 16.13; 17.3; 19.11; 20.1, 11; 21.1), which regularly marks the beginning of new visions. Again, the phrase *meta tauta*, 'after this,' often advances the narrative to a new scene (e.g., 4.1; 7.1, 9; 15.5; 18.1; 19.1). Sometimes (e.g., 18.1) we find both phrases together. While all of these structural markers can indicate narrative movement, they cannot be completely relied on as clear and consistent indicators of the book's overall structure, as the myriad proposals on offer attest.

At a broader level of focus, more promising are the obvious sequences of seven that seem to structure the book as a whole: seven oracles (2.1–3.22), seven seals (6.1–8.5), seven trumpets (8.6–11.19), and seven bowls (15.5–16.21). In some accounts, there is also a less obvious sequence of seven unnumbered visions in the book's closing chapters (19.11–20.15). The structure of this commentary largely adopts these broad section divisions, as the chapter headings indicate. A crucial question any interpreter of Revelation faces is how these units (however delineated) relate to one another and to the overall structure/plot of the book. Here, I have refrained from offering a more precise overall linear narrative structure, for reasons that I will now explain.

These cycles of seven are particularly important for discussions about whether Revelation has a linear or nonlinear structure. Linear readings essentially view the events of Revelation's narrative proceeding in a continuous, successive fashion, such that the end of the seven seals leads to the start of the seven trumpets (as 8.1–2 seems to suggest), and so on through the book. Other variations of the essentially linear approach might have the seven trumpets contained within the last seal and the seven bowls within the last trumpet, such that the sequences are linear but telescoped together. Nonlinear readings, on the other hand, prefer to view at least some of these sequences as essentially recapitulative, such that they describe the same events from different perspectives. Such approaches might maintain a degree of linearity, with cycles moving forward, and/or with increasing intensity, like a spiral. Recapitulative readings, which come in various forms, can be traced back as far as the earliest full commentary on Revelation that we possess, that of Victorinus of Petovium (mid to late third century), who says the following concerning the trumpets and bowls:

> The 'trumpet' is the word of power. And although there is a repetition of scenes by means of the bowls, this is not spoken as though the events occurred twice. Rather, since those events that are future to them have been decreed by God to happen, these things are spoken twice. And therefore, whatever he said rather briefly by way of the trumpets he said more completely by way of the bowls. Nor ought we pay too much attention to the order of what is said. For the sevenfold Holy Spirit, when he has passed in revue the events to the last time, to the very end, returns again to the same times and supplements what he had said incompletely. Nor ought we inquire too much into the order of the Revelation. Rather, we ought inquire after the meaning, for there is also the possibility of a false understanding. And therefore, those things written concerning the trumpets and the bowls are either the devastation of the plagues sent to the world, or the madness of the antichrist himself, or the blasphemies of the peoples, or the variety of the plagues, or the hope for the kingdom of saints, or the ruin of cities or the ruin of Babylon, that is, of the city of Rome. (Victorinus,12, commenting on Rev 8.2)

Which is to be preferred, a linear or nonlinear approach? Does Revelation's plot trace out a relatively continuous narrative arc from beginning to end, or does it present us with a more nonlinear cycle of visions? Reaching a decision on this matter can be aided, I think, by recognising that there is a distinction in narrative analysis between 'story' and 'discourse.' This is a distinction that goes back to literary critic E. M. Forster in the 1920s (classically, in his book *Aspects of the Novel* [London: Edward Arnold, 1927]) but can arguably be traced back as far as Aristotle's *Poetics*. It became more important for biblical studies through the work of Seymour Chatman, in works such as *Story and Discourse: Narrative Structure in Fiction and Film* (Ithaca: Cornell University Press, 1978). The basic distinction is that a text's 'story' is its underlying sequence, usually progressing in a linear fashion and in chronological time, distinguished from its 'discourse,' the arrangement of the story in the flow of the text itself, which can align with its story but does not need to. This is a simple but profoundly helpful distinction when it comes to analysing the structure of Revelation. I want to suggest that the book has a *linear story* (concerning God's purposes for creation) but is arranged with a *nonlinear discourse*. This allows us to affirm the insights of nonlinear readings emphasising the recapitulative and cyclical arrangements in the book's *discourse* without completely jettisoning the linearity of its overall *story*. Recapitulation and linear progression theories are thus not entirely incompatible but can be seen as describing the discourse and the story, respectively. For example, when John says 'after this' he is indicating a forward movement in his discourse, but not necessarily in his story or his chronology (Blount 2013, 140). This nonlinear narrative technique is regularly used with powerful, if disorienting, effect in Revelation, and we will regularly observe its theological purposes throughout.

This can be helpful in making sense not only of Revelation's recapitulations but also of its otherwise vexing non sequiturs. For example, some of Revelation's key characters are introduced in the discourse before we know anything about their role in the story. Take the character of Babylon. She enters briefly and confusingly in 14.8, where an angel proclaims that she is fallen before we have any idea who she is. There, her fall is the second of three angelic messages, the third being the judgement of the Beast, whom we met a chapter earlier. The insight that Babylon is a city isn't suggested until 16.19, and here we are told briefly that she is the object of God's wrath. A full description of the character isn't really provided until the vision of chapter 17, which makes her the narrative focus, but by now we have already understood something of her role in the story. Chapter 18 repeats the proclamation of her fall, describes her judgements, and details the laments of the merchants at her burning. The discourse of Revelation thus disrupts the story timeline of the character Babylon, and her fall is recounted several times from different perspectives.

The same sort of nonlinearity is characteristic of other narrative features of the book. In 8.7, all the grass is burned up but is then there again to be protected in 9.4. In 6.13 the stars fall, but in 8.12 they are darkened by a third. The mountains are removed in 6.14, yet people can still hide in them one verse later; they are removed again in chapter 16, yet the woman sits on seven mountains in 17.9 and John is carried away to another in 21.10. Heaven and earth, or parts thereof, flee away at least three times (6.14; 16.20; 20.11). A number of important themes and ideas from the end of the story are introduced early in the narrative without explanation: the 'tree of life' (2.7/22.2), 'second death' (2.11/21.8), 'book of life' (3.5 (also 13.8;

17.8/20.12), and 'New Jerusalem' (3.12). And, in what some consider a clear indication of Revelation's nonlinearity, 11.15 declares, at the blowing of the seventh trumpet, that 'the kingdom of the world has become the kingdom of our Lord and of his Messiah.' The twenty-four elders celebrate that the day of God's judgment has come (11.16–18), and yet this marks only the halfway point of the book.

All of this is very confusing if discourse and story are taken to be essentially synonymous. As Koester (2014, 788) notes, 'non-sequiturs in the visionary world make it difficult to translate these scenes into coherent sequences of events in the readers' world.' But this 'translation' is made easier (in theory, at least) if we recognise the distinction between the two, viewing Revelation's discourse (and therefore its structure) as largely nonlinear while affirming the linearity of its underlying story. The same events in an essentially linear redemptive story are sometimes shown 'out of order' in the discourse or repeated from different perspectives, with growing intensity and with depictions of God's final triumph closing each major visionary cycle (and in this way I adopt the recapitulative approach in respect of narrative). Readers of Revelation accompany John and experience these discontinuities and repetitions. We share his disrupted experience of cause-and-effect and are invited to piece together the story from the shuffled plot we are given. We are displaced and confused, and that's part of the point. In due course (e.g., in the introduction to chapter 12), we will have more to say on how John's nonlinear plot relates to his view of time and space and to the eschatological victory of God. Here, though, I have largely followed Victorinus's advice not to 'pay too much attention to the order of what is said.'

This focus on Revelation's nonlinear discourse should not, however, cause us to forget that the book does have an underlying ordered and linear story, or (to be more precise) several underlying linear stories. These stories are expressed in the book of Revelation in something of a nested arrangement, like a *matryoshka*, a Russian doll of stories-within-stories. We can trace at least three levels to this complex nested story, each with its own setting in time and space. First, there is the story of John's visionary experience on Patmos and his prophetic oracles to the seven churches, with which the book begins and ends. Second, within this narrative frame but at a wider temporal one, there is a story of his heavenly ascent and his visions of the cosmic throne room and judgements on the earth. Third, nested in the middle of the book, we find this temporal frame expanding still further, with visions set in an innermost heavenly location with a primordial story involving cosmic war, the victory of Christ, and the final judgement of God's enemies.

This threefold narrative analysis is similar to that proposed by David Barr, whose own structural proposal identifies three 'scrolls' in Revelation (the 'Letter Scroll,' 1.1–3.22; the 'Worship Scroll,' 4.1–11.18; the 'War Scroll,' 11.19–22.21). These, Barr argues, are 'three distinct and interrelated movements set in a common frame' (Barr 1998, 13). I think Barr's analysis has much to commend it, but I want to suggest a couple of adjustments. First, I do not see the three stories separating quite so neatly or so sequentially in the narrative structure of the book. Instead, they are rather shuffled together, John's narrative moving between them in complex ways. I will comment on this further in a moment. Second, while the three stories share themes and characters, in Barr's analysis they 'do not form a causal sequence' (Barr 1998, 13). Again I'm inclined to disagree: once the three stories are viewed not sequentially but in a nested arrangement, like a *matryoshka*, a number of causal connections between them can be observed. Events at one level have causal effects at the other levels, though the imagery used may be different. Since these effects are shuffled into the narrative rather than laid out successively, some work will have to be done to see these connections. Cause and effect might be out of order in the narrative, or events might be repeated in order to depict them at different levels, but the three stories are nevertheless causally connected rather than each having its own discrete logic.

Keeping track of which story we are in is challenging (perhaps deliberately so) but is guided by indications of the book's threefold 'geographical' setting; John's is a 'three-storied world' (Resseguie 2009, 32) in both senses of the term. First, there is John's vision on earth, the setting for the story of his encounter with Christ in the opening three chapters and the epilogue. Second, there is his ascent and vision in heaven, where much of the book's material happens. There is action on earth but it's usually described from a heavenly point of view. Third, there is also a story that happens in relation to an innermost space, 'the temple in heaven' (11.19) or 'the temple, the tent of witness in heaven' (15.5). The three stories that correspond to this three-storied universe are nested, like a *matryoshka*.

As with space, so with time. John's experience of time bends and stretches depending on 'where' he is. John's visionary experience on Patmos 'in the spirit on the Lord's day' (1.10) may be the widest narrative frame, but it is not the widest temporal frame of the story. That is found, I think, in the innermost setting, in chapter 12's vision of the dragon, the woman, and a war in heaven. This vision, preceded by the observation that 'God's temple in heaven was opened' (11.19), tells the story of a primeval conflict between God and God's enemies, led by the dragon. The temporal setting of this vision is somewhat unclear; we are not told exactly 'when' the war broke out (if that is even a sensible question to ask), but I take Bauckham to be essentially correct in placing this vision 'chronologically earlier than any previous part of his visionary narrative' (1998, 15). Yet it is also, somehow, contemporaneous with and causally related to the first-century churches of Asia Minor. In this innermost layer of the vision, the dragon is defeated and 'thrown down to earth' (12.9) and a voice proclaims that God's victory and kingdom have now come (12.10). This is a depiction of a victory 'already' completed, but only on the timeline of this primordial innermost vision. There, as in 11.15, heaven rejoices, but there is still woe for the earth because the effects of this victory are yet to be fully seen on the earthly timeline, where the dragon continues to make war, knowing that his time is cut short. Subsequent chapters of Revelation play out this victory on the other timelines, as the setting cuts between heaven and earth, before ultimately converging in the final vision of the New Heaven and New Earth. But it also echoes backward to the churches of Asia Minor, whose conflict with the powers of evil is now understood as an earthly outworking of this cosmic battle. There is thus a causal connection between the three stories, though it is not always presented in a linear way by the narrative. The devil's defeat in this cosmic frame, completed in 12.10, is related in complex ways to his defeat in the other heavenly visions and, ultimately, the church's participation in this victory in earthly time.

Use of Imagery and Liturgical Setting

By now, it should be clear that reading Revelation requires the engagement of the reader's imagination in ways that many other texts do not. This is nowhere truer than in handling its imagery. Here again, poor reading strategies and a lack of appreciation for literary form are often the cause of problematic interpretations. The most common error, I think, is when Revelation's symbolic imagery is treated as a problem to be solved rather than something to be embraced for what it is. Too often, this book is approached as if it were a code to be cracked, whether the 'answer' concerns events of the past (often the strategy adopted by 'preterist' readings) or events still to come (usually the strategy of 'futurist' readings, especially those done within a dispensational framework).

There is an element of truth to this decoding approach, to be sure. Some images, such as the number 666 or the name 'Babylon,' do seem to be encoded references inviting the reader to decipher them, and doing so is an important part of interpretation. However, this is sometimes understood (wrongly, as I shall argue) as the end of the interpretative task, as if the goal of reading Revelation's imagery were to turn it into a series of propositions. In such approaches, once the symbolic code has been cracked, the imagery can be safely discarded, leaving only prosaic statements, which (by implication) are where the 'real' meaning lies. A conviction throughout this commentary is that this 'decoding' approach does poor service to Revelation's literary genius. This is not only an act of aesthetic vandalism but also regularly leads to missing (or misunderstanding) the theological meaning of the book's imagery.

A better way of handling Revelation's images is to read them in such a way that their nature *as imagery* remains hermeneutically significant, and not merely a question of literary form. One thing that images can do, which propositions usually cannot, is express multiple things at once. Whereas a prosaic code is univocal (image X = statement Y), poetic imagery can express more than one idea simultaneously; imagery is by its very nature polyvalent. Often it is in this very polyvalence that Revelation's theological meaning is to be found. Interpreting apocalyptic imagery requires that we engage a 'double vision,' thinking two things at once.

As such, symbolic imagery is the perfect form of expression for the sociopolitical function of apocalypses (discussed above), since it allows the writer not only an encoded reference to political or social power but also simultaneously to express prophetic judgments about them. For example, 'Babylon' is not merely a cipher for Rome but simultaneously imbues the reference with a prophetic critique, recasting Rome as the oppressor of the people of God. Again, the number '666' is not merely a coded way of saying 'Nero' but simultaneously expresses the theological significance of the reference (on which see the comments on 13.18).

Expressed through visionary imagery, these prophetic judgements do not only inform the reader of what God says but also counter the images of the world in order to effect a radical 'purging of the theological imagination' (Bauckham 1993, 17), changing *how* the world is perceived in its past, present, and future. It is not only that heavenly mysteries are revealed on earth but that the manner of this revelation transforms the way earth will henceforth be seen. And, we should note, more than just 'seen.' John's apocalyptic symbols are expressed not only through his visionary encounters but through his auditory and even (as we shall see) gustatory and olfactory ones. It is a book not only of sights but of sounds, smells, and tastes. It is the whole body that inhabits the world, and Revelation is a 'whole-body' text, effecting and affecting John's (and therefore the reader's) embodied response to the world. We should therefore also recognise that symbolic language is not just cognitive but also affective. This transformation of the imagination is not only a shaping of the mind, or even the body, but also of *desire*. Apocalyptic imagery transforms both *what* we know and *how* we know and also what we *love*.

Once again we should note that Revelation was intended for oral enactment (1.3), to be experienced aurally and in its entirety rather than segmented and meticulously dissected as written text (and so when Revelation says 'let anyone who has an ear listen' it really means '*listen*'). This orality, David Barr has argued, has a lot to do with the structure of the book and 'is an essential element of its hermeneutic' (Barr 1998, 171–180; Barr 1986, 243). There are good reasons to think that the intended context for this oral (re)enactment of John's visions was a liturgical one, not least that John's narrated experience is set 'in the spirit on the Lord's day' (v. 10). Much of the book depicts scenes of worship, and the narrative is regularly interrupted by 'liturgical' elements, such as prayers and doxologies (e.g., 7.10; 11.15; 16.5; 19.1, 5). There are seven blessings (1.3; 14.13; 16.15; 19.9; 20.6; 22.7; 22.14), and eight songs of praise (4.8; 4.11; 5.9–10; 5.12; 5.13b; 7.12; 11.17–18; 15.3–4). Revelation ends with a repeated refrain 'come,' a benediction, and an 'Amen.' We don't know enough about the content of early Christian gatherings to be certain, but with a little historical imagination it is not unreasonable to suggest that these liturgical elements might have involved call-and-response participation by a gathered congregation, or that the closing visions of the wedding supper of the Lamb might be followed by a Eucharistic meal. This Barr considers not only appropriate but probable, and supported by the frequent Eucharistic imagery in the book (Barr 1998, 172; Barr 1986, 254).

It is intriguing to note in this connection that even today, every year on 'Bright Saturday' (also known as 'Apocalypse Saturday,' the Saturday of Easter), the Coptic Orthodox Church reads the book of Revelation aloud in a liturgical setting. It is read aloud in its entirety as part of a Paschal vigil, with incense raised whenever the book mentions it and the lighting of sevenfold lamps. The reading is interrupted by chanted call-and-response from the people at the refrain 'he who has an ear, let him hear, what the Spirit says to the churches' in chapters 2–3, at the counting of the twelve tribes in chapter 7, at the 'Alleluias' in chapter 19, and at the cycle of foundation stones in chapter 21. It ends with a chant of 'Amen, Lord have mercy' and a priestly anointing using the oil of the seven lamps. Though this liturgical reading practice has a venerable tradition (reaching back centuries), it does not constitute evidence for the use of Revelation among its earliest readers. However, it does seem, to me at least, that this reception of the Apocalypse is very much in keeping with its original purpose as a book to be read aloud in a liturgical setting.

Whatever form it once took, this kind of oral 'reenactment' of John's visions dramatically increases the book's power to shape the imagination in a range of ways. First, liturgy has its 'own' sacred time and space, where there is access to transcendent reality, and uses this experience to imbue the ordinary with theological meaning. Second, the act of worship not only names authority and allegiance but ascribes honour and shapes desire. Third, therefore, worship shapes not only the religious but also the political imagination (and, as we shall see, the two were intertwined in the ancient world). Worship is a political act. Much like its imagery, then, Revelation's implied setting has multiple layers of meaning.

Western modern readers may find all this—John's narrative nonlinearity, his symbolic polyvalence, and his liturgical setting—somewhat disorienting. But John is neither modern nor Western, and he does not share a commitment to monovalent, linear, propositional discourse (Yong 2021, 18–19). Those of us from that world should adjust our approach to his images accordingly, rather than forcing him into our modern, Western procrustean bed. Treating John's images as encoded propositional language forces him to speak our language and does poor service to Revelation's literary and theological power; his images cannot be reduced to mere propositions without serious loss of meaning. Apocalyptic imagery involves a complete transformation of the theological imagination and requires a reading strategy suitable to this.

Since this is not only a narrative but also a theological commentary (on which more shortly), we pause briefly to observe a deeper theological significance of both the liturgical setting and the apocalyptic polyvalence of this remarkable theological book. First, worship is not merely a major theme or a literary setting but is the appropriate *environment* for theological reflection. After all, where else but in worship can one speak appropriately about God? Second, Revelation's polyvalent imagery is also not merely a literary feature but is an appropriate *language* for theological reflection. This second statement warrants further discussion. Simple monovalent propositions do poor service to the task of interpreting apocalyptic imagery, to be sure, but they are also ill-fitted to the task of theology. The 'double vision' of apocalyptic imagery is, in some senses, a far more appropriate discourse for speaking of God, for to speak of God properly we must 'speak twice.' This is a theological instinct expressed most recently in the work of systematic theologian Katherine Sonderegger, who uses the idea of '*redoublement*' in theological language, an idea borrowed from Bonaventure and Thomas Aquinas (via Gilles Emery) to describe the need always to 'speak twice' when speaking of God (Sonderegger 2020, 210–14). For Sonderegger, this 'redoubling' is not merely a function of the limitations of human language but is the appropriate—even required—form of theological speech since it echoes the life of God, of whom we must say the two words 'One' and 'Three.' This 'conceptual "two-ness"' (433) must be expressed simultaneously, not as a 'countable' two-ness but as an expression of the 'doubling' in the oneness of God's relations. Sonderegger traces this 'doubled identity' in the Old Testament, which she considers 'an instance, the prime literary instance of *redoublement*' (xxviii). This is no less true, I suggest, of Revelation's redoubled apocalyptic imagery, which, in its inherent polyvalence, is also a literary world remarkably suited to theological discourse. There is a place for prosaic propositions in the writing of theology, but poetic imagery can rise to the challenge of theological language in a way that propositions cannot, and those who would speak of God need both kinds of speech. Revelation's imagery, with its 'double vision,' provides a linguistic form well suited to theologian's task, namely that 'to say it fully, we say it twice' (Sonderegger 2020, 211). This is not the only place where we will observe an integration of Revelation's form, function, and content. In the closing section of this introduction, I will say more on the theological significance of this. And in the commentary that follows I will, from time to time, offer reflections on Revelation's apocalyptic and theological 'double vision,' attending to the redoubled way John's images, and combinations of images, express two divine words at once. In places my written style may be more poetic than is usually found in a book like this, and in places it may even sound like worship. I have tried not to get too carried away, but I trust that the reader will now grasp why I consider this to be a theologically appropriate form of commentary.

Revelation's Use of the Old Testament

Much of Revelation's symbolic imagery is not entirely novel but is itself Old Testament imagery, drawn from a rich prophetic and apocalyptic tradition. It is impossible, therefore, to appreciate the rich theological meaning of these images (and not only the images, as we will see) without attending closely to the way John echoes and adapts the Old Testament. This raises the question of *intertextuality*. To read Revelation as literature is to read it not only within its historical world but also within its literary world, part of a universe of other texts.

Almost every line of the book of Revelation is shaped by this textual universe. Though John never explicitly quotes the Old Testament, he alludes to it constantly. Some count as many as 600 or more allusions, ranging from near-quotations to broadly suggestive echoes of images or turns of phrase. John draws on a large corpus of Old Testament books, but, as we noted earlier, he has a particular fondness for his 'comrades the prophets' (22.9).

The book of Isaiah is regularly alluded to, as it often is in the New Testament, but a distinguishing feature of John's use of the Old Testament is his frequent allusions to Ezekiel, Daniel, and the minor prophets (on which see Moyise 1995, 14–16), as well as to noncanonical apocalyptic texts such as *1 Enoch*.

Since there are no explicit citation formulae or direct quotations to compare, the question of which version of the Old Testament John uses is a thorny and complex one. In places, he seems to be working with Greek versions (whether the Old Greek or the Septuagint). In other places, it appears he is translating from a Hebrew source. While it is hard to be precise, we seem to be able to say with confidence that John worked with various textual sources in different languages, and even perhaps that these sources were themselves pluriform. As such, the subtitle 'Revelation's use of *the* Old Testament' is an imprecise shorthand. This may seem unusual and disorienting, but this kind of scribal activity was very much in keeping with textual culture in the second temple Jewish period (on which see Allen 2017). John wrote at a time when there were multiple forms of his Old Testament sources in circulation, and not in our modern textual world of (relatively) stable canon and concordance.

Most commentaries on Revelation will observe that John's use of the Greek language is 'irregular,' suggesting to some that there is Semitic influence on his translation or writing style or that his skill with Greek isn't particularly high. To others, however, these solecisms (errors of grammar and syntax, which number in the hundreds) are evidence of a deliberate rhetorical or stylistic decision, perhaps John's way of imitating the apocalyptic or prophetic tradition upon which he draws. For example, in commenting on the textual challenges of the 'garbled' inaugural vision of Ezekiel, Daniel Block notes its 'incomplete sentences, erratic grammar, confused vocabulary, and incoherent structure' (1988, 433), which he attributes not to a lack of capacity with Hebrew but to the seer's emotional state when narrating his ecstatic visionary experience and the limitations of human language to describe it. The opening vision of Ezekiel is one of John's main Old Testament sources (exercising a profound influence on Rev 4–5 in particular, but see also the 'prophetic commissioning' of Rev 10–11), and it is a reasonable hypothesis that in his own visionary account he might echo not only the content of Ezekiel but its apocalyptic literary style, too, speaking, as it were, in 'Ezekiel's voice' (on which see Best 2021). Perhaps both emotional and literary explanations are compatible, such that the language used not only reflects the seer's affective revelatory experience but also replicates it in the oral reading of the book. In any case, these proposals suggest, perhaps, that we should credit John with more literary skill than his 'clumsy' Greek initially suggests.

Whatever his sources, John is by no means a derivative writer, simply reproducing Old Testament motifs or arranging them into a textual collage. On the contrary, his allusive method is one of the more innovative and theologically generative features of his writing, in at least two respects. First, there is the way in which John combines multiple allusions together to forge new meanings. Sometimes the question of Revelation's use of the Old Testament is treated in a rather flat-footed 'concordance' fashion, identifying a singular source text, using that to control a univocal 'meaning' for John's allusion, and then moving on. But, as Steve Moyise puts it, 'an allusion is not simply a footnote to a previous work' (1995, 110). John's allusive method is far more complex than that, and far more interesting. He does not treat the Old Testament simply as a box of source texts to be drawn from but rather forges new connections between texts by weaving together multiple allusions, placing them in unlikely juxtaposition or in fresh contexts, adapting and combining features of multiple images, or otherwise creating interactions between texts drawn from a wide range of Old Testament writings. Here, John's approach is similar to aspects of ancient Jewish exegetical strategies, not least the principle of *gezera shawa* ('equal category'), in which the presence of shared terms in different texts is exploited to relate them together and to forge mutually interpretative connections. This was especially popular in later rabbinic interpretation, but the practice likely predates the rise of Christianity and is attributed in rabbinic writings to Hillel (d. AD10; see Longenecker 1999, 19–20). It is also found at work in the Dead Sea Scrolls (Moyise 1995, 106). In Revelation, such connections regularly involve two images, one seen and one heard, that allude to different Old Testament texts. For example, in chapter 5, John juxtaposes the auditory image of the 'Lion of the tribe of Judah, the Root of David' (itself already a combination of allusions to Gen 49 and Isa 11) with the visual image of a sacrificial Lamb. As we will see in more detail in the commentary on that chapter, the result of this intertextual combination is not the replacement of 'Lion' with 'Lamb' (so Caird 1984, 75) but a newly forged—and *redoubled*—Christological image, as each allusion interprets the other. New combinations and contexts, then, create something fresh and surprising, something that is both the same and very different to the source texts and that returns us to those sources with a transformed interpretative universe.

Second, and more briefly, John not only alludes to Old Testament phrases or images but also echoes broader theological and narrative patterns. This, too, is a feature of ancient Jewish scribal practices, which made use of verbal correspondences between source texts and of correspondences in narrative structures, theological themes, and motifs (and possibly, as we have already seen, stylistic features). John demonstrates a similar affinity for such allusions, for example, in the use of Ezekiel 38–48 in Revelation's closing chapters, which pick up Ezekiel's eschatological temple imagery and trace a similar narrative arc at a broader level. In some accounts (e.g., Moyise 1995, 74–5), the structure of Ezekiel *as a whole* is echoed across the twenty-two chapters of Revelation. To bring in a more contemporary analysis, Michelle Fletcher reads John's multivalent allusive practice through the lens of *pastiche*. Though the label is sometimes used disparagingly (to imply a hodgepodge or clumsy imitation of traditions), it more accurately describes how a text imitates and combines parts of a tradition in intertextual and multivalent ways, forging new meanings that are simultaneously alike and different and inviting the reader into this universe of 'hypertextuality' (Fletcher 2017, drawing on the work of Gérard Genette), or into what Moyise calls a dialogue with and between texts. There are important differences between these proposals, and many other options besides, but the basic interpretative conviction remains clear: we must resist flat, prosaic, univocal readings and instead seek to expound the multiply resonant nature of John's creative use of the Old Testament. Revelation is a remarkable work of literary and theological creativity, and this commentary will attend to these allusions and combinations throughout, though we will, inevitably, merely scratch the surface.

A final comment is in order on the question of Revelation's intertextual relationships, not with the Old Testament but the New. In this commentary, I will regularly observe theological and thematic connections between Revelation and other New Testament writings; as such, this is something of a canonical reading. Here we are much more in the realm of considering intertextuality as a readerly phenomenon rather than an authorial one. Comments on theological connections between Revelation and other New Testament texts, then, are not intended as suggestions of common authorship (in the case of other Johannine texts) or implications of historical derivation. Rather, they are an attempt to hear the dialogue between Revelation and all the voices of Scripture, and not just those of the Old Testament. If Revelation is to be read in the literary and theological universe in which it is now found (namely, the New Testament as part of the whole Christian Scriptures), we are well served, I think, by noting such connections unapologetically. This is, after all, a narrative *and theological* commentary. And so my final task in this introduction is to explain more fully what I mean by that.

Introduction

Reading Revelation Theologically

The apparently simple statement that 'God reveals himself' is certainly one that John of Patmos would affirm, and here it will be the touchstone for what we mean by a *theological* commentary. Already in this introduction we have indicated a range of important theological themes and some of the ways these intersect with our narrative approach to Revelation. We close here with a reflection on what it means to read Revelation theologically. Once again, John's opening paragraph will serve as our guide (such that, again, form and content meet, and our theological method aims to correspond to Revelation's message).

> The revelation of Jesus Christ, which God gave him to show his servants what must soon take place; he made it known by sending his angel to his servant John, who testified to the word of God and to the testimony of Jesus Christ, even to all that he saw. Blessed is the one who reads aloud the words of the prophecy, and blessed are those who hear and who keep what is written in it; for the time is near. (Rev 1.1–3)

'Revelation of Jesus Christ': Reading Revelation as Divine Self-disclosure
First, *God* reveals himself. An apocalyptic reading of Revelation, at least as I understand the term, does not merely acknowledge the book's literary connections to the Jewish and Christian apocalypses but also begins with the theological claim that it is God who is the source of this apocalypse, who gave this revelation. Theological commentary is, then, an act of response to divine self-disclosure. Too often this theological goal is framed in addition, competition, or even outright antithesis, with the tasks of historical analysis. But for those who approach the text as Holy Scripture, as I do, this need not be so. The historical artefact that is the text of John's Apocalypse is not merely a work of literature that can sufficiently be accounted for with the tools of literary analysis but is, within the divine economy, the creaturely locus of God's self-revelation. Because this is true, a theological reading is by no means a secondary 'layer' of interpretation (as if one could begin somewhere 'neutral,' and comment on Revelation's historical or literary features, before offering some subsequent 'theological interpretation') but is the proper response to what the text *is*. This is not, then, a literary commentary accompanied by theological reflections, as if those were two logically separable movements, but a literary *and* theological commentary (and it is literary because it is theological). In the pages that follow, therefore, you will not find a separation between comments on the historical/literary aspects of

the text and its theology (as one often finds in commentaries). Rather, these two will be interwoven throughout.

Because the emphasis falls on the text as the locus of God's self-revelation, reading Revelation is not so much an act of analytical reading and writing as it is one of proper hearing and testimony. This commentary is an attempt to hear 'what the Spirit is saying to the churches' (Rev 2.7, 11, 17, 29; 3.6, 13, 22) and to respond appropriately. The interpreter does not seek to become a 'master' of the text through technical skill and analytical dissection but (following the example of John, who himself follows Jesus) 'testif[ies] to the word of God' (1.2, cf. 22.20). The goal of interpretation, as I understand it, is to enter into relationship with this speaking God, to be faithful in receiving the gift of divine address, and to be faithful in responding as a witness to it. This is by no means the only way of reading Revelation, but it is a fitting hermeneutical stance when reading and writing on this book, for, as we shall see, 'faithful witness' is a theme that runs throughout.

Second, God *reveals* himself. This is certainly an apt theological starting point for a book that begins with the word *apokalypsis*, 'revelation' (Rev 1.1). God *reveals*. The book of Revelation is a 'word of prophecy' (1.3) not merely in its generic form but in its theological purpose, as a divine word of address. As John's apocalyptic brother Daniel confesses, 'there is a God in heaven who reveals mysteries' (Dan 2.28). Divine revelation is the epistemological *sine qua non* of all apocalyptic thought, and to say this is not merely to make a literary/generic claim but a theological one, with a number of implications for the task of commentary.

Because God reveals—and as he reveals—God also redeems, and by his Spirit God enables human ears to hear what he is saying. Any theological reading, then, begins with this double confession: God has spoken, and he has, by his Spirit, enabled 'his servants' (and not only 'his servant John') to hear. This commentary, then, begins by understanding the book of Revelation within the divine economy as an act of revelation and redemption. The foregoing comments on reading the book of Revelation as literature are therefore to be understood not only as an analysis of human writing, culture, and tradition but also as the proper disciplined attention to the text as a created instrument, medium, and locus of divine communication. This theological posture is by no means an excuse for laziness, passivity, or confessional circularity. Commentary, as I have said, is an act of attempting to hear and to confess 'what the Spirit is saying to the churches' through the text, and so this act of hearing and confession is a creaturely act, involving all of the skills of grammatical analysis, historical enquiry, and literary sensitivity that one finds in modern commentary. But these rational acts of the commentator as creature are also (or at least should be) understood within and directed toward the divine economy of revelation and redemption. Commentary, therefore, must attend to such matters of language, history, and literature, but it must do more. As vital as those matters are for faithful reading, and for taking seriously the human character of the text, they are, theologically speaking, penultimate and insufficient. To limit commentary to such things restricts the commentator to the task of description rather than interpretation (and too many modern commentaries, it seems to me, stop short at description). If this is truly to be a literary *and theological* commentary, we must not merely describe but interpret and thus engage in the task of God-talk, guided and constrained by the text of Revelation.

Third, God reveals *himself.* God is both the source of this revelation and its chief subject matter. Revelation is a book that speaks of many things, things past, present, and future, but it is primarily a book about God—how easily we forget this! Divine revelation is divine self-revelation, God's self-expression in and through his Word. The book of Revelation wonderfully encapsulates this truth in the ambiguity of the book's opening genitive construction: *apokalypsis Iēsou Christou,* 'revelation of Jesus Christ' (1.1). I will shortly offer an interpretation of this ambiguity from a grammatical and syntactical perspective, arguing that the book's first verse indicates that Jesus is the source of the revelation. As a rubric for the book as a whole, however, we may interpret the 'revelation of Jesus Christ' as both a genitive of source and an objective genitive. This book is a revelation that comes *from* Jesus Christ, as its source, but that is also a revelation *of* Jesus Christ, as its object. In respect of the latter, Christian commentary on Revelation must attend to what the text has said, and what it says, about Jesus. To state briefly what is explored in more detail at various points in the commentary, Revelation depicts Jesus as participating in the identity of God. As such, the 'revelation of Jesus Christ' is divine self-revelation.

'What Must Soon Take Place': Divine Sovereignty and Eschatology

So far this introduction, including these comments on the task of theological interpretation, has taken the form of an extended reflection on Revelation's prologue. However, two phrases in that prologue have yet to receive our attention: John tells us his book is a revelation to God's servants of 'what must soon take place' (1.1) and then pronounces a blessing not only on the reading but also the hearing and keeping of this prophecy, because 'the time is near' (1.3). We will close by attending to both of these phrases in turn.

'God reveals himself' is by no means Revelation's only apocalyptic theological conviction. A crucial theological question that runs through the book is 'to whom does the sovereignty of the world belong?' This was a fundamental theological question raised by Ernst Käsemann, who saw it as the driving question of apocalyptic thought (1969, 135). Though Käsemann's attention was largely focussed on the theology of the apostle Paul, this generative apocalyptic question is also at the heart of the book of Revelation. The book makes its answer abundantly clear in every cycle of images: though the world is a site of cosmic battle, its sovereignty is not in doubt, for it belongs to God. As we will see, there are various depictions of idolatrous claims to usurp this sovereignty on the part of a range of figures, but through all of this Revelation does not depict a comic dualism, a world in which the equal and opposite forces of 'good versus evil' or 'light versus darkness' are locked in conflict, with the outcome hanging in the balance. From beginning to end, it is clear that God is on the throne, ruling the world with justice and righteousness. There are certainly apocalyptic battles playing out in heaven and on earth, but these are set against this backdrop of the essential cosmological truth of a divinely ruled world, a theme that frames each visionary cycle.

'Apocalyptic,' Käsemann famously claimed, is the 'mother of all Christian theology' (1969, 102). By this he meant the more specific issue of apocalyptic eschatology in post-Easter faith, but I think it applies more broadly to apocalyptic thought in all its dimensions: not only eschatology but cosmology, epistemology, soteriology, and more. Revelation has much to say about all of these things and illustrates the importance of the texture of apocalyptic thought, apocalyptic eschatology in particular, in early Christian theology. Though Revelation is clear that God is sovereign, the cosmic battles against the powers challenging his rule are very real, and so the promise of a divinely ruled world remains, at least from an earthly perspective, in the future. The subaltern martyrs express this eschatological tension when they declare the truth of God's sovereignty while also confessing their desire for that sovereignty to be fully realised in an unjust world: 'Sovereign Lord, holy and true, how long will it be before you judge and avenge our blood on the inhabitants of the earth?' (6.10). This question 'how long' is the apocalyptic eschatological question of the church living under the conditions of the end. Revelation's answer is as simple as it is perplexing: 'the time is near.'

Thus the book of Revelation, like much of the New Testament, is shaped by an eschatological tension: the declaration of God's sovereign rule and the imminent anticipation of its coming. For Käsemann, it was exactly this eschatological imminence that birthed all Christian theology, and in some accounts it is the fundamental theme and heartbeat of apocalyptic thought (though, as we have seen, this honour perhaps belongs more to the theme of divine revelation). This apocalyptic eschatology is often expressed as a dualistic tension between 'two ages,' a present age characterised by sin and injustice in the world and a glorious 'age to come' in which God's sovereign rule is made fully and finally effective. The apocalypse of *4 Ezra* expresses this eschatological dualism: when it says 'the Most High has made not one world but two' (*4 Ez* 7.50). In Christian adaptations of this Jewish apocalyptic eschatology, the inauguration of God's rule in the Christ-event creates an 'eschatological tension,' usually encapsulated in the phrase 'now and not yet.' Although this 'inaugurated eschatology' is certainly a major feature of the New Testament's apocalyptic thought, Revelation included, we do well to note that it is not only a Christian phenomenon, though one regularly hears this claimed. The situation is complex, since there were various eschatological schemes in the writings of the second temple period, but in some Jewish apocalyptic literature we find expressions of a similar 'eschatological tension,' the presence of the 'age to come' amid the present age. Though undoubtedly Revelation's Christological shaping of this theme is a uniquely Christian one, present and future intertwine in various ways in the eschatological hopes of John's Jewish contemporaries, too.

In contrast to many of his interpreters, John of Patmos is not driven by an interest in eschatological speculation or in setting a timeline for the end. He is, however, very concerned with the imminence of God's coming and with faithful living in the light of that imminent arrival. The hope for an imminent coming of God's righteous judgement and rule is one that also profoundly shapes the message of the minor prophets. Joel, Amos, and Malachi provide the language of the 'last days' and the 'Day of the Lord,' as well as the apocalyptic imagery that fills the eschatological discourse not only of Revelation but also of the Gospels (e.g., the synoptic apocalypse, Mt 24 // Mk 13 // Lk 21), Acts (e.g., Peter's speech in Acts 2), and the Pauline letters (e.g., 1 Thess 5). Though long expected, it is a Day that comes suddenly, like a thief, like the sounding of a battle-trumpet, with the darkening of sun and a moon turned to blood. It is a Day, soon coming, when there will be justice and restoration on the earth, and suffering, injustice, and all kinds of evil will be dealt with once and for all. And, at the heart of all this, it will be a Day of the Lord's presence on earth, come to conquer his enemies and bring in his righteous rule. This prophetic hope shapes the eschatological vision of Revelation (as it does much, if not all, of the New Testament) and constitutes the definitive answer to the question 'to whom does the sovereignty of the world belong?'

But if John's vision concerns 'what must soon take place,' what does this 'soon' mean? Here we join the subaltern voices in asking 'how long?' Like an impatient child on a long car journey, we receive the same (non) answer they did: 'a little longer' (6.11). Here we find ourselves in need of a proper theology of time and of the relationship between earthly time and divine time. This relationship cannot be expressed with a timeline, however 'inaugurated' it may be or however we might extend it into the future, for there is an 'infinite qualitative distinction' between time and eternity. The 'time of God' (the 'soon' time of his coming) intersects with the time of earth but cannot be marked on our calendars or plotted on our timelines. Rather, despite the infinite distinction between our life and God's, in the incarnation of Jesus Christ (his 'first' coming), God has gathered human time to himself—human time assumed into the life of God—and in this way we may speak of the 'nearness' of the Day of the Lord. In order to speak of such things we must, once again, maintain a 'double vision,' viewing this eschatological 'soon' from both earthly and heavenly perspectives. As we have already discussed, the apocalyptic imagery and nonlinear narrative of Revelation provide us with a unique combination of imaginative resources with which to do this. We will see visions from the perspective of heaven, which display God's 'already' rule. And we will see visions of the 'not yet,' of God's rule contested on earth as his enemies seek to oppress and to conquer his people. These images can be seen simultaneously, doubly. We will also, however, see visions of the consummation of God's rule, the uniting of those two realms, of heaven and earth come together in a final embrace, and the Day of God's coming and his sovereign presence in the world. And such images shape the theological imagination of the church as it lives in the 'time that remains between time and its end' (Agamben 2005, 62), which is, as we will now discuss, a time for faithful witness.

'Keep What Is Written . . . for the Time Is Near': The Church as Witness in the Time that Remains

Although the prologue to John's book pronounces a blessing on 'those who hear and who keep what is written in it; for the time is near' (Rev 1.3), what Revelation will not give us is a timeline. We will not be provided with an answer concerning the quantity of the 'end time,' though we are told much about its quality, and it is this that informs Revelation's message to the churches, both in first-century Asia Minor and throughout the world today. The revelation of the 'soon' coming of God transforms the present time, the time that remains between the coming of Christ and his glorious return, into a time of eschatological anticipation, of *expectation*. It is the time of expectation in which the church lives, and Revelation will have much to say about what that means for its life. However, this time of expectation is not to be understood as a time of quietistic *waiting* for the end, but rather a time for faithful *witness*. As John goes on to describe in the vision of chapter 6, the subaltern martyrs are 'told to rest a little longer, until the number would be complete both of their fellow servants and of their brothers and sisters, who were soon to be killed as they themselves had been killed' (6.11). This word 'witness' (*martys, martyria, martyreō*) is ubiquitous in Revelation and central not only to its depiction of Jesus but also of the people of God. Like John, who was on Patmos 'because of the word of God and the testimony (*martyria*) of Jesus' (1.9), the church's calling in the 'time of the end' (Agamben 2005, 62) is to bear witness to Jesus, indeed to share in his faithful witness, and through this testimony also share in his victory (12.11). This is by no means an endorsement of Christian dominionism, as the nature of the various visions of God's people will make abundantly clear, for this witness on earth is depicted as a suffering witness. In God's mercy, this time of suffering witness is a time 'cut short for the sake of the elect,' as Jesus put it in his own apocalyptic discourse (Mt 24.22; Mk 13.20) and as Revelation's imagery expresses in various ways. The eschatological 'soon' does not mean that God's sovereignty is deferred. Rather, he remains sovereign over even the length of these days of witness, which will not last a moment longer than he desires. The 'time of the end' will be cut short, and then it will be the time of the coming of God, which is the end of time. Revelation is a message for those who live in the interlude between those two 'times.'

Revelation echoes the prophets and speaks regularly of God as *the one who comes*, but it does so in ways that frustrate human attempts to plot the life of God on our timelines. We can trace the contours of this theological challenge in another short phrase in the prologue, which names the Lord not as 'the one who is, who was, and *who will be*' (although that would have been more grammatically symmetrical) but as the one 'who is, who was, and who is *the coming one (ho erchomenos)*' (Rev 1.4 AT). This threefold 'time signature' (itself repeated three times, 1.4, 8; 4.8) rhymes with the threefold life of God, as one who has come, comes, and will come again. Seen from the earthly perspective, these three distinguishable 'comings' might be intelligible as different 'events' on a chronological timeline, as past, present, and future. But when viewed from a heavenly perspective (and Revelation will give us this perspective too), they are not three separate events but three interrelated forms of the one 'coming' of God. God's past coming in the incarnation of Christ, his present coming by the Spirit, and his future coming in consummation are all united as the one and the same apocalyptic event. Seen from this perspective, it is clear that the threefold divine life cannot simply be plotted straightforwardly with the three tenses of creaturely history. Rather, God simply is 'the coming one' who comes to history and assumes it.

Likewise, Revelation bears repeated witness to Christ as 'the coming one.' He is the Son of Man who comes on the clouds of heaven (1.7 cf. Dan 7.13), the one who warns the seven churches that he will come to them (2.5, 16, 25; 3.3, 11, 20), and the who closes the book with his thrice-repeated promise 'I am coming soon' (22.7, 12, 20). Again, whatever this 'soon' means, we must not attempt simply to plot it on the chronology of this world but seek to understand it with the life of God who is 'the coming one,' who came in the incarnation of Jesus, comes to us now by the Spirit, and will come again as sovereign of the world. These three 'tenses' of God's coming are, theologically speaking, three ways of saying the same thing: he is, as Revelation 1.4 puts it, the one 'who is, who was, and who is to come.' In the end, Revelation's primary message for the church, which is the appropriate theological response to Jesus's words 'surely I am coming soon,' is not to ask 'when?' but to bear faithful witness to his soon coming and to give voice to the church's cry, 'Amen. Come, Lord Jesus!' (22.20).

Prologue and Opening Vision
Revelation 1.1–20

Prologue, 1.1–3

The first verse of a biblical book often provides us with its title, or some formulaic opening appropriate to the genre. A psalm might open with 'a Psalm of David,' a prophecy with 'the words of Amos' or 'the vision of Isaiah,' and the New Testament letters regularly begin with epistolary greetings naming author and recipients. Though it might appear similar, the opening verse of the book of Revelation is not such a formula. Although (as we will see in v. 3) John sees himself standing within the prophetic tradition, he does not open his book with 'the words of John' or 'the vision of John.' And although he will soon deploy the standard greeting formula of a letter, that too is deferred, so that his own name does not come first. Revelation's first three words are not, then, a title or a formula but rather an encapsulation of the theological purpose of the whole book: *apokalypsis Iēsou Christou*, 'Revelation of Jesus Christ.' We have already reflected on the importance of this opening phrase, and indeed the whole of this opening paragraph, for the task of theological commentary and for theology in general. John begins textually where we must all begin theologically: with *apokalypsis*, with revelation.

Later scholarship would identify a family resemblance between this book and other similar literature written in the second temple period and would borrow this first word 'apocalypse' to label this revelatory genre of literature. But it is not what John means when he begins this way, and we miss too much of the power of the first line if we reduce it to a formulaic genre label. It is, rather, a statement of the book's primary theological purpose: the disclosure of hidden things. The book of Daniel, the other canonical apocalypse, indicates the theological foundation of such writings when it declares that 'there is a God in heaven who reveals mysteries' (Dan 2.28). John would agree, but what he is about to write is more specific about the source of this revelation: this is a revelation of Jesus Christ. The hidden things that will be revealed are the hidden things of Jesus.

There is a measure of grammatical ambiguity in this opening phrase, since one might take 'revelation of Jesus Christ' to mean either that Jesus is the object of revelation or its subject/source. Careful attention to how this phrase fits in the whole of this first verse, however, makes it clear that we are dealing with some version of the latter. Jesus is the source of the revelation, or rather it is he who has received this revelation from God and shows it to his people through an angelic intermediary and his servant John, forming a chain of revelatory transmission (see Bauckham 1993, 1) that connects the reader to God. It is important to remember, as we journey with John and his angelic guide, that they form two links in this revelatory chain that joins them to Jesus and to the God in heaven who reveals mysteries. Toward the end of the book, John will be reminded by the angel that he too is merely a fellow servant (19.10), testifying to Jesus. Likewise, John's role, and that of the churches to whom he writes, is to testify, to bear witness 'to the word of God and to the testimony of Jesus Christ.' Like his namesake in the Gospels, John's role is to 'bear witness to the light,' to point his finger at Christ and declare, 'behold the Lamb of God' (Jn 1.7, 29). The Greek word *martyres*, from which we get 'martyr,' is only derivatively to do with death; first and foremost it is about testimony. There are some whose testimony will lead to death (like Antipas in 2.13, whom Jesus calls 'my witness, my faithful one,' or those beheaded for the 'testimony of Jesus' in 20.4), but all are called to be witnesses. As we will soon see, the theme of faithful testimony will run like a thread through the whole book and is one of the primary ways in which the churches are joined to Christ. Jesus is the faithful witness, and John's vocation as a servant of Jesus Christ, a vocation shared by the whole church, is to bear witness to him.

But this witness of John concerning what he saw, and the witness of the church to Jesus, is first a testimony to the witness of Jesus Christ concerning himself, and it is perhaps this sense that comes to the fore here in verse 2. In Revelation 19.10, John's guiding angel will echo these opening words and tell him that 'the testimony of Jesus is the spirit of prophecy.' In the book as a whole, Jesus is not only the source of John's revelation but also its primary object and content, and the power behind the words of this prophecy. He is both the revealer and the revealed, the source and content of the divine mysteries. What John will hear and see is both the testimony of heaven and earth concerning Jesus and Jesus's testimony about himself, but the former is logically and utterly dependent on the latter. We are well served in interpreting this bewildering book if we remember this double Christological focus.

Having said all that, the opening verse of the book also declares more specifically that what is given to Jesus to show his servants concerns 'what must soon take place.' Unlike Daniel, who is told to seal up his book since it concerned a distant time of the end (Dan 8.26; 12.4), John's vision concerns that which is coming 'soon.' Revelation's numerous allusions to Daniel, Zechariah, Isaiah, and others make it clear: the 'last days' about which the prophets spoke are not a distant hope but are near, and as such the book is meant to have immediate significance for John's contemporary churches, not some distant generation. However, what is meant by 'soon' must be understood in the light of the theology of the book as a whole, including its construal of time and the relationship between heaven and earth. Several possible errors present themselves, and the contested history of Revelation's interpretation is partly a function of how one interprets 'soon.' We might take it, simply and unambiguously, to indicate the months and years that followed the book's composition. Seen in this way, what is to 'take place' are the tumultuous events occurring among Christ's followers in late first-century and early second-century Asia Minor, *and nothing more*. We might believe that these things were fulfilled, or we might read the book with hindsight as a witness to a misplaced Christian millenarian hope, but in either case there is the error of reading 'soon' as a mere chronological designation. An opposite error, however, would to parse it as some kind of 'spiritual' metaphor, without any connection to the timeline of earthly history, and explain it as something like the ever-present 'soon' of Christian experience. Or we might view 'soon' as really meaning 'in another two thousand years,' however unlikely it is that John's first hearers would reach that conclusion (usually bringing in a somewhat tortured exegesis of 2 Pet 3.8). A proper account of what it meant for John to say 'soon' must take seriously the world of his contemporary audience without limiting the meaning of the visionary time of the book to a this-worldly, immanent (or imminent!) chronology. It will also recognise that the 'soonness' of John's view of time has more to do with its theological quality than its chronological passage (Yong 2021, 30). We will have much more to learn about Revelation's complex understanding of time as his visions unfold.

The book of Revelation pronounces seven blessings in its pages (1.3; 14.13; 16.15; 19.9; 20.6; 22.7, 14; see, e.g., Aune 2017, 22f.; Mounce 1998, 43). We find the first in verse 3, as the prologue closes, and it is echoed (like so much in this opening chapter) at the end of the book, in the penultimate blessing of 22.7. Two categories of people are named in this benediction, beginning with 'the one who reads aloud.' As discussed in the introduction, the book would likely have been read aloud by an individual to a gathered church, an exercise that takes about an hour. It's difficult to reach any convincing conclusions about what such a reading may have been like, but the form and content of the book, combined with a certain amount of historical imagination, suggest a liturgical setting, such that the book functioned as part of the church's worship. Worship is certainly an important theme of the book, and there are many indications of what might be its liturgical use (the use of songs, prayers, call and response, and so on). The liturgical reading of the book in its entirety is, sadly, rare in the church today, but it is a practice that is still found in the Coptic Orthodox Church, where one will hear such a liturgical/performative reading of Revelation each year on 'Apocalypse Saturday' (the Saturday of Easter; see introduction). In any case, the reader/performer of the book is blessed here by John.

Along with the reader, the second group upon whom a benediction is pronounced are those 'who hear and keep what is written.' The proper response to the reading of the word of God is both hearing and keeping, a double response that brings blessing, as Jesus himself declared (Lk 11.28) in one of many beatitudes he pronounced during his earthly ministry. This blessing reminds us that the revelation in these pages is not primarily a puzzle to be solved (though it will certainly invite the engagement of the reader's mind) but a word to be heard and kept. It is not merely a coded prediction of future events (though it will also speak of such things) but a call to a life of obedience and to the faithful witness and endurance of the saints in the present. This is what it means to 'keep' these words.

In this benediction, John's book is explicitly designated as a *prophecy*, and the prologue closes, echoing its opening verse, with the words 'for the time is near.' John's book is intended to be read not merely as a participant in the great prophetic tradition but as its climax (hence the title of Richard Bauckham's collection of essays on Revelation: *The Climax of Prophecy*). In most prophecy, the primary audience is the contemporary inhabitants of the world of the prophet, and Revelation is no different. His first-century hearers are blessed because they are those who have a share in these climactic days: hearers who are, as Paul puts it, those 'on whom the ends of the ages have come' (1 Cor 10.11). But Revelation, also in line with the biblical prophetic tradition, has a meaning that spills over from that contemporary time and place to times and places beyond the prophet's horizon. The pronouncement 'the time is near,' with which John closes his benediction, was an important part of Jesus's message when on earth (Mk 1.14–15). Again, this is not simply a chronological statement, as if Jesus were merely announcing that the sands of time were running out, but an eschatological and theological pronouncement: the appointed *kairos* time has come near. God, who hold all times in his hand, is acting decisively in and through his Son. In him, the chronological history of this world is embraced and taken up into the divine life, and thereby transformed. This is not so much 'time running out' as 'time being fulfilled.' As such, we can no longer read the 'nearness' of what is revealed in the book of Revelation in such a way as to plot its events on the linear schemes of earthly chronological time. Instead, we must become and remain sensitive to its claims concerning divine eschatological action and the fulfilment of God's purposes for his world, as in Christ time's fulfilment has come 'near' to the world of the first century and the twenty-first.

Epistolary Greeting, 1.4–8

As well as signaling some of its key theological themes, the prologue of the book of Revelation has indicated something of the genres in which it participates. It is an apocalypse and a prophecy. But in this next section we find the hallmarks of a third genre of writing: the letter. As was customary in contemporary letter-writing, John identifies himself as the author and names his audience, the 'seven churches that are in Asia.' Unlike most of the letters of the New Testament, Revelation is not addressed to one church or individual but to seven: it is a circular letter. But the historical identification of these seven churches in what is now southern Turkey does not do justice to the way language works in this book. The number seven speaks also of totality or completeness, and as such we can consider this to be something of an 'encyclical' that addresses the whole church, not just these seven. That is not to say that we have nothing to learn from attention to the historical situation of these specific communities: far from it. We will dig deeper into these historical details further below, but for now it suffices to make the point that Revelation's nature as a letter means that attention to the historical situation of sender and receiver is an important part of interpreting the book. Whatever else it may have to say, this is an address to a particular group of early Christian communities in first-century Asia Minor and would have had significance for their time, not only the distant future.

There then follows a familiar epistolary greeting, 'grace to you and peace.' Familiar, that is, to those who know the New Testament letters. The standard Greek greeting would likely have been simply *chairein*, 'greetings,' though in many Christian correspondence the related (but more theologically significant) word *charis*, 'grace,' is used. The combination of this with 'peace' (*eirēnē*, suggestive of Hebrew *shalom*) is a particularly Christian innovation.

But even in this most formulaic of Christian epistolary greetings, there is remarkable imagery and theological depth. As one commonly finds in Paul's letters, the source of this 'grace and peace' is named as God, but the manner in which John does this is characteristically complex. John embroiders the stock fabric of his epistolary introduction with images that will be developed later in the book. In so doing, the grace and peace invoked by John are not merely deployed as a standard greeting formula but are put to profound theological service. His greeting is connected to a threefold designation of God, the ultimate source of grace and peace. Each designation both alludes to the Old Testament and foreshadows the visionary material to come.

First, grace and peace are from 'him who is and who was and who is to come.' This designation foreshadows the benediction at the end of this greeting (1.8), and John will repeat it in various ways elsewhere in the book (e.g., in 4.8; 11.17; 16.5). Two worlds collide in this phrase. For many of his readers, the phrase would have echoed a common praise of Zeus ('Zeus was, Zeus is, Zeus shall be,' Pausanias, *Descr.* 10.12.10), and in so doing challenged its validity. It is also an allusion to the divine name revealed to Moses in Exodus 3.14, though John expands it to include two more phrases. In this expansion (and not for the last time), his expression seems to be straining against the rules of Greek grammar and style to express the eternality of the One God of Israel. It is interesting that the phrasing, which adds notions of past and future, changes the expected 'who is'/'was'/'shall be' to 'who is'/'was'/'is *to come*,' though perhaps a better translation of this last word (*erchomenos*, a present participle in the Greek) is 'the coming one.' God is not simply the one who 'will be,' enduring eternally and apparently disinterested in this ephemeral world, but the one who is, who was, and who is continually coming to us.

Second are 'the seven spirits who are before his throne.' John's greeting is the only one of this sort in the New Testament to include the Spirit. We have not yet seen the throne or met the 'seven spirits' who are before it; John is again foreshadowing the visionary material to come. The phrase 'seven spirits' will be used four times, here and at 3.1, 4.5, and 5.6. The naming of seven spirits, rather than one, might suggest it is not the Holy Spirit who is in view here but some other figures. But again this is to misread the way numbers work in Revelation. The aim is not to enumerate but to convey the theological significance of the imagery. John is alluding to the seven lamps on the singular lampstand in the vision of Zechariah 4, a chapter that will be significant in various places, not least in the throne vision of chapters 4–5 and when John is describing the activity of the Spirit of God (4.5; 5.6; cf. Zech 4.6). When read together with similar imagery elsewhere in the book of Revelation as well as the seven lamps in Zechariah, the 'seven spirits' speak of the totality of the vision, might, and power of the Spirit of God in his churches and throughout the earth, indicated by its fourfold use (see Bauckham 1998, 35). The grace and peace pronounced on the sevenfold church comes from the sevenfold Spirit who is at work among them.

Third, the one named as the source of grace and peace is Jesus Christ himself, who is described in a threefold pattern foreshadowing Christological imagery from elsewhere in the letter: 'the faithful witness, the firstborn of the dead, and the ruler of the kings of the earth.' Jesus will soon speak of himself as the one who was dead and is alive (1.18) and the 'faithful and true witness' (3.14). The declaration of his rule over the 'kings of the earth' is significant, for in the later chapters of the book these characters will ally themselves with God's enemies and take the field against Christ. Yet here in John's opening greeting there is a signal that even these are, in the end, subject to the true king. As we will see, challenges to his rule are no challenges at all. Like the 'kings of the earth' of Psalm 2, their conspiracy against the Lord's anointed is in vain, for his son is already installed on the throne. These three designations thus summarise the career of Jesus, speaking of his earthly ministry as witness, his death and resurrection, and his present reign. The sequence of testimony, death, resurrection, and rule is also Revelation's pattern for Christian discipleship, as we will see.

This discussion highlights John's remarkable theological and literary artistry in making a standard epistolary formula rich with intertextual allusion and theological depth, naming the singular source of grace and peace as the creating, covenant God, the life of the Spirit, and the risen king Jesus. We should be wary of imposing anachronistic patristic and Trinitarian categories here, but John's threefold designation sets the mind on a trajectory to consider the implications of this for his understanding of the identity of the one God.

John's prologue and greeting are then followed by a doxology, the only one in the whole New Testament explicitly offered to Jesus. He is blessed for his love, for his work of deliverance from sin by his blood, and for his establishment of his people as a kingdom of priests. There are early indications here that Revelation will show how Jesus's twofold office of king and priest is one that he shares with his people (cf. 5.10). This connection between the life of the church and the life of Jesus will shape much of what is to come.

We have already encountered a tapestry of Christological themes in the opening verses of this book: Jesus is both the revealer and the revelation, the faithful witness, the deliverer of his people, and the ruler of the world. It is this Jesus who comes to his people. John expresses this eschatological hope as he closes his prologue, greeting, and doxology with a hymn of praise. John's language here is thick with allusions to the vision of Daniel 7.13–14, which concerns the judgement of idolatrous kingdoms and the Son of Man 'coming with the clouds of heaven' to receive dominion, and to Zechariah 12, which speaks of the coming 'day of the Lord' and the resulting lament over 'the one they have pierced.' The hymn, then, concerns the hope of God's coming to unseat idolatrous rule and bring justice to his world through his anointed. No wonder John ends with an 'Amen.' This hymn is not a dislocated acclamation, with John suddenly pivoting to the future and a hope postponed, but a song of praise to the almighty God whose reign is both present in Jesus and remains the hope for a world abused by idolatrous kingdoms.

Forming a pair with verse 4, verse 8 bookends the passage with a restatement of God's 'name' as the one who is, was, and is perpetually coming to his people. This is now combined with a second self-designation: 'the Alpha and Omega,' the first and last letters of the Greek alphabet and a clear image of God's nature as the beginning and end of all things. The eternal God does not have a 'beginning' or 'end' in the way that earthly time does, being characterised by such limits. But nor should we view his eternity as perpetual timelessness. Rather, his eternity is the gathering together of beginning, middle, and end into the pure duration of his life. He does not have limits but simply *is* the Alpha and Omega because he possesses all endings and all beginnings without being conditioned by them, and is the ground and Lord of time as we know it.

These two phrases in 1.8, and one more similar one, are found in various combinations at either end of the book of Revelation. As well as this expression here near the beginning of the book, the phrase 'first and last' is found on Jesus's lips in 1.17. At the other end of the book, in 21.6, God speaks again and names himself as 'the Alpha and the Omega, the beginning and the end.' And finally, as the book closes, it is Christ who describes himself with a combination of all three: 'I am the Alpha and the Omega, the first and the last, the beginning and the end' (22.13). This fourfold self-designation forms a pattern that speaks of John's understanding of the identity of Christ: in short, he is who God is (see Bauckham 1993, 25–26). The implications for how we understand 'eternity' in the light of these Christological self-designations are profound. In Jesus Christ the eternal God has taken earthly time, including the tensed experience of past, present, and future, into himself, embracing it and making it part of his divine life.

Vision of Christ, 1.9–20

Instruction to Write, vv. 9-11

At this point, the complex braided genre of the book of Revelation takes another turn. After the epistolary opening of verses 4–8, John now shifts to a first-person account of a visionary experience, the standard fare of much apocalyptic literature. We do well to remember, though, that this visionary report nests within the letter form opened in the preceding verses. Though the majority of the book will be characterised by the imagery and literary conventions of the prophetic and apocalyptic literature, John is still writing a letter to the churches of Asia Minor.

Right at the start of this section, however, he departs from apocalyptic convention in a significant respect. Usually an apocalypse is composed pseudepigraphally, written under another name. Often the name chosen would be that of a long-departed saint (such as Enoch or Baruch) in order to give the vision a character of ancient revelation concerning the far future, which is now the present and imminent future for the recipients of the book. John does not use this narrative technique. As he did in the letter opening, he identifies himself as the recipient of the vision, and there are a number of reasons for this. First, as we will see, this vision does not primarily concern the far future. Though visions of the end will come to John, his revelation is not one that is to be sealed up for a distant generation; it speaks to the church of his day. Second, it is likely that John was well known to these churches as a prophet, and so there is no need to appeal to the authority of an assumed authorial voice. His solidarity with and pastoral concern for his churches are evident here, and John immediately describes himself as their brother and a 'co-sharer.' He does not stand over his communities but stands with them. He wants the churches to know that he shares their experiences. John is no detached seer, dispensing sage advice and profound visions from the blissful seclusion of an island retreat. His vision comes to him in the trenches with the churches, as he shares with them the call to testify to Jesus and notes the persecution that sometimes comes with it. John is careful to indicate that his 'co-sharing' with the churches is no mere human solidarity. It is 'in Jesus' that John and the churches share the persecution, the kingdom, and the call to endurance. Their union with Christ, the true witness and true king, is the theological reality that underpins their existence, and it is in him that Christian fellowship transcends mere human affection or solidarity.

Persecution and patient endurance are not the only thing he shares with them, however. Sandwiched between these two is a reminder that the church also shares in the kingdom as a present reality. This incongruous combination should catch our attention: patient endurance and persecution are not the opposite of participating in the reign of God but are its very character in this world. As Revelation will show repeatedly, in a world seemingly run by powers opposed to Christ's reign, suffering and the kingdom go together; the primary response required of those who recognise Jesus's reign is therefore 'patient endurance.' Indeed, in the Greek here there is only one article attached to all three words, and so a better translation would be 'the persecution, kingdom, and patient endurance.' The three come as a package deal, both grammatically and theologically. This is the first of seven mentions of *hypomonē*, 'endurance,' in Revelation, and, together with *thlipsis*, 'persecution,' it is a major theme running through the book, not least in the messages to the seven churches. The translation 'patient endurance' (NRSV) might imply that the saints of God are called to something like passive waiting, as if the kingdom of God were a train that is delayed. But this does not do justice to Revelation's account of 'endurance.' It is a far more determined disposition, an unbending refusal to abandon the witness to the lordship of Jesus, even in the face of opposition, exclusion, or physical violence. As we will see, it is this determined nonviolent resistance and faithful witness that form the very character of victory in Revelation's theology.

It is because of such witness, John tells us, that he is on Patmos, an island thirty-seven miles off the coast of Asia Minor, to the southwest of Ephesus. First-century Patmos was not, as is sometimes thought, a deserted island or a penal colony. Archaeological evidence tells us that it was well populated, having an athletic society, active worship of the goddess Artemis, and a military garrison guarding a busy shipping lane. Again, our image of John the secluded seer needs some correction. But why was he there? His explanation is at once vague and theologically profound. 'Because of the word of God and the testimony of Jesus' is all he tells us. Though it is possible to read this 'because' as an indication of a purposeful, voluntary act (John sailing to Patmos in order to hear from God or to proclaim the message), the usual interpretation (beginning in patristic interpretation) has been that John's witness to Jesus resulted in some form of exile or imprisonment on the island, perhaps sentenced to years of hard labour (see Aune 2017, 77–79, for a discussion of the various forms of exile), and John may have had something like this situation in mind when he says that he shares in the persecutions of the churches. It is certainly the case that such punishments were occasionally handed down by the Roman justice system, particularly for those found guilty of the politically seditious crime of *stasis* or of participation in unsanctioned religious 'superstitions' (Koester 2014, 243). While such politically disruptive crimes may have carried the death penalty, those of higher status could choose banishment instead.

John, however, provides no such explanation, and so we cannot be sure. Indeed, his choice of words refuses to identify such legal processes as the decisive rationale for the course of his life. His explanation names neither himself or these political systems as the true agent of his arrival on the island; he says neither 'I went' (naming his own agency) nor 'I was sent' (ascribing it to others). Instead, he simply says 'I was on the island,' leaving the agent of the action unstated. Perhaps we might translate it in a way that captures the delightful ambiguity of the Greek middle voice, 'I found myself on the island called Patmos.' This stylistic decision suggests a profound theological claim: for John, the real reason for his present circumstance is 'the word of God and the testimony of Jesus.' Whatever Caesar and his courts might think, sovereignty over the world and its affairs belongs to God (Mangina 2010, 48). If John finds himself on Patmos, whether as exile or not, it is because the Lord willed it.

Having introduced himself and established his connection to the churches, John begins to give an account of his vision on Patmos, which will occupy the rest of the book. He was, he tells us, 'in the spirit,' the first of numerous occurrences of this phrase. This is not a mere figure of speech, suggesting a vague 'spiritual experience' such as a trance. The numerous connections to the prophetic witness make it far more likely that John here indicates that his vision, like that of Ezekiel (3.12; 11.24) or Zechariah (7.12), is the result of the activity of the Spirit of God. The vision happens on 'the Lord's day,' a symbolic naming of the calendar that evokes the day of Christian worship and of the resurrection of Jesus. This may again be a signal of the intended liturgical situation for the reading of this book. In any case, as with all worship, time and space are given new theological significance. What may seem to be another Sunday on the island of Patmos is transformed, for John and his readers, into an experience 'in the spirit on the Lord's day.' This is not the last time John will experience a 'temporal' and 'geographical' transformation in the spirit. While his ecstatic vision begins on Patmos, he will soon be guided into the heavenly places (4.2; 17.3; 21.10).

I say 'vision,' but what comes first is an 'audition.' As will frequently happen in the book, John describes what he hears almost as often as what he sees, and the two sensory experiences are regularly made to interpret one another. Revelation is a noisy book, and it begins at high volume. What John hears, coming from behind him like the sound Ezekiel heard (3.12), is 'a voice like a trumpet,' a sound that will regularly guide John's visionary journey as the book progresses. The trumpet was one of the loudest known sounds in

John's world, and it had both military and cultic associations. More specifically, the sound of a trumpet was often associated with moments of divine revelation (especially Exod 19.16, but see Aune 2017, 85, for many others). Readers (hearers?) would likely expect John to encounter such a theophany.

The voice speaks and instructs him to write down what he sees in his vision. This act of writing will make John's visionary experience both accessible and permanent. Usually in the prophetic tradition, such writing is instructed because the vision pertains to a distant generation (e.g., Dan 12.4, and Isa 30.8). Not so with John's vision—the written account is to be sent at once to the seven churches of Asia, now named as those in Ephesus, Smyrna, Pergamum, Thyatira, Sardis, Philadelphia, and Laodicea. John's vision is not one to be sealed up for a day to come but is of immediate significance for those churches in their present day.

We have already commented on the significance of the numbering of the seven churches in Asia, but why are these seven named? Though they are all real historical Christian communities (not abstract ciphers, as they are sometimes read), there is no obvious historical reason for this list. That has not stopped interpreters proposing all sorts of hypotheses, ranging from John's familiarity with different communities to the workings of the ancient postal service. We can perhaps say with some confidence that it is not a list based on importance. There were equally if not more important churches in the region. Colossae, Miletus, and Troas, for example, were significant for various reasons but are not named. Though our knowledge is fragmentary, the practicalities of the book's transmission might also add to our interpretation. If one were to consult a map and trace the route a messenger might logically take from Patmos to each of the seven cities, in the order named, one would find that Revelation is, quite literally, a circular letter. This interpretation requires a fair amount of historical imagination about what routes a messenger might take, and it is doubtful that this alone explains the choice of these seven churches. In any case, the significance of the number seven as a symbol of completeness renders any historical explanation ultimately secondary to the more important theological insight that this is a single letter with a visionary message for the whole church, represented by these seven communities.

Christ among the Lampstands, vv. 12–16

Having heard these instructions, John tells us that he 'turned to see the voice.' How does one *see* a voice? Perhaps John's Greek is stumbling here, as it so often seems to be. Or perhaps this is simply a metaphorical way of speaking, whether synecdoche (Koester 2014, 245), or metonymy (Beale

1999, 207). Some English translations seem to read it as such and clean up the awkwardness of the Greek phrasing to make John see not the voice but the one 'whose voice it was' (NRSV). But John, I think, writes in this way with more artistic and theological intention. In this phrasing he intends, I think, to confuse the senses and thus relay something of his own experience in encountering a voice so powerful as to be practically 'visible.' This idea of a 'visible voice' was not unheard of in contemporary Jewish apocalyptic thought, and not merely as a metaphor (see Charlesworth, 1986). Daniel 7, which is echoed throughout this first chapter, also speaks of a voice that can be seen (7.11 LXX, altered by Theodotion, which is followed by English translations). John's form of expression here is, moreover, another allusion to the Sinai theophany, where the people 'saw . . . the sound of the trumpet' (Ex 20.18 LXX, AT) or, as Deuteronomy describes the encounter, they 'saw not the appearance but the voice' of God (Deut 4.12 LXX, AT; see Koester 2014, 244).

John will use this 'I heard / I saw' device a few times in the first half of his book, and each time the expectations raised by what he hears are radically transformed by the vision that follows. In this case, a reader familiar with the Hebrew Scriptures would expect the sound of trumpets to lead to a theophany, perhaps even the 'voice' of God made visible. Yet as John turns to look, he encounters 'one like a human being.' When John 'turned to see the voice,' what he sees is 'an embodied voice, a visible word, divine speech rendered in human flesh' (Mangina 2010, 49, cf. Jn 1.14; 1 Jn 1.1).

The first thing John sees, however, is not this figure but seven lampstands. The Old Testament allusion is to one of John's favourite passages, Zechariah 4 (see comment on 1.4–8 above). In Zechariah's vision the golden lampstand was singular, with seven lamps on it, much like the seven-branched lamp that the Israelites were instructed to make for the tabernacle (Ex 25.31–40 / 37.17–24). Here, however, there are seven separate lampstands, united by the figure who stands among them. There is a clear connection, made by allusive threads to Zechariah 4, to the earlier mention of the 'seven spirits' before the throne. Later, as John is given an interpretation of this image, we will see that the sevenfold descriptions of both Spirit and church are closely related.

In John's description of the 'one like the Son of Man' who stands among the lampstands, the imagery of Zechariah is combined with another prophetic vision that echoes through the book of Revelation, Daniel 7. In verses 9–14 of that chapter, Daniel sees a vision of 'one like a human being' who approaches the throne of the 'Ancient One' to receive an everlasting reign. We have already heard an echo of this passage in 1.7, where John deployed the phrase 'coming with the clouds,' alluding to Daniel 7.11b, and here he mines the whole passage for imagery to express the vision before him. But unlike Daniel's vision, here we recall that the one like the Son of Man is not 'coming on the clouds' but already standing among the lampstands, which are the churches, and already holds the angels of those churches in his hand. That the living God is the 'coming one' is no doubt a hope that sustains the church. But that Christ is present through the Spirit in the midst of them ensures that this is not a hope entirely deferred. He is the one who is, was, and is to come.

This phrase 'Son of Man' is, (in)famously, one that Jesus is fond of using in the Gospels, and a particularly significant comparison can be made with its use in the 'little apocalypse' of Matthew 24 and Mark 13, passages that also strongly echo Daniel 7. On one level it means simply 'one like a human being,' or even just 'human,' and thus is a poetic reference to humanity in general (e.g., Ps 8.4, but cf. Heb 2.5, where the psalm is interpreted Christologically). In some interpretations, this archetypal human figure represents the personification of the people of Israel specifically. In second temple Jewish interpretation, particularly in the apocalyptic writings (e.g., in *1 Enoch* 46, 48, or *4 Ezra* 12; see Reynolds 2020), the phrase was interpreted messianically, with such passages often combining imagery from Daniel 7 with echoes of Psalm 2 and Isaiah 11, 42, and 49. The most significant use of the phrase, for John and many others, is Daniel's. So we must not ignore the fact that, although he may well intend a reference to the people of Israel, the imagery with which Daniel describes this figure transcends humanity, opening up the interpretative possibility of the Son of Man as an exalted figure of angelic (even 'divine') identity. John exploits this possibility in his own reworking of the tradition.

But John, as usual, does not simply lift his images from the Old Testament and wheel them out as tired tropes. His complex tapestry of allusions skilfully reworks the source material for theological purposes. In this passage, composed of just two breathless sentences in the Greek, John weaves the setting from Zechariah 4 with visionary material from Daniel 7 and 10. Comparing his description of the figure among the lampstands with the imagery of his two Danielic source texts gives a fascinating demonstration of John's approach to intertextual allusion. Some of the details of his description of the Son of Man clearly echo (without precisely matching) the figure Daniel encountered by the river Tigris (Dan 10.5–6). The Son of Man in John's vision wears a long robe with a golden sash, echoing and adapting (respectively) the priestly and royal imagery of the linen robe and golden belt of Daniel 10. His feet are like bronze, reminiscent of the Danielic arms of bronze, and his fiery eyes, shining face, and voice like 'many waters' evoke

Daniel's description of the figure's eyes of flame, lightning-bright face, and 'voice like a multitude.' As usual, however, in order to appreciate the significance of John's reworking of this imagery, the reader needs to read more widely than one source text. As he does so often, here John threads multiple Old Testament texts together, with profound theological results.

For example, the sonic metaphor of rushing waters is borrowed not from Daniel but from the visions of Ezekiel (43.2), where it is the noise that accompanies the arrival of the glory of God. Again, John's description of the Son of Man's head and hair, white like wool or snow, alludes not to Daniel 10's glorious human figure but to the depiction of the Ancient One in Daniel 7.9 (see also *1 Enoch* 46.1). In this way John incorporates some of the attributes of God into his depiction of the Son of Man. Whoever this figure is (he will soon speak and identify himself), John's experience of meeting him was a combination of encountering someone at once human and 'divine.'

Many attempts have been made to identify the seven stars held in his right hand. Proposals have included particular constellations (the Pleiades or Ursa Major), or the planets, thought by some in the first century to be seven in number (lists vary but usually name the Sun, Moon, Mercury, Venus, Mars, Jupiter, and Saturn as the seven 'planets'). In first-century Asia Minor, it was widely believed (as it is still by some) that these heavenly bodies controlled human destiny. Coins minted in the early 80s during the reign of the emperor Domitian depict his son, who died in infancy, seated on the globe of the earth and surrounded by the seven stars (see Blount 2013, 45). The inscription on the coins reads *DIVUS CAESAR IMP[erator] DOMITIANI F[ilius]* 'Son of Domitian, Divine Caesar, Emperor.' This inscription reflects the common claim that deceased members of the imperial household, and sometimes the living emperor, had divine/divinised status (the term 'divus' is more complex than simply saying 'divine'), and the combination of this inscription with the astronomical imagery of global sovereignty is a potent example of imperial propaganda. If this sort of imagery is at least part of what John intended to evoke, then his reworking of it here sends a powerful message. The 'right hand' is a common Old Testament way of speaking of power, authority, and protection. As such, the placing of the seven stars in the right hand of the Son of Man makes a theological and sociopolitical claim: authority over human destiny, thought to belong to heavenly bodies and/or imperial powers, really belongs to him. However, while there may be some truth to such astronomical interpretations, they are not really the main point. The seven stars are closely connected with the seven lampstands and are, as John will soon be told, the 'angels of the seven churches.' An ecclesiological emphasis must be therefore be maintained in any interpretation. We will look in more detail at what that may mean shortly.

As John's description of this resplendent figure closes, we are given a final, impossible detail. A 'sharp, two-edged sword' comes out from his mouth, in place of a tongue. Up to this point the imagery used stretches but does not break the limits of human imagination. Now those limits are tested. This unlikely image will be repeated in the next chapter (Rev 2.12, 16) and then twice again in the violent imagery toward the end of the book (19.15, 21), and in each of these cases it is Christ who is being described. How are we to picture such a thing? As with much of the fantastical imagery we will encounter in Revelation, if one takes this to be a literal description of the figure among the lampstands, the image quickly collapses into the ridiculous. John has himself reached the limits of human imagination; he is trying to express the inexpressible and reaches for whatever images convey the power and significance of his visionary experience. What does this imagery mean to convey?

To be sure, this is an image of a warrior. But his weapon comes from his mouth. This is further reinforced by John's wordplay, describing the blade as 'two-edged,' *distomos*, literally 'two-mouthed.' John is not the first to use such imagery. Like the writers of other apocalypses in the second temple period, John draws Daniel and Isaiah together at this point. He echoes the language of Isaiah 11.4, where a conqueror strikes the earth with the 'rod of his mouth,' and the servant of Isaiah 49.2, whose mouth is made 'like a sharp sword.' In the New Testament, both Ephesians 6.17 and Hebrews 4.12 liken the word of God to a sword, in the latter case a two-edged one, sharp enough to divide soul from spirit and joints from marrow and to judge the thoughts of the human heart. The warrior-king who stands before John, therefore, wields in battle not a blade but his words, his double-edged testimony of deliverance and judgement.

Instruction to Write, vv. 17–20

As yet, the figure standing before John has not identified himself. First, John's reaction to the experience is described. He 'falls at his feet as though dead,' the usual reaction to supernatural encounters in the Bible. Ezekiel fell to his face on encountering 'the likeness of the glory of the LORD' (Ezek 1.28). Daniel fell prostrate before the angel Gabriel (Dan 8.17) and, more significantly, went 'deathly pale' and fell facedown before the angelic figure in Daniel 10.9. In the New Testament, in Matthew's account of the resurrection, there is a similar reaction when 'the angel of the Lord,' whose appearance was also 'like lightning,' appears at the empty tomb (28.2–4). This awestruck bodily response, then, is the appropriate reaction to the appearance of an angel or, sometimes, the presence of the glory of God. John's posture is not, at this point, the deliberate prostration of a worshipper (such as we find explicitly in Rev 22.8–9) but the involuntary response brought about by the appropriate human fear and awe when presented with such a holy and powerful presence.

As often happens in such encounters in apocalyptic writings (e.g., Dan 8.18, 10.10; *4 Ezra* 10.30), the one who has fallen prostrate is then encouraged in two ways. First, the one like the Son of Man lays his right hand on John, a sign of approval and strengthening, though unlike in some other visions of this kind, we are not told that John is lifted back to his feet. This is the same right hand that holds the seven stars, indicating authority over the destiny of humankind and the angels of the churches. No doubt the placing of *this* hand on John imparted strength and awe in equal measure. Second, as in both Ezekiel and Matthew, John is comforted with words, as the figure finally speaks, giving John the most common angelic command, 'do not be afraid.' After John's prostration and strengthening, there is then a third phase to the encounter, where further revelation is given and the visions explained. This follows the threefold pattern of many similar scenes in the apocalyptic literature, including Daniel's encounter with the angelic figure.

The revelation now given by the one John encounters concerns his own identity, beginning with the sort of 'I am' statement characteristic of the fourth Gospel: 'I am the first and the last, and the living one.' With these words, any notions we may have that John is encountering a mere angel are dispelled. Such a claim could only come from the mouth of God, and no angel would dare say such things of himself. His words echo Isaiah 40–48, especially chapter 44, which deals with the absurdity of idols and the exclusive divine claims of YHWH, in which the Lord of hosts says of himself, 'I am the first and the last; besides me there is no god' (44.6). Just two verses later in that passage, after throwing down a challenge to all would-be divine pretenders, the Lord then says 'do not fear . . . you are my witnesses.' Isaiah 44 and Revelation 1 are connected by a number of verbal threads.

There is likely a continued subtext of anti-idolatry polemic, therefore, when this divine figure next says of himself, 'I am the living one.' All other 'gods' are lifeless blocks of wood; only the God of Israel truly lives. Calling YHWH 'the living one' or 'the living God' was a common Jewish practice, attested throughout the Hebrew Scriptures, the second temple Jewish writings, and the New Testament (for a long list of references, see Aune 2017, 102). It not only a theological statement concerning the creator as the source of all life but also a not-too-subtle claim to exclusive monotheism. YHWH is *the* living one—and all other gods are not. But as this divine figure's speech continues, the designation 'living one' acquires another surprising layer of meaning. He goes on, 'I was dead, and see, I am alive forever and ever.' The 'living one' was dead but now lives eternally, literally 'unto the ages of ages.' The fulness of the quality of the divine life, and not only its quantitative duration, is what 'eternity' means. We can now finally identify John's 'one like a Son of Man.' There is only one candidate who meets the description of this human and divine, dead but eternally living one: Jesus Christ.

Because he is the one who has both conquered death and possesses all life, Jesus holds 'the keys of Death and Hades.' The latter is the name of the Ancient Greek god of the underworld, and of the place itself, the shadowy realm of the dead. It is also the usual Greek equivalent for the Hebrew *She'ol*, which was not the fiery punitive hellscape sometimes imagined but a place where the dead would go to await the coming Day of the Lord. The keys Christ holds are symbols of his authority over Death and Hades, an authority not merely delegated, as to an angel, but gained by virtue of his own death and resurrection. This is why John has no cause to fear. Though he has fallen down in fear as though dead, Death itself has no authority in the presence of the Living One.

It is not clear here whether John intends us to think of Hades the place or Hades the god, and there is little hope for clarity from the Greek grammar, which could be translated either as 'the key *to* Hades' or 'the key *belonging to* Hades.' Since Death is neither a place nor a god (or is it?), the combination of the two does little to remove the ambiguity. In any case, what is important in this aspect of the vision is that, whether place or power or both, Hades itself is under the authority of its key-bearer and will (as we will see in chapter 20) ultimately be annihilated by consuming fire. Since Revelation will later make use of both the spatial understanding of Death and Hades (20.13) and their personification (6.8, and perhaps 20.14), it is possible that John's ambiguity here is deliberate. Readers of Revelation should get used to such ambiguities and many-layered meanings.

Having comforted John, in verse 19 Jesus instructs him to write down the vision (surely a less than comforting task in itself!). He has already received an instruction like this in the command of the trumpet-voice in verse 11. This repetition of the command bookends John's vision of Jesus, and it is now clear that it is Jesus himself who commissions John's writing. We are reminded of what has been said from the beginning of the book, that Jesus himself is the source of John's revelation, and it is this fact that gives the book its authority. Here the instruction comes in a threefold form, spanning the tenses: 'what you have seen, what is, and what is to take place after this.' This formula has been taken by some commentators as giving a kind of key to the outline of the book as a whole. In this way one might identify this first part of the book as what John has seen, to be followed by 'what is' in the life of the churches of Asia Minor in chapters 2–3, before the rest of the book takes up the theme of 'what is to take place after this.' I do not find this reading particularly convincing, not least because the evidence is thin that Revelation can be so neatly divided into chronological sections. The whole book, and not just the first part, is 'what John saw,' and all of it speaks of what is and what is to come. Some of the visions in the later chapters of the book concern the past (e.g., chapter 12) and others the future. Such schemes, I think, owe more to assumed dispensationalist readings of Revelation than to any indications in the language and structure of the text itself. In any case, there is far greater significance to the phrasing here than a mere structural outline. The three tenses of the command echo the similar phrasing in verse 8, where the Lord God is identified as 'the Alpha and Omega' and the one 'who is and who was and who is to come,' as well as the self-identification of Jesus in verses 17–18 as 'the first and the last.' This theological and Christological principle should underpin our reading not only of the content but also the logic of the book. The vision that John is instructed to write comes from and bears witness to the exalted Jesus, who, though living a fully human life, is not bound by the linearity of time as we are. He shares in the eternal life of God, and as such this 'revelation of Jesus Christ' speaks at once to this world's past, present, and future, which have been gathered together in him.

Often in the apocalyptic literature, the seer (once restored from prostrate fear) is given an interpretation of a vision by his angelic interlocutor. Here, Jesus briefly performs this explanatory role in regard to the 'mystery' of the lampstands and stars, though (alas!) not many of John's visions will be given such clear dominical interpretation. The stars in Jesus's right hand, John is told, are the 'angels of the seven churches' (each of whom is about to be addressed in turn), and the seven lampstands are the churches themselves.

The explanation, however, only generates more questions. Who are these 'angels'? Their identity has been much discussed (the various options are outlined in a lengthy excursus in Aune 2017, 108–112). First, since Revelation certainly has no problem accepting the reality of various 'supernatural' beings, it is entirely possible that Jesus means exactly what he seems to say, that each church has its own angelic mediator. If a supernatural being can be allocated to the kingdom of Persia (taking this figure in Daniel 10 to be a 'supernatural' one), there is no reason not to think that Ephesus, Smyrna, Pergamum, and the rest might have their own designated 'guardian angels' of some sort. Elsewhere in Revelation's dozens of references, angels are angels. But there is a small grammatical clue, often obscured by English translations, that things are not quite so clear-cut. The singular 'you' of the address to the angels in chapters 2 and 3 is sometimes mixed together with the plural 'you' when Jesus speaks to the communities (e.g., 2.13–14: 'you [sg] did not deny your faith . . . who was killed among you [pl] . . . but I have a few things against you [sg]).' On the one hand, we will be repeatedly informed that these messages are '*to the angel* of the church in X,' but on the other we are also told, confusingly, that they are 'what the Spirit is saying *to the churches.*' As we will see, the seven messages to these angels often sound as if they are speaking not to angelic beings but to communities of believers, particularly when there are words of rebuke or correction. A straightforward identification of the seven 'angels' as singular spiritual beings is, therefore, unsatisfying.

A second option is the converse of the first, that the word *angelos* should be rendered with its other, more mundane meaning, 'messenger.' Read in this way, the 'messenger' of each church might be an emissary, resident prophet, overseer, or some such person, whose job it is to receive and pass on the word of the Lord for their community. This is a plausible reading, but in my view it turns these messages into rather pedestrian pieces of writing when compared to the visionary tenor of the chapter as a whole, and this usage of *angelos* would quite possibly be very confusing given John's normal practice of using of the term to signify mediating spiritual beings.

A third option, however, is to read these 'angels' as imaginative 'personifications' of these Christian communities, particularly in terms of their spiritual state (so Mounce 1998, 63), or as some sort of 'alter ego' (Aune 2017, 109). The linguistic confusion between the churches and their angels is perhaps, then, a deliberate literary and theological move by John. We should notice that we have two ecclesial images: the plural lampstands among which Christ stands and the seven stars that are gathered in his right hand. The two images do not collapse into one another, as though it were a matter of 'mere' personification. Not for the last time, John's apocalyptic imagery allows him to speak in two ways about a single thing, imbuing ideas with a deeper theological meaning. When Jesus addresses the churches with the plural, he speaks as one speaks to a gathering of people, offering encouragement and instruction for their community lives. He speaks, as it were, as the Christ among the lampstands, the churches depicted in an earthly frame of reference. But when John has Jesus addressing a church's 'angel' in the singular, he means for us to hear an imaginative reification of the spiritual life of that congregation as seen from the heavenly perspective, as a 'single entity' representing the transcendent quality of a community of faith in their shared life, a life held in Christ's right hand (Wink 1993, 69ff; see also Woodman 2013, 94). In this apocalyptic 'bifocal vision' of the 'inner' and 'outer' aspects of the life of the seven churches, each of them is given assurance by a profound and double theological truth—Christ both holds his churches with authority and walks among them in solidarity.

Prophetic Oracles to the Seven Churches

Revelation 2.1–3.22

The Seven Oracles Taken Together

Revelation began with a vision of Jesus Christ who is at once the 'Son of Man' and the 'Ancient of Days.' This same Jesus whom John has seen in this vision, both walking among them and holding them in his hands, now addresses each of the churches directly. But, as a repeated refrain will remind us, what Jesus says to the churches is also 'what the Spirit says to the churches.'

For a number of reasons, we will call this sequence the 'seven oracles' and not, as it is often called, the 'seven letters.' First, as we have seen, the whole book of Revelation is one unified circular letter to all the churches, and these seven prophetic messages are part of that whole. The selection of these particular seven cities is more about symbolism (with the number seven indicating the church in its completeness) than it is about their particular importance; otherwise there is no reason not to include other significant churches of Asia Minor such as those in Colossae, Troas, or Hierapolis. Chapters 2 and 3 are not to be treated as some kind of detachable set piece, for a number of verbal threads connect these messages to the whole book. For example, the message to Ephesus begins with mention of the seven stars (2.1), which we just discussed, and ends with the imagery of the 'tree of life' (2.7), which is part of the book's closing vision (22.2, 14, 19). Many more allusive threads like this will link the seven messages to the opening and closing chapters of Revelation.

Second, in their form the messages are more like prophetic oracles than letters. There are none of the standard epistolary features that would signal these as letters in their own right, but there are some clear indications that they bear greater similarity to the prophetic oracles of the Old Testament, not least the prophetic formula opening each address: *tade legei*, 'these are the words,' more traditionally rendered 'thus says . . . .' There are some important adaptations of this form, however, which will be discussed shortly.

Each church will read not only their own oracle but the messages to their sister churches. This is important, because the situation of the churches is varied. Some are almost entirely positive messages, some almost entirely negative, and some are a mixture. Not all are persecuted—indeed, there is rebuke for the over-comfortable. There are differences between the cities in which the churches are situated, though these are sometimes overstated, but the primary concern is not the cities themselves but the different 'spirits' of the churches found in them (see Koester 2014, 267). This does not mean that their urban locations are completely irrelevant since the nature of these seven churches is influenced, though not determined, by the culture of their host cities. Nevertheless, it is their response that matters.

With some notable exceptions, each oracle has the same basic structure, signalled by the word-for-word repetition of several phrases. Each opens with the words 'to the angel of the church in . . .' followed by a command to write. The mention of the 'angels' of the churches sends us back to the discussion of 1.20 above. This imagery expresses the fact that Jesus is addressing the spiritual condition of each church.

Next come the words *tade legei*, 'thus says.' It is worth spending a little time on John's significant use of this phrase, which echoes the standard opening of a prophetic oracle in the Old Testament. It is used over 350 times in the Septuagint, with by far the heaviest concentration in the prophetic books (especially Jeremiah and Ezekiel, which seem to use it in every paragraph). It also appears frequently in historical narratives when a revelation or prophetic oracle is being given or when an emissary is delivering a royal pronouncement (e.g., the various exchanges in 2 Kgs 9 or the speeches of the Rabshakeh in 2 Kgs 18–19). A cluster of uses of the phrase is also found in Exodus 7–11, opening of each of Moses's prophetic oracles to Pharaoh. In the Septuagint, it is almost always followed by naming the source of the oracle as *kurios*, the standard Greek rendering of the divine name YHWH, sometimes expanded to *kurios ho theos (Israēl)*, 'the Lord God (of Israel),' or *kurios pantokratōr*, 'the Lord of hosts' (especially in Zechariah). The phrase is not found anywhere else in the New Testament, with the sole exception of Acts 21.11 where the prophet Agabus addresses Paul with a word from the Holy Spirit. It is reasonable to conclude, therefore, that it is a somewhat archaic phrase that would have the effect of evoking the spirit and authority of the prophets of old, much as if someone speaking today were to use the language of the King James Version: 'thus saith the Lord' (Paul 2018, 79; Aune 2017, 141).

The ubiquity and stability of this formulaic prophetic expression makes John's adaptation of it even more striking by contrast. In the opening of the seven messages, John follows convention in writing 'thus says . . .' but then, instead of the expected '. . . the Lord,' he names Jesus as the source of each oracle through a series of allusions to the vision of chapter 1. Though we should not discount the possible royal connotations, echoing the use of this formula in the historical books of the OT, it is far more likely that John intends the phrase to carry the weight of divine address, which is the dominant usage in the Exodus narrative, Zechariah, and Ezekiel, to which he most frequently alludes throughout Revelation. In placing Jesus in the role of the God of Israel, John continues to make profound theological claims about the one who now speaks.

After these introductory formulae we have the body of the message itself, each of the seven usually containing four shared elements. First, Jesus tells each church that he 'knows [their] works,' followed by a positive description of the spiritual state of that congregation, a commendation for good works or an acknowledgement of a difficult situation. Protestant Christians can be unnecessarily wary of talking about 'works,' but John is not so works-avoidant, and each message records Christ's evaluation of his churches in accordance with their works. Second, Jesus gives the bad news, a rebuke introduced (usually) with the phrase 'this I have against you . . . .' Third, there are words of encouragement or instruction, as well as specific words of warning or promise, all tailored to the condition of each church, often with a call to repentance, and almost always a declaration that Jesus himself will 'come' to the churches. The eschatological coming of Jesus is a dominant theme in Revelation (e.g., 1.7), and the basis of hope for the future. But we are reminded here that his identity as the one who comes (cf. 1.8) is not merely a future hope but a reality of present and imminent importance in the life of the church. Jesus is the 'coming one' in both present and future senses (see Thomas and Macchia 2016, 91), a truth also expressed in the 'farewell discourse' of John's Gospel (e.g., Jn 14.3, 18, 23, 28). The imagery used in these promises and warnings foreshadows the Christological vision of Revelation 19.

Last, each of the messages closes with two more repeated formulae, 'let the one who has an ear hear what the Spirit is saying to the churches' and a promise 'to those who conquer.' As we will soon see, the ordering of the two elements in the first three messages is reversed in the last four, resulting in the seven messages having a 'three-plus-four' arrangement. The first of these two formulaic phrases, the call to hear, has clear connections with Old Testament prophecy (especially Isa 6) and is also found in the synoptic witness to Jesus (Mk 4.9, 23; Mt 11.15; 13.9; Lk 8.8; 14.35). Its significance there is that the message of Jesus will be received by some and rejected by others. In Jesus's oracles to the churches here in Revelation 2 and 3, what is being said to the churches will, likewise, be heard by those who are God's. It is significant that the oracles are introduced as the words of Jesus (through the 'thus says' formula) but closed with the implicit claim that this is also 'what the Spirit is saying.' There is a close relationship between the agency of Jesus and Spirit in delivering these prophetic oracles. As in John's Gospel, the Spirit is the one who leads the church into the truth of Jesus's words and, moreover, is himself the fulfilment of Jesus's promise to come to the church (Jn 14.16–18; 16.7–13).

The final element is a promise given 'to those who conquer / whoever conquers' (the phrasing varies slightly), which is accompanied by imagery foreshadowing the closing visions of the book in chapters 21 and 22 (see Minear in Beale 1999, 134–35). The theme of 'conquering' is an important one throughout the book of Revelation and is regularly connected to the theme of 'faithful witness,' which we have already signaled.

We can therefore summarise the shape of the seven messages in this way:

1. opening formulae
    A. address: 'to the angel of the church in X, write'
    B. oracular formula: 'thus says . . .' + Christological imagery from chapter 1
2. body of message
    A. assessment: 'I know (your works)'
    B. rebuke (usually): 'but this I have against you'
    C. encouragements/instructions/promises/warnings
3. closing formulae (order differs)
    A. 'let the one who has an ear hear what the Spirit is saying to the churches'
    B. 'to those who conquer . . .' + Christological imagery from chapters 21–22

Having established this basic pattern, we will see that it is often the details and subtle departures from it that are most interesting. We will now discuss each message in turn.

The Message to Ephesus, 2.1–7

The first three churches addressed were all in significant Roman cities, and Ephesus was certainly no exception. It was a city of political and economic importance, being a vibrant port with good transport links and administrative infrastructure, which made it an obvious choice for Roman provincial government. It was also a city of great religious significance. The city had no fewer than six temples honouring Roman emperors, including Julius Caesar, Augustus, and Domitian (Aune 2017, 154). For this, it was twice awarded the honorary title *neōkoros*, 'temple keeper' (Acts 19.35) in recognition of the city's importance as a centre for the imperial cult (on which see the introduction and commentary on 13.11–18). It was also, perhaps more famously, the home of the temple of Artemis, the patron goddess of the city, a building that was one of the seven wonders of the ancient world.

It was also a city of significance for the early church. Paul's preaching there led to a riot instigated by the silversmiths serving the Artemesian cult (Acts 19), illustrating that we must be wary of our somewhat anachronistic categories of 'economics,' 'politics,' and 'religion': these spheres of life were largely inseparable in the ancient world. The church in Ephesus remained an important 'mother church' and missionary base thereafter, and Paul's protégé Timothy is believed to have led that congregation (see 1 Tim 1.3).

As discussed above, the opening 'thus says' formula in verse 1 is followed by an aspect of the visionary material from chapter 1. The imagery chosen for each message usually indicates particular resonance with the specific situation addressed in each church, though here in Ephesus the decision to identify 'him who holds the seven stars' and 'who walks among the seven golden lampstands' likely reflects the fact that this is the first of the seven messages. The imagery reminds the churches, and this 'mother church' in Ephesus in particular, that Jesus is both among them and sovereign over them. The subtle changes to the language of chapter 1 drive this point home. He doesn't just 'have' the seven stars (the verb *echō* in 1.16 is fairly neutral); he 'holds' them (*krateō*, 2.1), a stronger way of indicating his sovereign and protective control over the churches. Again, Jesus is not just seen 'in the midst of the lampstands' (1.13) but 'walks among' them (2.1). Jesus's presence in solidarity with the churches is not passive but active (see Thomas and Macchia 2016, 87).

As the body of the message to Ephesus begins, there is first a generous commendation for their 'works,' which are soon explained as *hypomonē*, 'patient endurance,' a theme that is repeated not only in this message (1.3) but in the book as a whole (seven times in all; see the commentary on 1.9). The specific occasion for this patient endurance in Ephesus is the presence of 'false apostles.' In the two phases of this commendation, John makes a nice little connection (sometimes obscured in English translations) through a play on the word *bastazō*, 'to bear.' The Ephesian church is commended first for not 'bearing with' evildoers (v. 2) and then for 'bearing up' for the sake of Jesus's name (v. 3, see Aune 2017, 143).

It's not all good news, however. Jesus next rebukes the Ephesian church for having 'abandoned the love [they] had at first.' What does this mean? Two options present themselves. Perhaps they have abandoned their first love for God, as the zeal of a new convert fades with time. Certainly that is a common reading of the text. But we may read it another way. Perhaps their pursuit of doctrinal purity, while commendable, has led them to abandon the primary importance of love *for others*. This might make more sense of the following command to 'do the works you did at first,' those works being works of love for their Ephesian neighbours. As Jesus taught us in his earthly ministry, love for God and love for neighbour are equally primary and inseparable commandments (Mt 22.36–40). In any case, the rebuke to the Ephesian church stands as a reminder that, while the maintenance of doctrinal purity is both essential for the health of church and a commended spiritual practice, to do this and forget the 'first love' that we must have for God and for others is to risk the judgement that follows: 'I will come to you and remove your lampstand from its place, unless you repent.' No amount of 'orthodoxy policing' can substitute for that 'first love.' A commitment to the love of God in the gospel, to the love for each other, and to faithful witness are the marks of a church. Without these a church is not a lamp to the world and is no light at all. There will be echoes of this hard judgement later in the message to Sardis, a church that risks being blotted out of the book of life.

Here, Jesus softens the blow of his word of rebuke with a final brief commendation. To their credit, the Ephesian church has demonstrated hatred of a particular group, also hated by Jesus, called the 'Nicolaitans.' Proper love of God and others is not antithetical to appropriate hatred, it seems. It is hard to be confident about a precise identification of this group, however, since very little exists by way of historical record beyond the evidence of Revelation itself. A number of options have been suggested, including Gnostic heresies, Judaizing missionaries, and a connection back to the Nicolaus of Antioch mentioned in Acts 6.5 (a popular interpretation among the church fathers). Perhaps this verse simply gives a name to the 'false apostles' discussed earlier (though why the name should be reserved until this last section of the message isn't clear). There is a suggestion that their teaching involves syncretistic and idolatrous worship, especially in the form of ritual sex and the eating of food offered to pagan deities. These details are mentioned in the message to Pergamum, which also names the Nicolaitans (2.14–15) and connects them to another false teacher symbolically named 'Balaam.' Similar concerns are again expressed in the message to Thyatira and its clearly symbolic 'woman Jezebel' (2.20) who misleads the church into idolatrous behaviour.

Whether or not there was a group going by this name, these connections across the letters suggest that 'Nicolaitans' is also in large part playing a symbolic role here. It is another of John's theological puns, playing on the Greek word *nikaō*, meaning 'conquer,' which is also found in the closing promise of this and every message. Whoever this sect or group were, it is likely, therefore, that their teaching involved some claim to 'victorious living.' Here is perhaps the more useful literary and theological insight: whereas Revelation defines and praises true 'victory,' it does so in the face of false teaching by groups of would-be 'conquerors.' The church in Ephesus is called to be a church who shares in Christ's victory, and the Nicolaitans are no conquerors at all.

Jesus closes his message to Ephesus by promising to the true conquerors the gift of the fruit of the 'tree of life.' This promise of 'permission to eat' could well be taken as further evidence that idolatrous food practices may form part of the false teaching of the Nicolaitans. In any case, the connection between 'eating' and 'victory' is clearly established in Jesus's closing words. This is the first mention of the 'tree of life'—as with all these closing promises, the imagery chosen foreshadows the final visions of the book, in this case 22.2, 14, 19. Someone hearing Revelation read aloud for the first time has not yet heard those final visions. As such, for those familiar with the Hebrew Scriptures, mention of eating fruit from the 'tree of life that is in the paradise of God' would almost certainly evoke the garden of Eden (Gen 2.9; 3.22), where the fruit of that tree was forbidden. In Jewish apocalyptic writings this image is further developed. *First Enoch* 25, for example, speaks of a fragrant tree of life, the fruit of which is forbidden until the final judgement when it will be planted in the temple's holy place and the elect given permission to eat. On a second hearing of Revelation, however, these echoes of Eden and the temple would be fused thereafter with the imagery of the eschatological garden of the New Jerusalem. This doubly allusive imagery thus connects beginning and end with powerful imaginative and theological effect.

For those coming into the church from a pagan background, there may have been a different echo. Excavations of the lower levels of the site of the temple of Artemis have uncovered evidence of a 'tree of life' shrine that once stood there, and the image remained significant in the Artemesian cult, as well as being featured in the emblem of the city of Ephesus, at least before the Roman administration (Weima 2021, 49, Hemer 1986, 41–47). In our interpretation, we need not choose between these Jewish and pagan resonances. The book of Revelation regularly makes use of imagery that resonates with both the Jewish and the Greco-Roman world, and because it is imagery (and not prose) a multi-layered reading is possible, if not preferable. Jesus's promise to 'give permission to eat from the tree of life that is in the paradise of God' represents, therefore, both the eschatological reversal of the primordial sin of Eden *and* a prophetic challenge to the falsehood of pagan religion.

Message to Smyrna, 2.8–11

The second message to Smyrna is the shortest of the seven, at just 102 words. Its brevity is in large part a function of what is missing. Unlike most of the others, there is no rebuke introduced by the words 'but I have this against you.' There is also no call to repentance or warning about Jesus's 'coming.' As a result, it is the most positive of the seven messages. As we will soon see, they needed the encouragement. Smyrna (modern-day Izmir) was another important port city, about forty miles north along the coast from Ephesus. It was a wealthy and beautiful city, and inscriptions found there suggest it had a fierce political loyalty to Rome as well as a strong sense of its own place in history. The city had famously been destroyed in 600 BC and re-founded three centuries later, and it was later likened to the phoenix for its capacity for rebirth (Aune 2017, 161). Some who lived there called the city 'the crown of Asia' (Paul 2018, 83), perhaps due to the shape of its acropolis (Thomas and Macchia 2016, 94; Hemer 1986, 239f.) and the emblem of the crown featured on its coins. Certainly, like Ephesus, it was a place that aspired to the status of Asia's 'first city.'

Also like Ephesus, it was honoured with the title *neōkoros*, 'temple keeper.' It boasted the first temple in Asia Minor to the goddess Roma (the personification of the city of Rome), as well as temples to emperors Augustus and Tiberius (Smalley 2015, 65; Blount 2013, 53; Aune 2017, 160), making it a city of religious as well as political significance. As well as vibrant pagan and imperial religion, Smyrna also had an established and civically engaged Jewish population, and this combination would significantly shape the experience of the young church there, a congregation that may well have included Jewish Christians, though the relationship between the two communities (as we will soon see) was likely quite fraught. It would later become a church of great significance, famously being the home of Polycarp, bishop of Smyrna, who was martyred in AD 156. It is not too much of a stretch to imagine a young Polycarp hearing the book of Revelation read aloud in his church (Beale 1999, 243), with its closing call that 'whoever conquers will not be harmed by the second death.'

The theme of 'death and life' features prominently in this short message. As before, John begins with a 'thus says' formula and an aspect of the earlier Christological vision, in this instance echoing 1.17–18 and Jesus's self-designation as 'the first and the last, who was dead and came to life.' This reminder of the sovereignty and resurrection of Christ is connected to the life of the church in Smyrna as the brief body of the letter begins. 'I know your affliction and poverty,' Jesus says. Hearing that their affliction is known by the one who is first and last would be a great encouragement on its own for the suffering Smyrnaean congregation. It is clear that their experience was far from the self-satisfied and wealthy status of the city as a whole. This suffering, it appears, was of two kinds: persecution (*thlipsis*) and poverty (*ptōcheia*). No doubt the two went hand-in-hand in a society where economics, religion, and politics were inextricably connected. It is therefore quite possible that the poverty of the church is Smyrna is the result of the economic exclusion that sometimes came from an uncompromising refusal to participate in the pagan sacrifices that accompanied Roman commerce. It may, however, simply be a statement of a preexisting state of affairs, the Christians in Smyrna coming largely from the poorer sectors of Smyrnaean society. Whatever its cause, however, their poverty is quickly reframed and reversed as Jesus reminds them that they are not poor but truly rich. This revealed inversion of an apparent earthly circumstance is a common theme in the seven messages and throughout the book. What Revelation reveals is that earthly appearances can be deceptive. Wealth can be poverty, and vice-versa, and defeat can be victory. This sort of visionary reversal is particularly evident here in the message to Smyrna.

The principal source of their persecution appears to be the local Jewish population. The description of this group is again characterised by apocalyptic reversal: they are 'those who say they are Jews and are not, but are a synagogue of Satan.' This phrase, repeated in the message to Philadelphia in 3.9, raises the question of who counts as a 'true Jew' in the most polemical terms. There are echoes here of John 8.44, where Jesus tells some *Ioudaioi* that they are children not of Abraham but of the devil. What are we to make of this? We must tread carefully, sensitive to the dangers of supersessionism and anti-Semitism that have long accompanied such rhetoric. We do well to remember, however, that the question of who counted as a 'true Jew' or a member of the 'true Israel' was at this time very much an internal Jewish debate, not one that was violently imposed on the community from outside. Evidence of similar polemical language in intramural Jewish debates over community identity can be found, for example, in the Dead Sea Scrolls (e.g., the *War Scroll* [1QM] and the *Hodayot* [1QH]; see Koester 2014, 276). This language, and the similar expressions in John's Gospel, are to be read similarly. John of Patmos was a Jew, as was Jesus. The 'slander' (*blasphēmia*) of which this group is accused must, therefore, be read as intra-Jewish, not as anti-Jewish polemics.

Having said this, the realities of life as a Jew under Roman rule meant that the definition of the boundaries of the Jewish community was a concern for the imperial administration, too. Special provisions were made for Jews in the empire, notably exemptions from participation in the imperial cult, and these provisions were a source of tension, particularly when the new Christian sect emerged, increasingly populated by ethnic non-Jews who claimed to follow a Jewish messiah. The presence of the church in Smyrna, therefore, may have represented a threat to the fragile status quo on which the Jewish community relied for its influence, or even its survival. There were both internal and external pressures, therefore, for them to police the boundaries of their community. In this environment, it is possible that the persecution experienced by the church in Smyrna took the form of being accused by the Jewish community and reported to the Roman authorities (Koester 2014, 274). After all, the name 'Satan' means 'accuser' (cf. 12.10). Just as in the former life of the apostle Paul, those doing such things probably believed they were acting righteously, out of zeal for the law and the covenant (Phil 3.6; Rom 10.2; cf. 1 Macc 2.24–27), considering the Christian claims about Jesus's divinity to be blasphemy against the God of Israel. But Jesus's words expose the reality that it is their accusation of the church that was blasphemous. In doing such things they were excluding themselves from God's true people. In John's worldview, as in much apocalyptic thought, there is no 'neutral ground' on which one might stand in the cosmic war between God and God's adversaries. If this group is not with Christ, they have become 'a synagogue of Satan' collaborating with the deceit and idolatry of the imperial systems.

Unfortunately for the church in Smyrna, it seems there is more of this affliction on the horizon, including imprisonment and execution. In the face of this, they, like John, are commanded by Jesus not to fear (v. 10; cf. 1.17). There is no 'but I have this against you' here, and no words of rebuke for this beleaguered church. Though he has just identified the 'synagogue of Satan' as the agent of this persecution, its true source is now revealed. The earthly reality is that the judicial machinery of the Roman Empire will pass the sentence, but the devil himself, they are told, is the one truly responsible for throwing them into prison. We see here an early indication of an important literary and theological strategy in the book: the identification of Satanic or demonic agency behind the apparently human systems that threaten the saints of God. As with the opening of the book of Job, we the readers are shown the true theological reality of what is happening, the true agency of 'the accuser' at work behind the scenes of earthly suffering. This is characteristic of apocalyptic writings. As also in the book of Job, the purpose of this persecution is revealed to be a 'testing.' In the face of such a test, the call to the saints is what it always is in Revelation: a call to faithful endurance, even unto death. The reward promised to 'whoever conquers' is not the cessation of earthly suffering, or the restoration of worldly wealth, but the crown of life. This 'crown' is not the diadem (*diadēma*), the symbol of royal rule, but the *stephanos*, the laurel wreath given to a military or athletic victor. It is not for nothing that the first Christian martyr described in the New Testament (Acts 7) is named Stephen. Though Revelation does not expect that all Christians will be slain as martyrs, time and again the 'victory' to which the church is called is defined as conquering through faithful witness.

The closing words of the message underline this central idea by foreshadowing the final visions of the book: 'whoever conquers will not be harmed by the second death.' This 'second death' is part of the visionary judgement of chapter 20, depicting a final great reversal when the devil, who threw the Smyrnaean believers into jail and put them to death, will himself be incarcerated (20.2) and then thrown into the 'lake of fire,' which is the 'second death' (20.10, 14). The conquering saints, though they die, are not harmed by this death.

Message to Pergamum, 2.12–17

We continue our journey north for about sixty-five miles, turning inland and climbing a thousand-foot granite plateau to the city of Pergamum (sometimes called Pergamon, the modern city of Bergama). Just like Ephesus and Smyrna, this was a city of great religious importance, famous for its huge and elevated altar to Zeus, a temple to its patron goddess Athena, and the first and perhaps most important regional temple to the emperor Augustus and the goddess Roma, erected as early as 29 BC. There was a vibrant cult to the emperor in the city, a civic religious fervour that no doubt played a part in a long-running political rivalry between Pergamum and its two neighbours to the south. Enthusiastic participation in the cult of the emperor was one way a city could demonstrate its loyalty and value to the empire. It seems to have worked: Pergamum was awarded the title *neōkoros* no fewer than three times. Without making the distinction too hard and fast (recalling that religion and politics were always intertwined in the ancient world), we might say that if Ephesus was the city at the heart of Roman financial and administrative life in Asia Minor, Pergamum was its religious capital (Hemer 1986, 82).

What will Jesus say to a church in such a city? The opening 'thus says' formula, again echoing the Christological vision of chapter 1, is ominous in picking up the image of the 'sharp two-edged sword,' later adding that it comes from his mouth (2.16; cf. 1.16). We may already be expecting that these words will be words of judgement, cutting to the heart of the Pergamene Christian community. First, though, Jesus begins the body of his message to them with a dramatic recognition that they live 'where Satan's throne is' and 'where Satan lives.' There are a number of options for what this may mean, and they are not necessarily mutually exclusive. We recall, again, that Revelation's imagery has a remarkable capacity for multivalence. The high acropolis plateau on which the city stood may have seemed, to those approaching from the south, like a granite throne rising from the valley. This is a somewhat speculative interpretation of the language of 'Satan's throne' and requires a little imagination that may or may not have entered the minds of Pergamum's residents, but it could be part of the picture. Perhaps more significant, however, is not the city's geology but its religious life. Perhaps the 'Satan's throne' language refers obliquely to one of the shrines on the acropolis, such as the elevated altar to Zeus, or the *Sebastion* (the temple for the imperial cult). In any case, the theological significance of the imagery is clearer. A 'throne' is, after all, not just an elevated place but a place of authority, and the Christians of Pergamum are said to be living in the place where Satan's own authority sits. No doubt this imagery would represent a radical reimagining of the fervent civic pride most Pergamenes placed in the religion of their city and its subsequent standing in the empire. But, as we have seen, such reversals and conversions of the imagination are how the book of Revelation works. In the face of this Satanic rule, the church at Pergamum is praised for 'holding fast' to the name of Jesus while living right at the heart of this idolatrous system.

Apart from John himself, the only named believer in the whole book of Revelation is Antipas, who is now held up as a paradigmatic example of Christian witness. He is described by Jesus as *ho martys mou ho pistos mou*, 'my faithful witness,' words that echo the description of Jesus himself as the 'faithful witness' (*ho martys ho pistos*, 1.5). Antipas was evidently put to death, a reminder again that bearing faithful testimony to Jesus, even to the point of death, is at the heart of Revelation's doctrine of union with Christ and its vision of Christian discipleship. While the Greek word '*martys*' does not yet carry the sense of 'martyr,' it would one day mean exactly that. Antipas is not called a *martys* simply because of his death, but his death comes because of his *martyria*, his witness to Christ.

Given the clearly traumatic situation in which they live, it is something of a shock that Pergamum is not granted the reprieve given to Smyrna. Their rebuke, however, will not be as severe as the Ephesian one; Jesus only has 'a few' things against them. Despite their faithful witness, their community has become a place that tolerates false teaching, named here as 'the teaching of

Balaam.' This is almost certainly not the teacher's real name and may not even signal an individual so much as invoke this archetype and personification of false teaching (as in 2 Pet 2.15–16 and Jude 11). In any case, the allusion to Numbers 22–24 is primarily meant to signal theological errors, the 'stumbling blocks' that this teaching places before the people of God. John assumes his readers are familiar with the story (suggesting that there were at least some Jewish believers among them). Balaam, son of Boer, was summoned by Balak, king of Moab, to curse Israel. Famously, however, Balaam delivered a series of blessings, not curses, on Israel and gave an oracle of impending doom to the Moabites. It might seem odd, then, that his name appears here as a byword for false teaching. The subsequent idolatry and sexual infidelity at Peor (Num 25) are not clearly the result of Balaam's teaching. But this did not prevent later tradition holding him at least partly responsible for it. For example, Josephus's account of these events (in *Ant* 4.6.6 [126–30]) fills the narrative gap by having Balaam suggest the seduction strategy to Balak and the Midianites so that God might become angry with Israel. It is likely this sort of tradition that lies behind the statement that Balaam 'taught Balak to put a stumbling block before the people of Israel' (Rev 2.14). Although we are told that Balaam returned home after delivering his oracles, in Numbers 31 he reappears in the story only to be slain, along with the kings of Midian (31.8), by the armies of Israel. On returning from war, we are told, the people engaged in betrayal of the Lord, apparently at Balaam's instigation (31.16). Despite his words of blessing, Balaam thus became the poster child for false teaching that led Israel astray, particularly into idolatry connected with idol food and improper sexual relations (Num 25.1–3).

The evocation of Balaam's name, and the subsequent explanation, make it quite possible that food sacrificed to idols and sexual sins are connected to the false teaching in Pergamum. However, throughout the Old Testament prophetic tradition the image of sexual immorality is used, by extension, to signal unfaithfulness to God more broadly (see esp. Isa 1.21–23 and Ezek 16.1–58, which use the imagery of a sexually unfaithful city that Revelation will later develop). Sex work is a suitable metaphor for idolatry and infidelity to God because it is complicit in reducing a covenant relationship to a commercial transaction. This imagery will feature heavily in the prophetic challenges to faithful allegiance found in the later visions of Revelation, and this is arguably the far more serious issue here and throughout the book.

Alongside this contemporary 'Balaam,' the Pergamene church is rebuked for its tolerance of the 'Nicolaitans.' As we saw above, this group was also active in Ephesus, and so we can now add to that earlier discussion. The causal connection assumed here between Balaam and the Nicolaitans (note the 'thus' of v. 15) makes it possible that the teachings of this group also involved idolatrous behaviours around food and sex. Certainly there were plenty of opportunities for both in Pergamum: sacrificial meals and ritual sex were common features of Greco-Roman civil religion, and how to deal with the commercial aspects of this was a perennial challenge to the churches, as the extended discussions of this issue in Paul's letters to Corinth demonstrate. Perhaps the would-be 'victorious' Nicolaitans, like the strong and knowledgeable ones in 1 Corinthians 8, are guilty of teaching a libertarian approach to idol food that has become to their Pergamene brothers and sisters a 'stumbling block' (*skandalon*, v. 14; cf. 1 Cor 1.23 and 8.9, which use *proskomma* but make a similar point). This is more serious than the problems in Corinth, however, since it concerns false teaching and not just the exercise of Christian freedom. Lest the message to Smyrna lead us to think that persecution is always a sign of purity, the message to Pergamum shows us that it is possible to be simultaneously afflicted for holding fast to Christian witness while also being morally and spiritually compromised.

The proper response to this situation is repentance, and Jesus calls for it. If they do not repent, he says, he will come to them as a warrior. But his warfare will be waged with the sword from his mouth (cf. 1.16), a conquest of words that judge and divide not only false teaching from truth but even soul from spirit. The message to Pergamum then closes with the familiar formula 'let anyone who has an ear listen to what the Spirit is saying to the churches' and a closing promise to 'everyone who conquers.' The promise is twofold, though only one of the two images involves the usual foreshadowing of Revelation's closing visions.

First, there is the promise of 'hidden manna.' The allusions to Exodus 16 are obvious, and there are also connections to the earlier rebuke concerning food. Instead of corrupted idol feasts, those who conquer through faithful witness are promised the true divine food that comes from heaven. Subsequent to Israel's wilderness wanderings, a jar containing a supply of manna was stored in the ark of the covenant in the tabernacle (Ex 16.32; Heb 9.4). Jewish apocalyptic tradition maintained an eschatological hope that this hidden treasury of manna would be given to Israel at the consummation of time (*2 Bar* 29.8). Jesus's promise to distribute this 'hidden manna' suggests, therefore, his authority to bring about that eschatological consummation and open the treasuries of heaven to all who conquer.

Second, there is the promise of the gift of a 'white stone' inscribed with a new, secret name. The significance of the white stone is hard to pin down. One suggestion is this evokes the common practice of voting using small pebbles of different colours (see Acts 23.10, where the word for pebble, *psēphos*, is used by extension to speak of the casting of a vote), with a white stone signifying acquittal and therefore the vindication of the saints. This seems theologically appropriate for a symbol of an eschatological divine gift, and it resonates clearly with the theme of judgement that accompanies the sword of Jesus's mouth. Another option, however, is that this stone is something like an amulet, popular in antiquity to ward off evil, which often bore a secret inscription. This reading is less likely, since there is no suggestion here of protection from evil. Moreover, the secret inscription on the stone is the part of this image that echoes more clearly through the rest of the book. The 'new name' known only to the recipient is a feature of the promise to Philadelphia in 3.12, where it is not the name of the believer but Jesus's own name. This, as we will see, foreshadows the vision of Christ in chapter 19, where he appears as a rider on a white horse having 'a name inscribed that no one knows but himself' (19.12). In the closing vision of Revelation (22.4), the worshipping servants of God see the face of God and the Lamb, and they are given his name on their foreheads (cf. 14.1). It is most likely, therefore, that the name promised to the Pergamene conquerors is also to be read as Jesus's own name, indicating not protection but worship and allegiance. Though they may live in the very seat of Satan's power, threatened by violence and undermined by false teaching, the eschatological gift of God promised to those who hold fast to Jesus's name is this: to eat from the treasure stores of heaven, to receive acquittal on the day of judgement, and to bear the name of Christ.

Message to Thyatira, 2.18–29

Thyatira marks both a geographical and a literary turning point in the series of seven messages. From Pergamum, the road turns inland and heads southeast through the remaining four cities. As the fourth message, it is the middle one of the seven, but there are features of the message that signal that this structural turning point is more than a mere accident of ordering. As noted in the earlier discussion, each of the seven messages closes with some version of the phrase 'let anyone who has an ear listen to what the Spirit is saying to the churches' and a promise 'to everyone who conquers.' As we will see, however, the order of these two closing formulae in the last four messages is the reverse of the first three, and that shift begins here with Thyatira.

As well as being structurally central, it is a much longer message than those we have seen so far, which is surprising as there is nothing particularly significant (humanly speaking) about the city of Thyatira, especially in comparison with the regional importance of the first three coastal cities. It lay forty-five miles southeast of Pergamum, at the intersection of two major trade routes. In the New Testament, it was the home of Lydia, a dealer in purple cloth who came to faith in Jesus after hearing Paul preach in Philippi (Acts 16.14–15) and who opened her home to the apostles (Acts 16.40). The dyeing of purple cloth was a significant trade in the city, serving a growing market for that luxury commodity. In addition, a number of other artisanal guilds were to be found in the city. Thyatira is marked out as significant in the region largely because of its importance as a centre for trade and commerce, rather than, say, its temples. Again, as we will see, we must not follow this to the conclusion that there was no religious significance to such activities.

The opening formulae follow the established pattern, beginning with a 'thus says' and an aspect of the Christological vision. In this instance Jesus is identified as 'the Son of God, who has eyes like a flame of fire, and whose feet are like burnished bronze' (v. 18). Jesus's eyes and feet are thus described in 1.14–15, imagery that draws heavily on the Son of Man in Daniel 10, as we saw in that earlier discussion. Again, the eyes of fire signal the penetrating vision that Christ possesses, particularly in respect of the spiritual condition of his churches. Jesus is, as he will later say, 'the one who searches minds and hearts' (v. 23), echoing the words of God in Jeremiah 17.10.

While this imagery is taken from the earlier visionary material, continuing the Danielic echoes, the designation 'Son of God' is a new addition. This is the only use of the phrase 'Son of God' in the whole book of Revelation. There is a Jewish tradition of treating 'Son of Man' and 'Son of God' as somewhat interchangeable, due in part to reflection on the book of Daniel (Beale 1999, 259). The 'son of (the) god(s)' seen in the furnace with Shadrach, Meshach, and Abednego in Daniel 3.25 was connected to the 'Son of Man' with limbs of burnished bronze in Daniel 10.6. Both are essentially royal titles.

Jesus, with penetrating spiritual vision, next declares what he sees in the Thyatiran church. There is first some praise, for love, faith, service, and 'patient endurance,' the *sine qua non* of discipleship in Revelation. In contrast to the Ephesian church, who was abandoning its first love, the church in Thyatira are growing in good works, their last being greater than their first (v. 19).

It is not all good news, however. Jesus has a rebuke for them, and again it concerns the tolerance of false teachers in the church. This time the source is identified as 'Jezebel,' who is named, as with 'Balaam' in Pergamum, for symbolic rather than literal purposes. The historical Jezebel was Ahab's wife, and although her name has become something of a byword for sexual temptations, her primary acts of transgression in the biblical narrative are inciting the people of God to idolatry, engaging in false prophecy, and incorporating

Baal worship into the life of Israel (1 Kgs 16–19; 2 Kgs 9). Unlike her Old Testament namesake, the 'Jezebel' of verse 20 even calls herself a prophet, though John immediately declares that she is a false one, leading the people of God astray. The primary similarity between them, and thus the suitability of using her name, lies in the common theme of temptation to idolatrous worship, the expression of which in Thyatira is idol food and 'fornication.' The similarities with the false teaching of the Nicolaitans suggest that they may well be the same group, or at least teachers with similar messages concerning food and sex, perhaps here having some connection with the trade guilds (recalling again that commerce and religion were not neatly separate areas of life in the ancient world). Whatever its precise source and nature, Jesus declares this teaching false, a mortal danger to the health of the church in Thyatira. He later labels this teaching the 'deep things of Satan,' perhaps alluding to the claim that this teaching had to do with the 'deep things of God' (cf. 1 Cor 2.10) and reversing it.

As we saw earlier in the message to Pergamum, such idolatrous worship is often described as sexual infidelity in the Bible, and it is possible that the image of fornication and adultery in this extended rebuke of 'Jezebel' goes beyond a simple identification of sexual impropriety. It is important to remember that the primary problem here is not sex but false teaching, which is described with the familiar biblical metaphor of adultery. Though it may have included accommodationist errors in respect of sexual behaviour (as well as diet, which ought to get just as much attention), the deepest issue is the false gospel at the heart of the teaching of 'Jezebel.'

The message notes that this false teacher has been given time to repent (an important step in church discipline for such problems), suggesting that there has been an earlier word from Jesus on this matter in Thyatira. The words that follow are some of the harshest expressions of judgement one will find on Jesus's lips, but it is important throughout Revelation to note that the purpose of judgement is repentance. This will be important to remember in the chapters that follow. Repentance, however, has clearly not been forthcoming, and the punishment for such idolatrous 'adultery' is that Jesus throws 'Jezebel' down, echoing the demise of her namesake, who was killed by being thrown down from a window (2 Kgs 9.33). Here, though, the 'Jezebel' of Thyatira is thrown 'on a bed,' continuing the sexual metaphor. In my view, attempts to soften the sexual overtones of this word of judgement by rendering it 'sick bed' (citing a supposed Hebrew idiom) lack sufficient evidence. More importantly, they unhelpfully mix the metaphor with which John is consistently working here. Though the imagery is deeply disturbing, it is the appropriate judgement for the 'fornication' of false worship. Furthermore, as well as being a place for sexual activity, the other primary use of a *klinē* (the word translated 'bed' or 'couch') was for reclining at meals, making this judgement doubly appropriate in light of the specific sins named (see Koester 2014, 299, and see also Crossley 2003). As often in Revelation, the punishment fits the crime: divine punishment takes the form of allowing a particular transgression to take its course, allowing such works to receive what they deserve (v. 23), namely their natural results. Regrettably, sometimes the ones who bear such results are the children of those who sin. The children of Jezebel certainly met with horrific ends (2 Kgs 10.1–11). It is not clear here whether literal or metaphorical children are intended, though in light of how the imagery has worked so far, I am inclined to read these 'children' as metaphorical depictions of those who inherit the false teaching of 'Jezebel,' perhaps even her disciples. The reminder that 'all the churches' will know who Jesus is through this act of judgement perhaps underlines the structural centrality of this message to Thyatira and reminds us that, within these specific rebukes and encouragements, this is a letter to all the churches from the one who sees and judges.

Moreover, it is not just 'Jezebel' and her 'children' who receive this word of judgement. Jesus has a warning, and a call to repentance, for those who have shared in her unfaithful teaching and behaviour. The call to repentance is interestingly expressed here: 'repent of her doings.' How does one repent of someone else's doings? Revelation, here and elsewhere, captures the essentially participatory nature of the church's life. To bear faithful witness is construed as participation in the life and work of Jesus himself and is ultimately depicted with the metaphor of the union of marriage. Conversely, following the works and teachings of false teachers like this 'Jezebel' is construed as participation in her life and thus adultery. They may be her works, but the church in Thyatira is said to be sharing in them and thus actively complicit. We will see more of this sort of 'union' language in respect of fornication and sin in chapter 18 below. For now, it suffices to say that idolatry is a violation not just of the first commandment but of what the commandments express and safeguard: the covenant relationship between God and God's people. This union of deep fellowship is what gives the sexual metaphor its theological force, whether we are talking about the metaphor of marriage (in the case of faithfulness) or adultery (in the case of unfaithfulness).

Despite this extended word of rebuke, there are some in Thyatira who remain faithful and who have not participated in the adulterous false teaching of Jezebel. For them there are now some words of encouragement, as Jesus addresses them directly (using the plural 'you,' not the singular 'you' of the church's angel). No other burden will be laid on these already heavy-laden saints. John's language here sounds very much like that of the message from the Jerusalem Council in Acts 15.28–29, where the questions of food and fornication were on the agenda. Whether or not John knew Acts, it is quite possible that he was familiar with the church's established instructions for Gentile believers in these matters, and his instruction here may (intentionally or not) echo this apostolic decree (Aune 2017, 208; Beale 1999, 266). Given the surrounding threats of false teaching and idolatrous practice, it is enough for the Thyatiran saints to 'hold fast' until Jesus comes. Such an instruction may appear to commend a passive or quietistic ethic, but what follows immediately subverts such simplistic readings. This 'holding fast' to the end in the face of tribulation is what it means to 'conquer' in Revelation. This time the promise to the conqueror precedes the 'ears to hear' formula and also includes a call for perseverance to 'the end.' The content of the promise weaves royal and messianic imagery from Psalm 2 (the iron rod and shattered pots) into the usual foreshadowing of one of the closing visions. The enduring saints, far from being passive, are promised a share in Jesus's authority to judge the nations (cf. Rev 20.4). In addition, there is a promise of the 'morning star,' a share in who Jesus is (Rev 22.16), and another image of authority.

This central message to the church in Thyatira then closes with the call to listen to what the Spirit is saying to all the churches.

Message to Sardis, 3.1–6

The road continues southeast for another thirty to forty miles to Sardis. It was a splendid city with an illustrious history, once home to wealthy kings. The river Pactolus, which ran through the city, was said to contain gold dust and was connected in legend to Midas, who was believed to have washed off his curse in its waters. More prosaically, it made its name through a vibrant mining industry and a thriving trade in textiles. By the end of the first century, however, much of this former glory had faded. Its geology, a rocky plateau surrounded by sheer cliffs, made it a suitable place for a military stronghold that was thought by most to be impregnable. Impregnable, that is, until 546 BC, when a sneak infiltration of the walls, unnoticed by the guard, led to its capture. Subsequently, 'capturing Sardis' became a metaphor for achieving the impossible. When this happened a second time, hubris and a lack of vigilance were blamed. The city was destroyed in AD 17, not by invaders but by a large earthquake, which extensively damaged a number of cities in the region, including the neighbouring city of Philadelphia. Sardis's subsequent reconstruction was completed with imperial support.

The opening address of this quite brief message echoes the imagery of the 'seven spirits' and 'seven stars' from the opening Christological vision (1.16,

20; cf. 1.4). Again the theological emphasis is on Christ's sovereignty as the one who holds the fate of the churches in his hands, held together (quite literally) with the all-seeing vigilance of the sevenfold Spirit. The phrase 'seven spirits' is found four times in the book (here and at 1.4, 4.5, and 5.6) and is, as discussed earlier in the commentary on 1.4, an image of the divine Spirit. In this opening address to Sardis, the Christological imagery is remarkable. As well as the assurance of God's protection and vigilant care for his churches in Christ (no doubt a message that would have hit home even more powerfully in a city famed for its history of hubris), we also see that the churches are held together, by Christ, with the Spirit of God.

Most of the time, the 'I know your works' formula introduces some note of praise, or at least a mixture of praise and correction. Here, an almost entirely negative rebuke follows (and hence there will be no need for a balancing 'nevertheless.') The problem in Sardis is not the presence of false teaching, tolerance of idolatry and moral transgression, or another such thing invading the community. Rather, the nature of the issue is at the heart of the spiritual condition of the church itself. Like their city of old, they have a good reputation, a 'name' for being alive. But the reality, from the point of view of the all-seeing gaze of Jesus, is that they are dead. Their 'works,' which are judged not to be perfect (lit., 'fulfilled'), aren't really works at all, it seems, but just a good name.

Once again, Revelation reverses the apparent state of things. As with Lazarus, Jesus commands the dead church in Sardis to 'wake up' and strengthen what remains of their near-death faith. Having thus been woken from the sleep of death, their instructions are threefold. First, they are to remember what they have been told. Second, they are to obey. And third, they are to repent. These three form the content of the kind of theological vigilance to which the church in Sardis is called, and it remains a potent theological stimulus for any church. Remembrance, obedience, and repentance are Christ's smelling salts for an unconscious church.

Like their twice-invaded fortress, the reputation of the church in Sardis is no substitute for such vigilance, and hubris will always be exposed. Jesus warns them that, unless they wake up and start paying attention, he will come to them unexpectedly, like a thief in the night. This last expression is found in the eschatological teachings of Jesus in the Gospels (Mt 24.43) and of Paul's letters (1 Thess 5.2–4). This image is often connected to Jesus's final return, but here the message is of a more imminent unexpected 'coming' with a wake-up call of judgement for a sleepy church. Similar warnings were given, we recall, to Ephesus (2.5) and Pergamum (2.16). The two 'comings' are theologically connected, for Jesus is the one who perpetually 'comes' to his churches, as Revelation will repeatedly indicate, and this is a down payment and guarantee of his final coming to the world to restore all things.

There is a small crumb of encouragement hidden in this severe rebuke, however. We are told that there are some in Sardis (lit., 'a few names'—the impression given is that we could easily list them) who 'have not soiled their clothes.' A small handful of faithful saints will not last long in a catatonic church, however, and so Jesus's wake-up call must be heard. The reward for these few whose clothes are not soiled is that they walk in white, one of Revelation's favourite images for the faithful church (e.g., 7.13–14; 14.4; 22.14). It is an image that has Old Testament echoes in Zechariah 3.1–5, and in the Roman world it was the clothing of both a military victor and a pure worshipper (again, Revelation delights in such multivalent images).

Like the few found worthy, this attire is promised to all who conquer, and with it the promise of a name in the book of life, foreshadowing the imagery of the closing visions (see 20.12, 15; 21.27). The 'book of life' was a widespread image in the Old Testament and second temple Jewish literature (Ex 32.32–33; Dan 12.1; Mal 3.16; *Jub* 19.9; 30.22). Being blotted from the book of life meant, quite logically, death (e.g., Ps 69.28). It may also indicate the ledger of heavenly citizenship. As with Ephesus, and the threat of the removal of its lampstand, here there is an important theological question: is this erasure a real possibility?

This is not a question unique to this passage or even to the book of Revelation; some of the Old Testament passages cited above also include the suggestion that names can be removed from the book of life. This exact threat is also found in the *Birkat ha-Minim* ('blessing on the heretics'), a Jewish liturgical text taken by some to be roughly contemporary with Revelation and possibly involved in the early excommunication of Christians from the synagogue. It was the twelfth benediction (perhaps more accurately 'malediction') of the eighteen used in contemporary Jewish daily liturgy, and in some versions it is explicitly directed against 'the Nazarenes,' cursing them with (among other things) removal from the book of life. This connection is hotly debated but is at the very least an indication of the more widespread use of the 'blotting from the book of life' metaphor to denote not only physical death but also religious excommunication of those deemed heretical.

And so we return to the theological question. With Jesus's use of this metaphor, is the possibility suggested, then, that the church in Sardis, or any believer, can have their entry in the ledger of heaven removed? Is this a veiled threat from Jesus, and if so is it a real or empty one? In approaching these questions, we do well to note at the outset that God has already entered their names in this book from the foundation of the world (13.8; 17.8), purely by the grace of divine election. We also do well to note that Jesus himself holds all seven churches secure in his hands and promises to confess their names before his father and the angels. After all, he is the one who can speak even to dead churches and command them to wake.

That said, there are some indications in the text that this may not be quite the 'conditional salvation' text a surface reading might suggest. The worrying 'if' that begins the verse in most English translations, suggesting the presence of a conditional clause, is absent from the Greek, which simply begins 'the conquering ones will be clothed . . . .' This, like all the closing words to the 'conquerors,' is first and foremost a promise and an assurance rather than a threat. Moreover, the phrase 'I will certainly not blot out' is emphatically negative and quite possibly an instance of *litotes*, understatement for effect, often by negating the opposite of the positive one wishes to assert (Mathewson 2020, 43; also Beale 1999, 280). Read as such, Jesus's promise not to blot them out of his book is not a veiled threat that such a thing would be possible, but quite the opposite: the assertion of the permanence of that inscription.

Another option for reading this language is that there is here an implied contrast with the contemporary political practice of removing citizenship (often immediately prior to execution) by means of blotting names from a ledger (Koester 2014, 319–320). Unlike the books of earthly citizenship, a name in the book of life is indelible. However, just as with the Ephesian lampstand (and indeed with the witness of the whole New Testament), we must not forget that the indicative of divine election does not negate the imperative of human accountability. The failure to confess the name of Jesus is a serious matter.

Message to Philadelphia, 3.7–13

Twenty-eight miles further southeast is the city of Philadelphia. It was extensively damaged, though not as heavily as Sardis, in the huge earthquake of AD 17 and had since been substantially rebuilt, again with imperial assistance. Cracks in the city walls caused by tremors were commonplace, and many of the city's inhabitants therefore took to living outside the city itself. This local geological instability had a positive side to it, however. The volcanic soil was particularly fertile and especially good for nourishing vineyards, for which the area was famous. Its population was cosmopolitan, with people relocating there from all over Asia, Macedonia, and Rome, as well as a Jewish community.

The message to the church in Philadelphia opens, like the others, with a 'thus says' formula and allusions to Revelation's inaugural christological vision. This time, although there are a number of images clustered together, the connections to chapter 1 are less clear. That Jesus is the one who is the 'key of David' might allude to 1.18 and the 'keys of Death and of Hades,' but the far stronger allusion here is to Isaiah 22.22, especially when taken together with the phrase 'who opens and no one will shut, who shuts and no one opens.' The key is a symbol of authority, and in Isaiah's oracle the 'key of the house of David' is taken from corrupt officials and given to Eliakim son of Hilkiah, conferring upon him the authority to grant access to the king. In later Jewish reflection, this key was said to open the sanctuary itself (*Targ Isa* 22.22; cf. Beale 1999, 284; Koester 2014, 324), and as such there may well be a sense of this opening being to the divine presence. The designation 'holy and true' is predicated of the Lord God in 6.10, though 'Holy One' is a common divine name throughout the Scriptures.

Metaphors of open doors and other architectural features run through the body of the message. For a church in a city regularly shaken by geological tremors, the strength and security of buildings would be a common concern. Jesus first tells them that he has 'set before them an open door.' In the New Testament this metaphor usually indicates opportunities for evangelism. In the Corinthian correspondence, for example, Paul twice speaks of an open door for effective gospel work (1 Cor 16.9; 2 Cor 2.12; see also Col 4.3). It is possible that a similar sense is meant here, that in the midst of their difficulties, Jesus has opened a door for the preaching of the gospel in Philadelphia. However, in light of the allusions to Isaiah discussed above and in the context of the whole message, it is perhaps more likely that Jesus opens this door not for them to walk out in the work of evangelism but for them to enter into the safety of the house of God. As we often find with the imagery of the book of Revelation, a double meaning is entirely possible (so Beale 1999, 287).

As with Smyrna, there is no word of rebuke in this short and positive message to the Philadelphian church. There seem to be a number of similarities in the situations of both churches. Jesus knows that they are a church with 'little power,' who are bearing faithful testimony to Jesus in the face of opposition. It is another striking reversal that in these seven messages the 'little' and 'poor' churches are the ones who are great and rich in their faithful witness to Jesus. The connection between suffering and witness, and the visionary reversal of what appears to be success and failure, are common themes in the book and should give us pause when we try to evaluate the 'success' of any church on the basis of earthly appearances.

It is a sad irony that there should be such a family feud in the city of brotherly love (Blount 2013, 73). Again, as in Smyrna, the opposition comes from 'the synagogue of Satan,' apparently a Jewish group, 'those who say they are Jews and are not, but are lying' (3.9; cf. 2.9). Jesus sets himself in direct opposition to them. In contrast to such falsehood, he is the one who is 'true.' In contrast to these would-be Davidides, Jesus is the one who is the 'key of David,' the one with real authority to open the doors to the Davidic kingdom. The precise nature of the opposition, however, is not clear. There is no indication that they are suffering physical persecution or even the imprisonment and possible execution of Smyrna. It seems that the church in Philadelphia is to be spared such horrors. Reading in the reflection of what is promised to the church, however, we can at the very least surmise that some form of strong rejection of the believers was involved, perhaps community exclusion or even pressure to deny Christ.

Whatever its exact nature, the Philadelphian church is promised that their present situation of opposition will be reversed, as those in the 'synagogue of Satan' are compelled by Jesus to acknowledge them and recognise that they are loved by him. Here is another remarkable ironic reversal. In the Old Testament eschatological hopes, it is the Gentiles who are made to come, bent low, to recognise that God loves Israel. An example of this with clear connections to Revelation is Isaiah 60, where we read the following oracle:

> The descendants of those who oppressed you shall come bending low to you,
> and all who despised you shall bow down at your feet;
> they shall call you the City of the LORD, the Zion of the Holy One of Israel. (Isa 60.14)

This passage also informs the imagery of the New Jerusalem at the end of Revelation (there are clear echoes of Isa 60.11 in Rev 21.25–26, with the city's open gates and the nations coming in). Here in Revelation 3 the roles are reversed: it is those who 'say that they are Jews and are not' who will recognise that the (largely Gentile) church of Philadelphia contains God's beloved.

Jesus has been so intent to encourage the Philadelphian church with this promised reversal that he has not yet named their 'works.' This now comes in verse 10. Because they have 'kept' the 'word of patient endurance,' they themselves will be 'kept' from the trials to come. Jesus's promise to 'come' to them therefore strikes a hopeful note here, not a threatening one. The Philadelphian church are not instructed to repent or change their ways but only to continue in this testifying life, holding fast, like Thyatira, to their witness. We can safely assume, I think, that such holding fast is the content of what it means for the church to conquer, and the crown they wear is again the *stephanos*, the victor's wreath.

Those who conquer in this way are promised a reward, again described with imagery taken from the closing visions of the book. The message continues its architectural theme, taking a number of such details from the vision of the New Jerusalem in chapters 21 and 22. This church that has proven itself steadfast under pressure is fittingly to be made a permanent pillar in the temple, never to leave it. There are no tremors that can threaten the stability of this building; it is now safe to come inside. As with Pergamum, the promise to the conquerors also includes a promise of a new name, written now not on a stone but on the church itself. This is not three names but a threefold name. First, the name of God written on them indicates a new mark of divine ownership (cf. 22.4). Second, being given the name of the city of God both strengthens the Isaianic allusions (cf. Isa 60.14b) and marks the people with a new allegiance in the city that comes down from heaven (cf. 21.2, 10). Third, the name of Jesus himself confirms a new identity in him (cf. 14.1; 22.4).

Message to Laodicea, 3.14–22

Our circular journey of the seven churches of Asia Minor ends southeast of where it began, as the messenger carrying John's scroll descends into the fertile Lycus valley toward their last stop: Laodicea. It was a wealthy city, due in large part to its location at a junction of two important trade routes, the road south meeting the one heading east from the Mediterranean coast. There were a number of prosperous industries in the city, including banking, textiles (famously a local black wool), and medicine (there are indications that the city was known especially for a locally produced eye salve). Its fertility was due to the same volcanic geology that benefitted its neighbours to the north, and Laodicea had also been damaged in the earthquake of AD 17. Imperial assistance to repair the city had been offered and accepted. When a second earthquake struck in AD 60, however, the city was prosperous enough to rebuild without such assistance, and this became an occasion for great civic pride. It was a proudly self-sufficient and independently minded city. There has been much discussion of one aspect of Laodicean civic life: its water supply. Hot volcanic springs were nearby at Hierapolis, and cool, fresh water was available at Colossae. Laodicea, it seems, had neither and relied on an imported supply. Many commentators note how the aqueducts that brought water to the city from hot springs, while an impressive feat of engineering, left the water tepid and nauseating by the time it arrived at Laodicea. Though it presents an intriguing possibility, the archaeological evidence for this is thin, and there are a number of pieces of counter-evidence that suggest nothing particularly unpleasant about the water supply in the city (see Koester 2003). It is more likely, then, that the drinking water imagery alludes not to the specific details of Laodicean plumbing but more broadly to dining practices in the ancient world, where both hot and cold water would be served at meals. We shall comment on this again below.

The churches in these three cities of the Lycus valley were well established and had a close relationship both geographically and spiritually. The presence of a church in Laodicea can be traced back to the beginnings of Paul's gospel ministry in the region and is mentioned repeatedly in his letter to Colossae (Col 2.1; 4.13–16). Colossians even describes a letter written to Laodicea (Col 4.16), which has either been lost to history or (as some think) has been preserved as the letter we call Ephesians, a debate that goes back to the church fathers. The instruction to the church in Colossae to read the letter to Laodicea indicates their close relationship and reminds us that these epistles, though directed at specific churches, were at times also intended for wider distribution. Certainly this is true of the seven oracles in Revelation 2–3, which (we recall) form part of one circular letter to be read by all.

This oracle opens, again, with a 'thus says' and an aspect of Revelation's Christological vision. Jesus is designated 'the Amen,' an unusual title (though it is found as a divine name in Isa 65.16, the Hebrew sometimes imperfectly smoothed out as 'God of faithfulness') but certainly an appropriate one for this final message. Again Jesus takes for himself a name used for God. The repetition of such a practice in Revelation should not numb us to its profound theological significance. He is also then called 'the faithful and true witness,' recalling the words of 1.5. 'True' (*alēthinos*) is the translation option taken by the Septuagint for the Greek rendering of Isaiah 65's 'Amen.' The effect of both expressions is similar: it is a double self-declaration of the surety of Christ's testimony to the previous six churches as well as what is about to be declared to Laodicea. It is also an implicit reminder of the call to discipleship in all the churches, summoned to bear faithful witness to Jesus. This is a task in which the Laodicean church seems to be failing, as we will see.

The Christological title *hē archē tēs ktiseōs*, 'the origin (or better 'beginning') of creation,' is a tantalising one, not least because of the similar language found in the New Testament letter to neighbouring Colossae, describing Christ's cosmic and creative lordship (cf. Col 1.15–18). The word *archē* is also significant in the prologue of John's Gospel. It is evocative of the similar word *archōn*, 'ruler,' in Revelation 1.5, from where the first Christological title was taken, as we just saw. Again there is merit in allowing this ambiguity to have theological significance by reading both resonances simultaneously. Christ is 'first' in a double sense, as both the origin and the ruler of all creation. The two roles are theologically linked. Because Christ is both origin and ruler of all created things, the gospel that concerns him also concerns all things, and not just the souls of the saints. Likewise, this book, the revelation of Jesus Christ, will in due course turn its attention to much more than these seven churches.

As the body of the message to Laodicea begins, it becomes immediately clear that it is going to be the opposite of the ones to Philadelphia and Smyrna. The content is resoundingly critical, almost entirely lacking in praise or hopeful notes. The theme of water is evident from the start, with the church described as 'lukewarm, neither hot nor cold.' This metaphor is sometimes read as an assessment of their 'spiritual temperature,' but that makes little sense in the light of verse 15, where Jesus wishes they were 'either cold or hot.' If the point were to measure their zeal on a temperature scale, surely a lukewarm love of God would fare better than a cold one? Why would Jesus want them to be 'cold' in their faith? The metaphor, however, is not about fervour but about effectiveness. Cold water is refreshing, and hot water is soothing (or even medicinal); both have their positive uses, and both can be enjoyed with a meal. The lukewarm water of Laodicea, however, is neither one thing nor the other and is therefore spat out. We should note that this metaphor is deployed as an assessment of the Laodicean church's 'works,' not their spiritual passion, and the primary work to which they are called is to bear witness to Jesus. It is easy for water to become lukewarm. All it needs to do is sit around for long enough, and the ambient temperature will have its effect (Thomas and Macchia 2016, 128). The same has happened, it seems, with the gospel witness of the church in Laodicea. Having accommodated to the surrounding environment, their witness has become neither refreshing nor healing but altogether complacent and ineffective. As with the removal of the Ephesian lampstand, or the deletion of Sardis from the book of life, there is a warning here that they will be spat out.

The city of Laodicea had prided itself on its fiercely independent and self-sufficient spirit, a culture encapsulated in the self-funded rebuilding after the earthquake of AD 60. But this culture has infiltrated the church's discipleship in unhelpful ways. Just like their city, they think of themselves as rich, prosperous, and needing nothing. This assessment is dramatically reversed by Jesus's fivefold revelation: they are 'wretched, pitiable, poor, blind, and naked.' The church in the city that has grown wealthy from textiles and eye salve is, from Christ's point of view, both naked and blind. This apocalyptic reversal is the polar opposite of the one in the message to Smyrna, who thought themselves poor but were rich.

All is not lost, however: the reversal can be reversed. Jesus counsels them to acquire true wealth, to buy true clothes, and to receive true medicine directly from him. There is a call to humility here for the church in Laodicea to recognise its spiritual poverty, to acknowledge its sin of spiritual self-sufficiency, and to turn in utter dependency to Christ who alone is sufficient. Buried in the logic of this devastating rebuke, however, is the message's only positive note. Jesus's stern discipline of the Laodicean church is a demonstration of his enduring fatherly love for them (cf. Deut 8.5; Prov 13.24; Eph 6.4), intended to reveal the truth and bring about repentance and change. In performing this educative work, Jesus remains the one who holds the churches. Even the lukewarm church in Laodicea remains a star in Christ's hands, and he walks among them. This reminder of fatherly discipline stands as a word for all the churches, then. It is better for a church to be rebuked by Jesus than to be forgotten, as if the latter were even possible.

The words that follow are some of the most famous from the whole book, and they close the seven oracles to the churches. As such, they are worth a little more of our time. We have the usual call to repentance, accompanied now with a command to listen. Those who do so will hear two sounds: a knocking on a door and the voice of Christ outside. This famous image has often been put to powerful use in evangelism, as a call to open the door of our hearts to the knocking Christ. We might consider, for example, the famous painting *The Light of the World* by William Holman Hunt, which depicts Christ knocking on the door of the human heart, a door overgrown with weeds and having no handle on the outside, so that access must be granted from within. Without wishing to pour water on that particular evangelistic fire, we do well to notice who is being addressed: the church in Laodicea. The door at which Jesus knocks is not the door of an unbeliever's heart but the door of the church (Resseguie 2009, 102)—in all their self-sufficiency the church itself has shut its Lord outside! No wonder such loving reproof characterises this message, for a church that bars the door to Jesus is in danger of becoming no church at all. Thankfully, Jesus has not walked away from the closed door, and he longs to 'come in' and eat with his people.

As we have seen, in these seven oracles, Jesus has repeatedly promised (or warned about) his coming to his churches through a number of different images. He comes to remove a lampstand (2.5), and he comes as a warrior (2.16), a judge (2.22), a thief (3.3), or a protector (3.10). Here, lastly, he comes as a dinner guest, waiting to be invited in. The imagery thus connects to the dining metaphor associated with the hot and cold water at the start of the message. Perhaps, though, as in the gospel *parousia* parable (Mk 13.33–37; Lk 12.35–38), he is not a guest but the owner of the house, returning home and expecting his servants alert and ready to welcome him—but instead finding a closed door.

This 'coming' of Christ is usually interpreted as a future event (and sometimes as one in the past), but here the image of the knocking Christ speaks urgently of Christ's 'coming' to his church *in the present*. This does not mean, however, that we should reduce future hope to a moment of imminent existential decision. To do so would be to engage in a false zero-sum logic, often at play in such discussions. Emphasising the present does not negate the future eschatological force of the *parousia* of Jesus, nor does an emphasis on the future constitute a downplaying of the present. Against this, the image of Christ as 'the one who knocks' unites the two apocalyptic moments. As Swiss theologian Karl Barth puts it, 'the eschatological character of the divine reconciliation and revelation does not mean any negation of its presence . . . . If a man presents himself to me or knocks at my door, he is present as one who is "future" to me, that is, as one "who comes to me"' (*Church Dogmatics* I/2, 95). To speak of Christ as the one who perpetually knocks at the door of the church is to speak doubly, both of his present knocking and of his future entering in. Christ's future coming in glory and his present coming by the Spirit (and, for that matter, his past coming in the incarnation) are not to be set against one another in a zero-sum game. He is present to the church as the one who was, who is, and who comes.

The New Testament bears witness to this threefold nature of Christ's advent in his incarnation, his presence by the Spirit, and the promise of his return. When understood from the creaturely perspective, these three distinguishable 'comings' are indexed as separate events on the timeline of human history, past, present, and future. In this way, and only in this way, we can speak of interruption, discontinuity, and the delay of his *parousia*. When understood from the divine perspective, however, these are not three separate events but rather three interrelated forms of the singular advent of Christ. From this perspective, Christ's coming in incarnation, expectation, and consummation are united as one and the same apocalyptic event, and it is here that the continuity of divine promise and fulfilment is to be located. From this perspective, we might say it is a theological distortion to speak of a 'second coming,' since there is but one *parousia*, one advent of Christ in his effective presence, triply indexed to creaturely history and yet not circumscribed by it. We can perhaps see this idea expressed in narrative form in the farewell discourse of John's gospel, where Jesus says to his disciples, 'I am going away, and I am coming to you' (Jn 14.28). Here in Revelation 3, we see it in the image of the knocking Christ. Christ simply *is* the coming one, the one who perpetually knocks at the door of the church. To speak of this knocking is to speak of Christ's effective presence in the mode of expectation. As expectation, though, it also shares in the hope of his entering in, his presence in the mode of consummation. At the sound of the knocking Christ, expectation and consummation are joined. The book of Revelation ends with a vision that expresses this final hope, depicting Christ's coming to his Bride and with his eschatological *parousia* saying, repeated three times: 'I am coming soon' (Rev 22.7, 12, 20; cf. 3.11). The Spirit and the Bride respond, 'Amen, come' (Rev 22.17), but until that day of consummation Christ remains present to the church in the mode of apocalyptic expectation, present as 'the one who knocks.'

Instead of reading this image as Christ the guest hoping to be invited into our hearts, it speaks of Christ the master coming unexpectedly to his own house. We are not the householders, but he is—and he is indeed now already present as the one knocking at the door of his church. He is the one who knocks, the one who comes to us through the ages, and the one who is now present to the church in the mode of imminent expectation. And this effective presence as the coming one, the one already present in knocking expectation, contains within it the promise of his final coming in consummation, to enter in and eat with his Bride. His patient knocking remains striking, though, given the previous message to Philadelphia, where Jesus is described as the one with power to open and close doors (Paul 2018, 116–17). This same powerful one now waits to be invited in. He depicts himself as being just outside the door, ready to come in and eat with any who will open.

The closing promise to the conquerors, the last of the seven, again foreshadows the book's final visions. In 20.4–6 and 22.5, those who had been killed for their faithful testimony (which, we recall, is what 'conquering' means in Revelation) are given a share in the reign of Christ, the faithful witness, and authority to sit on thrones and judge. This is no self-sufficient enthronement, however, but a participation in Christ's throne and in his conquering, achieved at the cross. The church in Laodicea, with all the churches, is thus reminded that their victory through faithful witness, as always in Revelation, is bound up with his. This is the main goal of the whole book, to exhort and to resource theologically the church's faithful witness to Jesus Christ.

These final images, of a door and a throne, forge a connection between the seven oracles to the churches and the visionary material that comes next, where a door stands open to the heavenly throne room.

The Throne and the Lamb

Revelation 4.1–5.14

The Throne Vision, 4.1–11

John's Ascent to the Throne Room, vv. 1–6a

What follows in chapters 4–5 (which operate as a single unit) is perhaps the most important vision of the whole book, for it provides the answer to the apocalyptic question at the heart of the book of Revelation: 'to whom does the sovereignty of the world belong?' (Käsemann 1969, 135; see the discussion of this in the introduction). In terms of literary structure, these two chapters launch the series of visions that will run through the rest of the book, guiding and underpinning their proper interpretation. The end of the seventh message to the churches is a natural breaking point in the structure of the book as a whole, and the reader expects something new as soon as the message to Laodicea closes. This is reinforced with other structural markers in the text. The phrase 'after this I looked,' often used by John to indicate the beginning of a new vision, opens this section. In verse 2, John's comment that he was 'in the spirit' also indicates that a new visionary section is beginning, as it did in 1.10, while reminding us of the ecstatic nature of the visions.

But the start of chapter 4 turns out to be a far more major shift than one might expect. Up until this point, John's narrated experience has been set on Patmos, where he encountered a vision of Christ who dictated the seven messages to him. While the vision was 'in the spirit' and full of heavenly imagery, its setting was earthly: Jesus appears to John on Patmos. With the restatement of that phrase, then, one might expect the continuation of this setting, perhaps with further revelations from Christ. But instead, the setting now changes dramatically, as John sees a door standing open in heaven and is commanded to 'come up here.' From now on, John's narrative setting will be the courts of heaven, which gives the visions a new theological perspective.

John is not the first or the last prophet to see an open heaven and to narrate a heavenly ascent experience. Isaiah tells us of how he saw the throne room of God (Isa 6), as did Ezekiel (Ezek 1) and Daniel (Dan 7), and familiarity with those prophetic visionary experiences will enrich the reading of John's ascent to heaven. Beyond the canon, Jewish apocalyptic literature is full of narrated ascent experiences, in which the seer crosses the permeable boundary between heaven and earth in order to learn their secrets. There are too many texts to name them all, but examples include *The Book of the Watchers* (*1 Enoch* 1–36, esp. ch. 14), the *Testament of Levi*, and the *Ascension of Isaiah*. (For a masterful treatment of this subgenre and its emphases, see Himmelfarb 1993.) These ascents are often particularly focussed on the heavenly temple (or heaven *as* temple) and the divine throne, wheeled and glorious, with its angelic entourage. Within this visionary tradition, the images of palace and temple are two aspects of the same thing. The heavenly throne room was seen as a temple and the heavenly temple as a throne room. This insight helps us to understand the ways in which John's ascent to heaven, narrated here in chapter 4, deploys a mixture of throne room and temple imagery.

There are some differences, however, between John's ascent and the usual tropes of this tradition. One of these distinctive features of John's ascent, as we will shortly see, is that the voice that commands John to 'come up' is not an angelic guide (commonly found in such texts) but the voice of Christ himself. Another is the immediacy of John's ascent experience. Often (as in *1 Enoch* 14, for example) the ascending seer will journey through multiple doors, concentric rooms, heavenly tiers, and/or zones of purity before arriving, at length, in the heavenly throne room / holy of holies. Even then, there might still be a lengthy narrated mystical experience of the contemplation of the throne, its wheels and so on, before any comments (if at all) are made about its occupant. Not so with John. No sooner has he seen the open door in heaven than he is before the throne and the one seated on it, who is then promptly described. In comparison with the Jewish heavenly ascent tradition, John's narrated experience is arresting in its immediacy.

But, as important as this context might be, John's vision is not simply an account of his ascent to heaven and what he saw there. If we restrict our attention to that we will miss something profoundly important about this book, for it is also a renewed vision of earth, seen from a heavenly perspective. The things seen in heaven have a number of correspondences and implications for the things of earth, though John's perspective on that material will, from now on, be from 'above.' These visions are not just visions of heaven but a 'heaven's-eye-view' on the world and its history.

Before going any further, it is worth pausing to remind ourselves about the nature of the book's imagery and how that shapes the task of interpretation (on which see also the introduction). Two guiding principles may help us here. First, there is the theme, which we have already seen at work in the seven messages to the churches, of apocalyptic 'reversal.' In the chapters that follow, John will see remarkable heavenly visions that reverse earthly appearances. Earthly defeats will be seen as victories, power as weakness, beauty as horror. Time and space will be manipulated and imbued with theological meaning or, more accurately, will have their true theological significance revealed. One of the reasons John is commanded to ascend to heaven is so that he may gain this perspective of apocalyptic reversal: all is not as it seems. While the messages to the churches offer this reversal in specific targeted oracles, given by Jesus through John as his intermediary, John himself will now experience that perspective firsthand and on a global scale. While there is a clear and major division in the book at this point, this shared emphasis on visionary reversal (not to mention the numerous details of the visions themselves) unites the book as a whole.

Second, as with the imagery that we have already encountered in the opening chapters, the interpretation of these visions will often require us to think about two things at once: the immediate earthly situation that corresponds to the visionary imagery and the 'deeper' theological significance that, like heaven itself, transcends earthly space and time. There is, as it were, a drama playing out on two levels 'simultaneously' (the word is surely inadequate where heaven is concerned). Neither cancels out the other but are seen in their myriad relations. Correspondingly, interpretation of Revelation's imagery requires an exercise of simultaneous two-level thinking. Historical 'decoding' may allow us to see (again, like chapters 2–3) the immediate earthly situation of the churches of Asia Minor recast in revelatory terms. Such historical interpretation is by no means unimportant to a responsible reading of Revelation. But this act of historical analysis does not exhaust the task of interpretation, as if the book's imagery were a 'code' to be deciphered into flat prose, whereupon it can safely be discarded. As such, the literary form of Revelation is treated as a problem to be solved rather than something to be embraced for what it is. This is a danger that is present both in the 'prose' of rigorous preterist interpretation and that of futurist dispensational timelines. In such approaches the theological and imaginative power of the imagery is defused. Rather, we will need to hold those first-century historical insights together, simultaneously, with the theological 'surplus of meaning' that is expressed through the imagery and transcends that specific first-century context. If we can manage this, we will approach a reading that attends faithfully to the redoubled nature of the book's literary form and theological meaning. These two interpretative insights, 'reversal' and 'redoublement,' are necessary exercises of the theological imagination for the interpretation of the visions that fill chapters 4–22.

And so let us return to 4.1. The voice that commands John to ascend is, he tells us, the same trumpet-like voice that first spoke to him at the start of the Christological vision in 1.10–11. Though this is now a new vision, it is the same Jesus who speaks. Having just heard Jesus calling and knocking at the closed door of the Laodicean church (3.20), John now hears that same voice inviting him through a door that is open. Having conquered and sat down with the Father on the throne (3.21), Jesus now beckons John into that very throne room. In this way, the opening scene of chapter 4 is linked closely to the closing of chapter 3. This is important not only as evidence of the literary unity of the book but also for the integrity of its theological purposes. In the midst of the variously challenging historical situations that marked out the seven messages to the seven churches of Asia, the call to 'conquer' is not just an earthly exhortation but is linked, in the person of Christ, to the realities of heaven. Accompanying the promise that the victorious will share the throne is a vision of the throne room and a reminder, perhaps despite earthly appearances, that the sovereignty of the world belongs to God, and God's reign endures.

As in the book's opening verse, Jesus is the agent of revelation in this vision, and he will show John 'what must take place.' What is about to be revealed are the things that follow logically from the call to witness in the seven churches, though (as we will see) they are visions that also overflow the constraints of earthly cause and effect. They are things that 'must' happen because God is sovereign, and so it is appropriate that the first thing revealed is a vision of God on the throne. John stretches human language to the breaking point in an attempt to describe this divine vision. It is not the form of 'the one on the throne' that is here described, but his attributes. In saying that the one seated on the throne 'looks like' various precious stones, we should attend therefore to the theological appropriateness of the imagery for expressing these divine attributes. John draws the imagery from a deep well of Old Testament texts. The jewels, while certainly indicating that what is seen here is glorious and precious, evoke (without precise correspondence) the list of stones embedded in the priestly breastplate in Exodus 28.17–20. Jasper and carnelian are the last and first stones listed there, a detail that is perhaps significant for the one who is the first and the last.

Surrounding his throne is an emerald-like arc. It is possible to translate the Greek word *iris* as 'halo,' but it is better to render it 'rainbow' due to the clear allusions to the throne vision in Ezekiel 1.26–28. There this image expresses 'the appearance of the likeness of the glory of the LORD' (1.28), described in terms that maintain the appropriate distance from God. No doubt this emerald rainbow also evokes the story of Noah (Gen 9.12–17) and reminds John, with all God's people, of God's everlasting covenant faithfulness to the earth.

John's eye is drawn outward from this focal point. Surrounding the throne are twenty-four other thrones, occupied by elders wearing crowns (again, not the royal diadem but the laurel wreath of the victor) and white robes. A wide range of interpretations has been proposed for this image, including the Old and New Testaments, angelic figures, and the twenty-four Roman *lictors*, attendants who accompanied the emperor Domitian. All of these interpretations lack clear supporting evidence from the text. There are possible connections to the twenty-four orders of priests (1 Chr 24.7ff.), but if there are echoes of that here they are very faint: the elders of Revelation 4 wear no clear priestly attire and perform no obvious priestly role (they engage in worship, as we will see shortly, but that is something done by all the people). Rather, they are robed in white, sit on thrones, and wear the crowns of victors. Thus what we are told about their attire and posture has a clear and immediate echo in the promises to the conquerors in the last three messages: to Sardis (white robes, 3.5), Philadelphia (crowns, 3.11; cf. 2.10), and Laodicea (throne[s], 3.21). These ecclesial connections suggest, I think, that these twenty-four elders are to be viewed as a picture of the church. It is not, however, a picture of the church replacing Israel, or even of a clear division between Jew and Gentile within the singular people of God. The number of them, two times twelve, evokes the twelve tribes of Israel together with the twelve apostles. We will see the same numerical imagery used in 21.12–14, where the architecture of the New Jerusalem is described in terms that suggest the whole people of God, its twelve gates interpreted as the tribes of Israel and its twelve foundations as the apostles of the Lamb. Here, then, the twenty-four elders likely represent the church in a similar way. But the image should not be interpreted so as to maintain a division of Jew and Gentile in the people of God. For one thing, this is not a vision of 'two twelves' but one group of twenty-four, without division. For another, we should remember that the apostles themselves were Jewish. Instead, we should not forget that these are 'elders,' the founders of the people, simultaneously evoking the twelve patriarchs and the twelve apostles in one combined image. The 'old' covenant established with the patriarchs and the 'new' covenant established with the birth of the church are here brought together into one image of God's covenant people, enthroned and victorious, surrounding God's throne.

John does not dwell long on this aspect of the vision, however, merely noting the presence of the elders before moving on quickly. It is as if he is trying to take it all in at once and is unable to pause to reflect on any one aspect of the vision. And no wonder, for it is a scene that overwhelms the senses. In addition to the visual splendour of the jewel-like occupant of the throne and its surrounding rainbow, there comes from it the sight and sound of a great storm. Here there are echoes of many Old Testament theophanies. Like Moses on Sinai (Ex 19) or Ezekiel by the Chebar (Ezek 1), from the throne in heaven John sees and hears 'flashes of lightning, and rumblings and peals of thunder.' This storm-theophany language will be repeated at key moments throughout the rest of the book (and each time expanded: compare 4.5 with 8.5; 11.19; and 16.18–21), particularly in connection with the visions of judgement, reminding the hearer of God's power and sovereign presence in the midst of all the apparent chaos.

Before the throne are seven torches, like those that lit the tabernacle (Ex 25.37) as well as the lamp in the tent of meeting that Aaron and his sons kept perpetually burning (Ex 27.20–21). In Ezekiel's vision of heaven, flaming torches are seen moving around among the living creatures (Ezek 1.13), and we recall that it was common in the Jewish apocalyptic literature, particularly those that involve heavenly ascent, to conflate the imagery of throne room and temple/tabernacle. It is not surprising, in this context, to find John's vision of the divine throne room populated by tabernacle or temple imagery, such as the seven torches. Unlike the rest of the scene, we are given the interpretation of this image: it is the 'seven spirits of God,' one of four uses of this phrase in the book (1.4; 3.1; 4.5; 5.6). They have sometimes been interpreted as angels, mediating 'spirits of God,' but in line with the interpretation offered earlier, it is to be read as a depiction of the divine Spirit (Bauckham 1998, 162ff.). Speaking of the Spirit of God in such sevenfold terms is disconcerting, to be sure, but we recall the numerical symbolism explored in the commentary on this phrase in 1.4. The point of this image is not to enumerate the divine form but rather to indicate something of his nature, in this case the totality of the perpetual light of divine presence.

The phrase 'seven spirits who are before his throne,' we recall, was foreshadowed in the book's inaugural blessing (1.4) and then again in the message to Sardis (3.1). A similar phrase also occurs in 1.20, to depict the churches themselves, but there the image is of lampstands (*luchnia*), whereas here we see seven torches (*lampas*). Certainly we should attend to the important distinction between the two images. But there is also an important theological connection between them. We recall that an important text for interpreting the imagery of that earlier passage was Zechariah 4, and it remains important here. In Zechariah's vision, the one golden lampstand (*luchnia*, Zech 4.2 LXX) is composed of seven lamps (*luchnoi*) and represents the presence of God in all the world. In John's interwoven tapestry of images, the seven lampstands that are the churches are connected to the sevenfold Spirit of God. In 1.12–16, the Son of Man is seen in the midst of the seven golden lampstands (*luchnia*) holding the seven stars, the angels of the churches. Revelation 3.1 echoes this image, but here he holds both the seven stars and 'the seven spirits of God,' the two being brought together in his right hand. Now those seven spirits are cast as torches burning before the divine throne. In this way, John weaves imagery with powerful theological effect. From the earthly perspective, it speaks of the presence of God in the world by his Spirit in and through the churches, who are both sovereignly held by Jesus's right hand and also assured of his presence in their midst. Now, from the heavenly perspective, we see the other side of that theological reality, with this picture of the presence of the Spirit and the churches in God's throne room. There is, then, an inextricable connection between Spirit and churches, and these two theological poles are joined in the imagery of the 'seven spirits of God.'

In front of the throne is a crystalline sea of glass. This image, like so many in Revelation, is doubly evocative. Throughout the Hebrew Scriptures, the sea is a common image for chaos and evil, and it features as such in the apocalyptic vision of Daniel 7. Just like that vision, later in Revelation the sea will be the place from which bestial powers emerge (13.1) before being ultimately removed from the new Jerusalem (21.1). Here, however, it is described not as a raging tumult but stilled waters, like glass. But this sea is placed in the presence of God, a setting that casts doubt on whether it is appropriate to read it as an image of primordial chaos. It is more likely, therefore, that this sea evokes a different Old Testament image, again associated with the tabernacle furniture. There was in the tabernacle, between the tent of meeting and the altar, a bronze washing basin (Ex 30.18), which in Solomon's temple was developed into a more impressive item and called the 'sea' (1 Kgs 7.23–26; 2 Chr 4.2–6). In this way the throne room of God is cast in terms that evoke the temple (cf. 15.2).

The Four Creatures, the Twenty-four Elders, and Their Songs of Praise, vv. 6b–11

John's vision continues to move outward from the throne at the centre, and what he sees next is a strange thing indeed. Around the throne and on each side are four living creatures, like a lion, an ox, a human, and an eagle. They each have six wings and are covered in eyes. What are these four living creatures? Patristic interpretation often read them as images for the four Gospels, usually citing some broad assessment of each Gospel's emphasis to make the connections. For example, Victorinus of Petovium, one of the earliest commentators on Revelation, saw Matthew as the man (due to his 'human' genealogy from Mary), Mark as the eagle (since his Gospel begins suddenly, 'in flight'), Luke as the ox (citing his sacrificial emphasis) and John as the lion (due to the roaring of his proclamation). Other accounts of this kind vary the associations and the rationales for making them. Augustine, for example, saw Matthew as the lion, Mark the human, Luke the ox, and John, with his soaring theological account of Jesus, the flying eagle. In any case, despite the lack of agreement on who was who, it remained an important tradition and can still be seen in imagery and iconography of the four evangelists.

A more prosaic option for the four creatures is to read them as representative of all living things, numbering four to signify all creation (as in the 'four corners of the earth'). More specifically, the lion could stand for the wild animals, the ox for domestic creatures, the eagle for birds, and the human for, well, humans. Read in this way, the four living creatures can be seen as a symbol of all creation. The division into these four categories seems somewhat arbitrary, however; it is not clear why these four in particular should stand for all creatures, or indeed why humans should be among them. And what about the conspicuously absent sea creatures?

A far more productive line of interpretation is to read this image alongside its clear Old Testament parallel, Ezekiel 1. There have already been a number of allusions to that chapter in John's vision of the throne and the rainbow that surrounds it, and the presence of these 'four living creatures' intensifies those connections still further. As usual, however, John does not merely copy an image from his source but creatively reworks it for his own purposes. Ezekiel's four creatures were the *cherubim* (cf. Ezek 10), angelic beings that supported the throne and allowed it to move on wheels (with which they have a close spiritual connection) ranging throughout the earth 'wherever the spirit would go' (Ezek 1.20). In John's vision, however, the four living beings (and perhaps that is a more helpful translation for *zōon*) surround the throne in praise. In Ezekiel's vision, the four living beings each had four faces (Ezek 1.6), of a human, a lion, an ox, and an eagle (Ezek 1:10). John's vision lists the same four animals, though here each of the four living beings has but one face and a different appearance (Rev 4.7). Ezekiel saw wheels covered with eyes (Ezek 1.19), indicating watchfulness and freedom to move about the earth. In John's vision there are no wheels on the throne, and the eyes cover the beings themselves (Rev 4.8). Whereas Ezekiel's beings each had four wings (Ezek 1.6), John's have six. In accounting for these details, as so often in the book of Revelation, it is not enough to trace just one thread of Old Testament allusion: John's intertextual tapestry is more complex. In noting their six wings, John combines the *cherubim* imagery from Ezekiel 1 with Isaiah's heavenly vision of the *seraphim* attending the Lord, each having six wings (Isa 6.2). The connection thus drawn between the two prophets makes it most likely that John's four 'creatures' are to be read as angelic beings, combining aspects of Isaiah's *seraphim* who attend the Lord with the *cherubim* supporting his throne in Ezekiel.

Like the *seraphim* in Isaiah (Isa 6.3), these composite angelic beings continually cry praise to the Lord of hosts in the words of the *trisagion*, 'holy, holy, holy,' while also echoing the divine title from 1.8, though here in a subtly different order, 'who was and is and is to come.' Songs of praise are very important to the book of Revelation and regularly punctuate the visionary material. In the introduction we discussed the likely liturgical setting for the public reading of the book, and that is reflected in the form as the sound of songs of praise now fills the remainder of the chapter. The continual praise of God is part of the job description for the angelic host, and we now see them doing so 'day and night without ceasing.'

In response to the praise of the four living beings, the twenty-four elders also fall prostrate in worship. The crowns that had been given to them for their victorious witness are cast in tribute before the throne, recognising the greater rule and victory of the one seated there. This physical act of praise is followed by their own song, declaring the worthiness of God for his creative power. The effect of this celestial scene is that of a perpetual call-and-response, as the angelic host and the church are united in praise of the one who sits on the throne and who alone is holy and worthy of such praise. This is not, however, a mere musical interlude, but contributes to and expresses the theology of the throne vision. The *Te Deum*, an ancient liturgical song, beautifully expresses this theological vision, here repeated as it appears in the *Book of Common Prayer*:

> We praise thee, O God; we acknowledge thee to be the Lord.
> All the earth doth worship thee, the Father everlasting.
> To thee all Angels cry aloud, the Heavens, and all the Powers therein.
> To thee Cherubim and Seraphim continually do cry,
> Holy, Holy, Holy, Lord God of Sabaoth;
> Heaven and earth are full of the Majesty of thy glory.
> The glorious company of the Apostles praise thee.
> The goodly fellowship of the Prophets praise thee.
> The noble army of Martyrs praise thee.
> The holy Church throughout all the world doth acknowledge thee;
> The Father, of an infinite Majesty;

Thine honourable, true, and only Son;
Also the Holy Ghost, the Comforter.
Thou art the King of Glory, O Christ.
Thou art the everlasting Son of the Father.
When thou tookest upon thee to deliver man, thou didst not abhor the Virgin's womb.
When thou hadst overcome the sharpness of death,
thou didst open the Kingdom of Heaven to all believers.
Thou sittest at the right hand of God in the glory of the Father.
We believe that thou shalt come to be our Judge.
We therefore pray thee, help thy servants whom thou hast redeemed with thy precious blood.
Make them to be numbered with thy Saints in glory everlasting.

The Scroll and the Lamb, 5.1–14

The Sealed Scroll, vv. 1–5

John's attention now returns to the throne itself and to the one seated there. In his right hand, indicating power and authority, is a scroll, 'written on the inside and on the back.' A large number of options have been proposed for what this scroll and its contents may signify, including divine judgements, the secret meaning of the Old Testament, God's plan for the world, or the content of the book of Revelation as a whole. Again interpretation can be guided by the multiple Old Testament allusions in this image, drawn from John's favourite passages in the prophets. In Zechariah 5.1–4, which immediately follows the vision of the lampstand, the prophet sees a flying scroll that represents a curse upon the land against those who steal (written on one side) and those who swear falsely (written on the other side). And the prophet Ezekiel, during his throne room vision, was given from the hand of the Lord a scroll written 'on the front and the back' (Ezek 2.10), symbolising his prophetic commission and the message of woe he was to deliver to the people of Israel. We can reasonably expect, then, that John's scroll also indicates a prophetic commission with a message from God written within. As so often in Revelation's use of the Old Testament, the allusions to Ezekiel's double-sided scroll are not precise quotations. John's expression 'on the inside and on the back' is a little awkward in its asymmetry (one would expect either 'inside/outside' or 'front/back') but does make sense for a scroll that (unlike Ezekiel's, which was spread out) remains rolled and sealed, so that the 'front' can legitimately be called the 'inside.'

Unlike a folded letter, a scroll will easily unravel if not secured somehow. Ancient scrolls were tied with a cord that was then sealed with soft wax or clay, bearing the unique imprint of the sender's signet ring to prove authorship and to guard against tampering. One could not read the contents of the scroll without first breaking this seal. The scroll John sees in the Lord's right hand is completely sealed with not one but seven seals, which will be broken in turn in the visions that follow in chapters 6–8. Some have suggested that this indicates a sevenfold progression of the revelation of the book's contents, but it is hard to imagine how that would work in the sealing of a scroll. Far more logical is that the scroll can only begin to be opened to reveal its contents once all seven have been broken. As such, the visions of judgement that accompany the breaking of the seven seals are not the contents of the scroll itself. The revelation of that will come once all seven are broken.

Next, John hears the voice of a mighty angel ask what might seem an odd question. Carrying over the theme of worthiness from the songs of praise in chapter 4, the angel asks, 'Who is worthy to open the scroll and break its seals?' Surely, the answer should be obvious—is it not the one on the throne himself, the Lord Almighty, who has just been acclaimed as 'worthy' (4.11) and who holds the scroll in his powerful right hand? Not so in John's vision, for no one in heaven or on earth or under the earth was found worthy to open this scroll. This alone is remarkable, that a scroll should exist that God Almighty is not worthy to open. No wonder John weeps, for if the Lord who holds the scroll in his right hand is not worthy to break its seals, all is lost. Why should the scroll not be opened by the Lord himself? We can only conclude that there is something about this act of opening the scroll that requires another agent, and this makes sense if the throne room scene is a prophetic commissioning, as in Isaiah 6. Though the voice that speaks in Revelation 5 is angelic rather than divine, the question posed echoes the commissioning of Isaiah, where the Lord asks, 'Whom shall I send, and who shall go for us?' (6.8). Isaiah could well have wondered why the Lord did not go himself, but instead he volunteered to be sent with God's word to his people. In Revelation 5, it is God's will that the content of the scroll be opened and its prophetic message delivered by a human being. This time, however, there is no volunteer, and a cosmic search for a candidate has apparently come up short. In his tears, John, like all creation in Romans 8 (Mangina 2010, 85), laments that there has been none revealed as worthy to proclaim the purposes of God to bring judgement and comfort to the world.

At this point another voice speaks. One of the twenty-four elders encourages John, telling him not to weep, for 'the Lion of the tribe of Judah, the Root of David, has conquered' and is thus worthy to open the seals and deliver the prophetic message within. In this way, the elder most appropriately performs the church's task: to comfort the weeping and to bear witness to the Lion's victory. The church in heaven comforts this weeping prophet with the reality of Christ's victory, even as he writes to the suffering church on earth. It is a scene that evokes the 'cloud of witnesses' in Hebrews 12.1. The phrase 'Lion of the tribe of Judah' has unmistakable Old Testament echoes. In Genesis 49, we read the story of Jacob giving his departing blessings to his sons. Judah is described there (vv. 9–10) as 'a lion's whelp,' and Jacob describes how he among his brothers shall be worthy to bear the sceptre and the ruler's staff. John combines this image of Judah's rule with another allusion to a prophetic image of the promised messianic ruler, the 'Root of David.' The clearest echo is in Isaiah 11, but there are also suggestions of the Davidic 'Branch' in Jeremiah (23.5; 33.15) and Zechariah (3.8; 6.12). It is a title Christ will claim for himself at the closing of the book (22.16).

At this point we note that, so far in John's throne vision, there is one character who has been conspicuous by his absence. Though it was his voice that summoned John through the open door of heaven, Jesus has yet to make an appearance in the throne room. This is about to change.

The Lamb, vv. 6–14
The vision that follows is arguably the most important in the whole book. The one we are about to see is the one who has been found worthy to open the scroll, and so how he is depicted will have a bearing on how we read everything else. Revelation began (1.1) with a Christological opening statement; this book is the revelation of Jesus Christ, given to him by God to reveal mysteries to his servants. This was quickly followed by John's vision of Jesus on Patmos, addressing the seven churches of Asia with a message of faithful witness. Now John has ascended to the heavenly throne room, where he will encounter the victorious Christ afresh. The words of the elder have raised the expectation that we are about to see Jesus cast in his role as the powerful ruler from the tribe of Judah, the promised king from David's line. His rule is legitimate because of this royal lineage, but he is also found worthy to open the scroll because he has conquered. This tapestry of allusions has led us, with John, to expect to see a prophetic warrior-king, a human being from the line of David who has the power and authority, and even the ferocity, of a conquering Lion. If the vision John saw of Jesus on Patmos was as the glorious Son of Man, what glories may await us in the heavenly throne room! What we see next, however, confounds these expectations.

Not for the last time, what John hears and what he sees are radically contrasting things. Having heard the voice announce the victorious Lion, John sees, standing between the throne and the four living beings, its polar opposite: a slaughtered Lamb. How are we to make sense of this strange juxtaposition? One option is to place the emphasis on what the elder has said and read this vision as a 'Lion in Lamb's clothing,' weak in appearance but in reality a ferocious king of beasts, his true nature only thinly masked in this present appearance. A second option is to resolve the juxtaposition in the opposite direction, allowing this vision to control or correct what was previously heard. With such a reading, we might then continue through the book glossing any violent lion-like imagery with straightforwardly lamb-like interpretations. In one case the hearing overcomes the seeing, and in the other it is the reverse. Neither approach, I think, does justice to the way John's audiovisual imagery works. Both aspects of John's encounter, the hearing and the seeing, must be allowed to exercise their appropriate force upon our imaginations, and we must resist the urge to resolve the paradox of this juxtaposition of lion and lamb in either direction. This, again, will require us to think 'doubly' about what is revealed. We cannot think of him with just one thought but must think two thoughts simultaneously, saying the two words 'Lion' and 'Lamb' without collapsing one into the other. As we saw in the introduction, to speak of the divine requires such redoubled speech, and not the simple univocity of a flat prosaic explanation. John's apocalyptic language and imaginative juxtaposition is an extremely well-suited discourse for this—they are examples, one might say, of 'double vision.'

How might we attempt such redoubled speech in interpreting this passage? As the elder has said, Jesus is indeed the true messianic king, from the line of Judah and David, who has conquered. The hopes of Israel for the rule of God are not transcended, superseded, or undone but rather brought to completion in this one man. But what it means to speak of his rule, and his victory, has now been radically reimagined through what John sees. The latent militarism and nationalism of the elder's words are placed in dialectical tension with the vision of Christ as the Lamb, looking as though slaughtered yet alive, ascended, and standing in the throne room. This is not a picture of defeat but a revelation of what Christ's victory looks like. He is indeed worthy because he has conquered, as the elder said and as the whole host of heaven will shortly sing (v. 9). The image evokes the lamb slaughtered at Passover, by whose blood the people of God were redeemed from slavery. It also speaks of the sacrificial lambs slain for atonement. Moreover, it echoes the suffering servant of Isaiah, who is led to slaughter like a lamb and thereby bears the transgressions of the people (Isa 53.7–8, 12). It is unlikely that we are meant to select any one of these lambs as the precise referent of this image, and the saving activities ascribed to the Lamb in this passage and throughout the book cover deliverance, ransom, redemption, sin-bearing, and atonement. However, here, and arguably in the book of Revelation as a whole, the salvation theme that comes most clearly to the surface is of victorious deliverance, like that achieved by lamb's blood at the exodus, a resonance confirmed by the many echoes of that event to come. This lamb is indeed victorious, but his victory over the forces that oppress God's people has been won not through power but through sacrificial death.

And yet power does not dissolve into sacrifice. Lest we begin to think we have resolved the imaginative tension, the slaughtered Lamb is seen, incongruously, to be standing in the throne room of heaven, having ascended to the presence of God. It is not dead but alive. It has not been consumed, or burned on the altar, but stands before the throne. The lamb is '*standing* as if it had been slaughtered.' We must take with utmost seriousness both the posture of the slaughtered lamb and the location of the vision: he is seen not on earth but in heaven, and he stands in the presence of the seat of divine rule. But the lamb is also 'standing *as if it had been slaughtered*.' The humiliation and suffering of Jesus was not an unpleasant but necessary earthly stage of his journey, now left behind and replaced with the glories of heaven. It remains part of his depiction in his heavenly rule. He stands in heaven in a *status duplex* ('double state'), in simultaneous humility and exaltation, without the two being arranged in a sequence or either collapsing into the other. John has not described a vision of the slain lamb on earth and the exalted Son in heaven, or of one image replacing the other. Instead, he sees here a 'double vision' of Christ in heaven, depicted simultaneously in both states, as lion and lamb. The lamb's sacrifice is not simply the means *to* the kingdom of God but the means *of* the kingdom of God. It is not for nothing that the Lamb is the most common title given to Jesus in Revelation: this vision of conquest through sacrifice is one of the book's most important themes.

As John begins to describe the Lamb's features in more detail, it becomes clear that we are not simply looking at the carcass of a cultic substitute but at something far more powerful and terrible. In the chapter that follows, we will even hear of the 'wrath of the Lamb' (6.16). Clearly, this is no ordinary lamb: it has seven horns and seven eyes. A lamb may have horns, of a sort, and in some rare cases more than two, but to spend time discussing ovine biology would miss the point of the imagery. Throughout the Bible, the horn is a symbol of God's saving power and rule (e.g., Ps 89.17; 2 Sam 22.3), though it was also a particularly popular image in the apocalyptic and prophetic literature in visions of enemy kings and kingdoms (e.g., Dan 7–8 and Zech 1), and a similar use of the imagery will be seen in the bestial visions of Revelation 12 and 13. Here the Lamb's horns are not given as much attention, being briefly noted, but it is significant that they are numbered in sevenfold completeness. There is more attention given to the Lamb's seven eyes, which, we are told, are 'the seven spirits of God.' There is a constant but mysterious presence of the Spirit in Revelation, here depicted in the juxtaposition of the seven torches before the throne (4.5) and the seven eyes of the Lamb (5.6). The eyes of the Lord, God's all-seeing presence by his Spirit, have been given to the Lamb. Perhaps this is why John did not earlier follow Ezekiel in placing the many eyes on the wheels of the divine throne-chariot. It is not by means of a wheeled chariot that God's Spirit has been 'sent out into all the earth' but by the Lamb. The echo here is again to the vision of the lampstand in Zechariah 4, the passage to which John often alludes when speaking of the Spirit and which describes seven lamps as 'the eyes of the LORD, which range through the whole earth' (Zech 4.10b). There may also be a faint echo of the previous vision that speaks of a single stone with 'seven facets' (Zech 3.9), using the Hebrew word *'ayin* that also means 'eye' (Richard Bauckham [1998, 164] suggests that John would have read this stone as a reference to Christ). The pneumatological importance of this section of Zechariah is likely due to the interpretative force of Zechariah 4.6, in which the Lord declares that his purposes will be accomplished 'not by might, nor by power, but by my spirit.' The combination of the seven horns and seven eyes alone suggests that power and might are here being spiritually redefined, and this is all the truer when embedded within the broader juxtaposition of the lion and lamb. The tapestry of John's imagery requires imaginative theological reflection on the way in which the agency of God, Christ, and the Spirit are closely interwoven.

The slaughtered Lamb now begins to perform the task for which he has been found worthy. He takes the scroll from the right hand of the one seated on the throne. Before he breaks its seals to reveal its contents, however, the scene climaxes again in praise, as the elders and living beings sing a new song in unison. In this rapturous celestial worship, it is easy to forget that we are still reading a letter from Patmos to the cities of Asia, bringing a word from the Lord to churches struggling to bear faithful witness under various difficulties. But it is the same book, and Revelation reminds us here of that connection between earth and heaven. The host of heaven are each seen to be holding golden bowls of incense, which, we are told, are the prayers of the saints. What an encouragement this vision must have been to the churches of Asia, to see that their prayers are not rebounding off the ceiling but are ascending as incense into the throne room of heaven. Even in the midst of celestial praise, the prayers of the saints are held in heaven. And yet these prayers are not held before the one sitting on the throne but before the Lamb. The saints are thereby shown that it is to the Lamb that their prayers are offered.

The new song of praise we now hear echoes the two songs of chapter 4 and ties the whole scene together. The Lamb not only receives prayer but also receives worship. The same chorus who first sang of God's worthiness now sing of the worthiness of the Lamb. And just as they fell prostrate before the throne, they now bow before the Lamb himself. At the end of the book (22.8–9), John will fall down before his angelic guide and be rebuked, since only God may receive such worship. It is remarkable, then, that such worship of the Lamb is described in heaven and that the prostrate worship and songs of praise in chapters 4 and 5 echo one another.

Once again, their song does not merely adorn but further expounds the theology of the passage. The Lamb is worthy not *despite* or even *through* but *because of* his slaughter. His blood ransomed the saints, not only from the people of Israel (which the Root of David would be expected to do) but 'from every tribe and language and people and nation' (5.9). The apparent redundancy of this expression expresses, in its fourfold form, the universal reach of redemption. In various forms, this fourfold formula will be repeated seven times in the book (5.9; 7.9; 10.11; 11.9; 13.7; 14.6; 17.15). All nations are not only redeemed through the blood of the Lamb but are also made to be 'a kingdom and priests' (cf. 1.6) and given dominion over the earth.

Again John's eye is drawn outward. He now sees that the twenty-four elders and four living beings are joined in their worship by a throng of angels surrounding them. Their number is 'ten thousands of ten thousands, and thousands of thousands,' but to try to count them would be an exercise in missing the point. The scene is of concentric circles of worshippers, and right at the middle the throne and the Lamb. This circle of praise then widens to its maximum extent, as every creature in heaven, earth, under the earth, and in the sea joins in a song of praise. Their song brings the vision of chapters 4 and 5 to its climax as they ascribe 'blessing and honour and glory and might' *both* to the one on the throne *and* to the Lamb, the two now united as the object of creation's worship. And the doxology of earth is met with the 'Amen!' of heaven.

The Seven Seals

Revelation 6.1–8.5

Introduction to the Seven Seals

We now come to the breaking of the seals of the scroll. We have already seen that there is commerce between earth and heaven, as the prayers of the saints are presented as incense in the hands of the elders (5.8), an image to which John will return at the end of the seal sequence, thus framing the whole section (8.3–4). As the seals are broken, these ascending prayers are now echoed by the descending divine judgements on the earth. The seven seals form a structural framework for the next three chapters of the book of Revelation, and they are clearly counted out in turn. This might lead us to treat these chapters as something of a detachable unit, but that would be wrong. It is important to remember that the seven seals should not be isolated from their literary setting, as an integral part of the vision of heaven that began in chapter 4. We must also remember that these seals are those found on the scroll that the Lamb has just taken from the hand of the one on the throne. We must not lose sight of this setting and these characters.

As was discussed in more detail in the introduction, following the series of seven oracles, this is the first of three 'sets' of seven judgements that shape the structure of much of the rest of the book of Revelation, the other 'sevens' being the trumpets of chapters 8–11 and then the bowls/plagues of chapters 15–16. As has often been noted, there is something of a shared pattern to each series of seven. The first six of the series are separated from the seventh by an 'interlude,' a vision or cluster of visions that interrupts the sequence, creating dramatic tension. As we will see, the two pairs of visions that interrupt the seals (and later the trumpets) are like a diptych, a two-panelled painting in which each panel interprets the other. At a more fine-grained level of analysis, we can see stylistic differences between the first four, which are handled quite briefly, and the others, which are more expansive in their description. As such, there is a clear 'four-plus-three' pattern to the seven seals, the seven trumpets, and (to an extent) the seven bowls. With the interlude visions interrupting the sequence before the seventh, the overall pattern we find is '4+2(interlude)+1.'

John uses the numerical symbolism of this 'four plus three' structure to powerful theological effect, since the visions themselves concern the relationship between earth (the number 4) and heaven (the number 3; see Resseguie 2009, Osborne 2002). The first four seals are very much concerned with judgements on the earth and the earthly threats of invasion, war, famine, and death, as the four horsemen are released. These are human phenomena, suggesting that the nature of these divine judgements is permissive, allowing the human thirst for conquest to lead to its consequence: war, which in turn often results in famine and death. As such, we should not read this as straightforward depictions of the acts of a vengeful God. But nor are they 'natural' disasters. They are manmade terrors that God often restrains but has here 'unsealed' so that the earth will feel the consequences of its injustice and will to power (Gorman 2011, 139). The fifth and sixth seals, however, are more focussed on activity in heaven, with the vision of the saints under the celestial altar and the cosmic imagery of sun, moon, and stars. The interlude visions of chapter 7, interrupting the sequence before its climactic seventh seal, speak about the nature of the people of God. The seventh seal, then, brings the sequence to a climax with a vision of God's final eschatological triumph. (Similar theological concerns will inform the shape of the seven trumpets, as we will see in due course.) The effect is that the church identifies itself as those standing in that 'interlude,' caught, as it were, between heaven and earth and called to a life of faithful witness in the 'interrupted' moment of apocalyptic tension between the present age of the revelation of divine judgement and the final consummation of the age to come.

The First Six Seals, 6.1–17

Seals 1–4: The Horsemen

There is a chain of transmission here that evokes the beginning of the book, where we saw that the revelation is given by God to Jesus, who directs his angel to show John what must take place (1.1). Likewise, here the seals have been handed by God to the Lamb, and his breaking of the seals triggers the angelic being to call out 'come!' (or 'go!'—the Greek is ambiguous). Although the living creatures are the immediate agents of the action, then, we are to remember that they are but intermediaries, and behind them stands the sovereign action of the Lamb and the one on the throne. This use of intermediaries is common in Jewish thought and has the effect of distancing God somewhat from direct involvement in the judgements that follow, without denying his ultimate sovereignty. A similar effect is achieved by the veiled references to God's ultimate agency through an unnamed voice that speaks from the midst of the four living beings in verse 6, as well as the frequent use of the divine passive voice to describe the horsemen and their activities (e.g., 'a crown was given,' v. 2; 'its rider was permitted,' v. 4; 'they were given authority,' v. 8).

As the Lamb opens the first four seals, and each of the four living beings calls out, we encounter four riders on horses (the number four echoes through this whole section, cf. 7.1). John is here continuing to develop his allusions to Zechariah, specifically the first (1.7–17) and last (6.1–8) of this concentric pattern of visions, in which Zechariah sees, respectively, four horses and four horse-drawn chariots in similar (though not identical) colours to those of Revelation. In Zechariah, both visions are interpreted by an angel, the horses/chariots representing the 'four winds of heaven,' sent by the Lord to 'patrol the earth' (1.10; 8.7). In Zechariah's visions, the report of these patrols is that all is at peace (1.11), leading Zechariah to ask how long the Lord will continue to hold back his judgement. In Revelation 6, we find something of an answer to Zechariah's question, which will soon be echoed by the saints (6.10), as the four horsemen are sent to the earth not just to patrol but to execute divine judgement.

The first seal is broken, and the first living being calls out 'come!' revealing the first horseman who is then sent to the earth. The horse is white in colour, and its rider holds a bow. For John's first-century audience, this image could have evoked the famous mounted archers of Parthia, to the east of the Roman imperial territory. The Parthians had defeated Roman armies three times in that century, and once in recent memory (53 BC, 36 BC, AD 62), and were often invoked in Roman propaganda as a symbol of the perpetual military threats that faced the empire from outside. This portrayal of the first horseman, then, would likely play on that fear of foreign invasion, especially in the borderlands of the eastern empire. John leaves us with little doubt as to this rider's purpose: he is given the victor's crown and sent out 'conquering and to conquer.' The imagery overflows such a simple historical correspondence, however, and as such speaks of the perpetual human thirst for conquest and fear of outsiders.

This is not the only rider on a white horse that we will encounter in Revelation. In 19.11–16, we will see another, called Faithful and True, the Word of God, who judges in righteousness and makes war. There, the rider is clearly an image of Christ, accompanied by the armies of heaven. Some, noting the similarities between the two riders, have suggested that the one who rides out here at the breaking of the first seal is also Jesus. There are enough differences in their depiction, however, to say that they are not the same figure. Nevertheless, their similarities allow a connection of a different sort, namely parody. We recall that what counts as true 'conquering' is very much a driving concern of the book. Though this rider may look a bit like the victorious Christ, and may think of himself as a conqueror, the vision reminds us that his authority to do so is ultimately not his own but lies with the Lamb and as such can be removed at his will. Moreover, we have already been told that it is he who has shown us what real conquering looks like. The conquest of this rider, then, is no true conquest at all but its parody.

The breaking of the second seal releases a rider on a red horse given not a bow but a great sword. He takes peace from the earth, reversing the red horseman's report in Zechariah 1.11. The result of this removal of peace is that the people turn on each other. Again this presses on deep-seated fears in the first-century context. The threat to peace in the Roman empire was not just an external one. There was an imminent concern about civil war, especially after the unrest of the tumultuous 'year of four emperors' in AD 68–69. The would-be eternal peace that Roman propaganda promised its subjects is here taken away. But, just as the conquest of the first rider is exposed as no conquest at all, Revelation offers a theological challenge to the would-be peace of Rome. It is not the only voice to do so. The historian Tacitus, in his *Agricola* (a chronicle of the life and death of his father-in-law, Julius Agricola, governor of Roman Britain), records these words from a Scottish chieftain called Calgacus, giving his perspective on the would-be Roman peace: 'to robbery, slaughter, plunder, they give the lying name of empire; they make a desert and call it peace' (Tacitus, *Agricola*, ch. 30). Just as the false victory of the first rider has been exposed, so too there is a challenge to the false peace promised by Rome, and indeed by any human power that sets itself up as the would-be bringer of peace.

With the removal of the divine restraints that hold back the human thirst for conquest and violence, there is war. And following fast on the heels of war, as history so often attests, are poverty, famine, and death. As the third seal is broken and the third living creature calls out, a rider on a black horse is sent out. No weapons are given to this rider, for none are needed. Rather than another military image, John now sees an economic judgement, though the two go hand-in-hand in the ancient world, as they often do today. The weighing scales in the rider's hand and his instructions from the divine voice make clear the nature of his economic task. The scarcity of food that accompanies war has led to uncontrolled inflation and thus poverty. A day's pay (a Roman *denarius*), which would usually buy about sixteen rations of wheat, now only buys one. Barley, the less nutritious crop, would usually be sold at around half that price. At these rates, then, a vineyard worker would need his whole day's pay just to feed himself (Koester 2014, 396). This economic crisis, however, is not equally distributed; the olive oil and wine (commodities with a higher profit margin than staple grains) are left untouched. Presumably, then, this would result in increased economic disparity, as the owner of the vineyard finds his wealth relatively undisturbed by the ravages of war while his workers live at the edge of poverty. This is a common pattern in history. Then as now, it tends to be the poor who suffer most at times of war and economic crisis, while the wealthy are relatively protected or even make a profit. We recall, however, that this situation, which might be described as the 'natural' results of the invisible hand of the market, is interpreted theologically through John's imagery. These are divine judgements, unsealed by the voice from the throne.

The fourth seal is now broken, and the fourth creature calls 'come!' The fourth horse is pale green in colour, the colour of sickly flesh. Unlike the other riders, this one is named Death. Following behind (as his hunting hound, perhaps?) is Hades, the name in Greek mythology for the realm of the dead and the god of the underworld. From an earthly perspective, Death might seem to be the one all-ruling power of the whole earth, a constant and unavoidable tyrant, especially in times of war, famine, and disease. But there is some hope in its portrayal here. Death has authority, yes, but (like the other horsemen) it is a delegated authority. We recall that Christ, who has tasted and conquered Death, has already been described as the one who holds the keys, and thus the sovereignty, to Death and Hades (1.18). Moreover, Death's remit is strictly limited here, to one quarter of the earth and not its totality. As such, the first four seals close with a reminder of the restrained nature of these divine judgements, which are intended (as we will see) to induce repentance. For those who belong to Christ, his earlier instruction still stands and encourages those who seek to bear faithful witness in the face of Death: 'do not be afraid' (1.17).

Seal 5: The Subaltern Saints

As the Lamb opens the fifth seal, the description becomes more expansive and the scene's focus of attention shifts. Instead of a fifth judgement sent to the earth, we now see a vision centred in heaven, where we see those who have died for their witness to Jesus. After having just met Death and Hades, it is significant that those who had been killed are not found there but are before the throne of God in heaven. The palatial imagery that John has been using to describe the celestial environment is now combined with imagery drawn from the temple, for John now sees in the heavenly throne room an altar, and under it are the souls of those who had died for their witness to Christ. It was not unusual for Jewish imagination to combine the two images of throne room and temple when speaking of heaven. Since the earthly tabernacle was modelled after the pattern of the heavenly sanctuary (see, e.g., Ps 78.69), heaven was understood to be a temple. But God was also regularly said to be 'enthroned' above the cherubim that adorned the cover of the ark in the holy of holies (e.g., 2 Sam 6.2; 2 Kgs 19.15; 1 Chr 13.6; Pss 80.1; 99.1; Isa 37.16), and so royal palace language naturally interweaves with the temple imagery. It is not clear which altar is being indicated. There were two in Jerusalem, one for incense and one for animal sacrifice, but it is perhaps unnecessary to be so precise. The thematic emphasis, however, is clearly sacrificial, as we will now see.

This shifting of the metaphor, and the placing of the souls of the martyrs under the altar, gives their deaths sacrificial meaning. John, we notice, does not simply say that they had been 'killed.' He tells us that these are those who have been 'slaughtered,' using the same word that described the Lamb in 5.6. Moreover, the reason for their deaths is given: they have been slaughtered because of the word of God and their testimony. They are thus intimately connected with Jesus himself, the slaughtered Lamb, the Word of God, and the faithful witness. When seen from this revealed heavenly perspective, the deaths of the Christians executed for their witness to Jesus are thus imbued with theological significance: their sacrifice is a participation in his.

This scene places the first four seal judgements in theological context. John hears the voices of the martyrs cry out in the presence of God with a loud voice, 'how long?' There is here an echo of the similar angelic question in Zechariah 1, and it is the eschatological cry of the church militant. Just as the prayers of the saints are held before the Lord as incense in the hands of the elders, so the cry for justice comes before him from the lips of the slaughtered saints (and perhaps in this way both Jerusalem altars are fused together in this heavenly one). Their cries for judgement and vengeance might appear to be less than Christian, but these are appropriate cries on the lips of those who are suffering. It makes all the difference in the world that this plea comes from under the altar, not from a position of power, and that it is a cry for God to judge and not for human vengeance. It is a cry that continues to echo in our world wherever there is injustice: 'how long?' It is not a question, however, that receives a precise answer. Instead of a timeline, they are given a white robe and an instruction to wait. We recall that a white robe was promised to those who conquer in the message to the church in Laodicea (3.5). Revelation thus signals that these subaltern saints are the true conquerors, since in their faithful witness unto death they have shared in the victory of the Lamb (cf. 12.11) and have gained their promised reward. Once again the constant theme of victory through sacrificial witness united Christ and his church.

Faithful endurance is what gained them this victory, and it will now characterise their ongoing heavenly role. How long will they wait? Until, it seems, 'the number would be complete' of their fellow martyrs, slaughtered as they were. The idea of a set number of martyrs that must be counted before the day of judgement is found elsewhere in apocalyptic literature (e.g., *4 Ezra* 4.35–37, in response to the question 'how long?'), and this sort of idea is clearly implied in many English translations of this sentence (e.g., NRSV, NIV, ESV). But the word 'number' is not there in the Greek, which literally reads 'until are fulfilled both their fellow slaves and their brothers, the ones about to be killed as they were.' This fulfilment, then, need not be read as some kind of heavenly 'martyr quota,' as if God were holding back judgement until the earth reached a predetermined body count. It is not their number but their work of witness that matters and must be fulfilled. In the message to Sardis in 3.2, the only other place where this word is used, it is unfulfilled works of witness that are in view (Blount 2013, 137). Thus, John's emphasis is not on the number of martyrs but on the fulfilment of their witness itself. God's judgement is held back until the completion of the testimony of the church. This witness must be fulfilled, whether in life or death, as indicated by this verse's twofold identification of the agents of witness as 'fellow servants' and the 'brothers and sisters who are soon to be killed.' Here, and throughout Revelation, it is the faithful witness to the word of God that is of primary theological importance, not the martyrs' deaths, for it is in this witness that the church participates in the victory of the Lamb and brings about the purposes of God in the world.

Seal 6: The Stars Fall from Heaven
And so we arrive at the penultimate seal, the breaking of which brings about a scene of cosmic destruction and sets our sights on the widest frame of God's judgement. John describes this scene with imagery drawn from a rich apocalyptic and prophetic tradition. Haggai prophesied the shaking of the ground (Hag 2.6), and in Joel the Day of the Lord (the prophet's main theme) is heralded by celestial signs of a darkened sun and bloodied moon (Joel 2.31; cf. 3.15–16). Ezekiel and Daniel use similar cosmic and earth-shaking imagery (e.g., Ezek 32.7; 38.19–20; Dan 7.11). Isaiah does too (e.g., Isa 13.10), and he also speaks of the Lord's judgement on the nations being accompanied by the skies rolling up like a scroll and the stars (the 'host of heaven'; cf. Dt 4.19) falling like withering leaves or fruit (Isa 34.4). John is not alone in the

New Testament in deploying this prophetic cosmic destruction imagery. In the book of Acts, Peter's Pentecost sermon quotes the same material from Joel (Acts 2.17–21). In particular, the synoptic Gospels draw from the same sources in describing the end of the age, the Day of the Lord, and the coming of the Son of Man (Mt 24.29–31; Mk 13.24–27; Lk 21.25–28).

What are we to make of this imagery? Is this a literal depiction of the collapse of the universe, of terrible earthquakes and meteors afflicting the earth? We must certainly resist such readings, for they are not in keeping with either John's use of imagery or the prophetic tradition on which he draws. Such cosmic destruction language describes the coming of the Lord in judgement in terms that capture the theological significance of that event. The supposedly fixed things of our world, like the orbits of the heavens and the stability of mountains, are undone at his coming.

If we insist on taking this imagery literally, we are next presented with an incongruous scene, for how can the kings of the earth hide in the mountains if the mountains themselves have been removed from their places? Having seen one group of people calling out to God from under the altar, we now see the supposedly powerful inhabitants of earth hiding in caves from the terror of the Lord (cf. Isa 2.19–21). Though they are singled out for specific attention, it is not only the powerful who are seen here, but everyone, slave and free. This vision of kings cowering in the same cave as their slaves exposes the falsehood of human definitions of power and importance. The lines drawn to separate people are thereby redrawn by this vision of the Lord's judgement. Instead of calling to the Lord that they might be saved (cf. Joel 2.32), the people call upon the mountains to fall on them and hide them from the one on the throne. In this cry for help, they also declare their terror at 'the wrath of the lamb,' a phrase that would almost be comical if not for its profound Christology. This day of wrath that has come with the breaking of the seal is the eschatological Day of the Lord, as the cosmic imagery makes clear, now recast as a day that belongs to both God and the Lamb. We must not divide the two, as if wrath belonged to the one on the throne and mercy to the Lamb. Rather, the two share both. Certainly this is a terrifying scene, but it is one released on the world as the Lamb breaks the sixth seal, and it remains in his hands. As such, we must allow the 'double vision' of the slaughtered but conquering Lamb to define what is meant by 'wrath.' Nevertheless, for the inhabitants of the earth the coming wrath is a terrible thing. Who can stand on such a day?

Interlude, 7.1–17

The 144,000 Sealed, vv. 1–8

An answer to that question comes in two visions that now interrupt the seal sequence, temporarily pausing the series of judgements. The effect of this interruption is to place the reader on the edge of their seat, caught between the sixth and seventh seals and eagerly awaiting the resolution of the cliffhanger in 6.17 and the completion of the seal sequence. It is as if the audience now shares something of the experience of the subaltern saints. Briefly to anticipate the interpretation that follows, this experience is the theological reality of the church militant. We live, as it were, in the tension between the sixth and seventh seals, a time of eager anticipation by the saints, a time for prayer and for asking 'how long?' But it is also a time in which we are reminded that God's judgement is held back so that the church's testimony might be fulfilled. The church is the people of God called to faithful witness in the interlude.

As with the vision of the lamb, this interlude has two interrelated phases, with John first hearing an announcement before he sees a vision, and so it is likely that we are meant to read the two in parallel. The global scale of the judgement released by the first six seals is underscored by what John sees next: 'four angels standing at the four corners of the earth.' Certainly these angels can stand on the day of the wrath of God, for they have a share in bringing it about, and we are told that they have been given power to damage the earth and sea. A similar sign of four angels sent to gather the elect from the 'four winds' is found in the synoptic apocalypse (Mk 13.27; Mt 24.31) as a portent of the Day of the Lord. For now, however, their only act is restraint, as they hold back the winds. We are thus reminded again that God is in control.

In addition to these four angels, another comes up from the east, holding the seal of the living God. John now hears his announcement. The angel issues instructions to the other four, holding them back until he has done his work. The seventh seal has been held back, the four angels hold back the winds, and the fifth angel holds back the other four. The dominant theme in this vision so far, therefore, is one of restraint.

The wordplay in the announcement is unmissable, for John writes that the four must wait until this angel with the seal (*sphragis*) has 'sealed (*sphragizō*) the servants of God.' Before the breaking of the seventh seal (*sphragis*, 8.1), there is first the sealing of the servants of God. Presumably this is the same instrument that was used to imprint the seven seals on the scroll. As we noted earlier, a seal like this would be used, like a signet ring, to make a unique mark in wax or soft clay, sealing scrolls in a way that authenticated the message and guarded against tampering. At this point we are told very little about the precise nature of this 'seal,' but later visions will give us more insight. We may reasonably conclude, however, that the seal is something like the name of God, or some other indication of the divine identity.

The servants of God are sealed, we are told, 'on their foreheads.' Some read this as a mark of ownership, indicating the ancient practice of a slave-owner tattooing or otherwise branding slaves on the forehead (the word translated 'servant' here can also mean 'slave'). This is unlikely here, however, for a different word (*stigma*) was used to indicate this practice (Koester 2014, 416). There is perhaps a faint echo of the mark of Cain, placed on him by God to protect him from retribution for the murder of Abel. Another allusion might be traced to Exodus 28.36–38, which describes the priestly attire. On the front of the priest's turban, like a signet engraving, are the words 'Holy to the Lord,' marking Aaron out on his forehead as set apart for priestly service. Both consecration and protection may therefore be in view. The latter is further emphasised not only by the context of this passage (the restraint of judgement) but also by a stronger allusion to the vision of divine judgement recorded in Ezekiel 9. In that passage, after his glory has left the temple, the Lord's judgement comes to the city of Jerusalem in the form of six armed executioners (9.1–2). Their judgement is sweeping and universal, as they are instructed to cut down men and women, young and old, beginning at the temple and moving out through the whole city. The only ones who are protected are those who have cried out against the city's abominations, who are first marked on their foreheads (9.4). Thus the marking on the forehead in Revelation 7 signals the setting apart of God's servants and their protection from impending judgement. While the seven seals on the scroll are being broken to remove protections from divine judgement, these servants of God will receive a new mark of protection.

Before he sees them, John hears the number of the servants of God, counted out by the twelve tribes of Israel in a manner that echoes the censuses frequently found in the Old Testament narratives, which are almost always taken in preparation for a battle. What John hears, then, is an assessment of the military strength of the people of God. The book of Numbers opens with a similar census, as the people of Israel prepare to enter the promised land, and others are found elsewhere, though none precisely match John's list of tribes either in the names or their order. There are some intriguing departures from convention in the details of this census. For a start, although this is a counting of the twelve tribes, one is missing: the tribe of Dan. In order to make the number still come to twelve, so that the symbolism of

Israel might be maintained, John adds a name. Instead of listing Ephraim and Manasseh as the sons of Joseph (so Num 1.10), John lists both Joseph and Manasseh separately. Moreover, it is interesting that the tribe of Levi is included. The priestly tribe, usually exempt from battle, is to be part of this army, thus sanctifying it. Ever since the exile, and the loss of the ten tribes, the counting of all twelve was a sign of eschatological hope, the ingathering of the whole people of God in anticipation of the final messianic holy war (the *War Scroll* from Qumran [1QM] is an excellent example of this tradition and also includes Levi). The census of Numbers 1, taken at God's command just before the arrival at the promised land, provided a powerful image for that eschatological hope.

This isn't a particularly large army, however, at only 144,000 men. For comparison, in 1 Chronicles 21.5, the combined fighting force of Israel and Judah (not including priests) is numbered at over 1.5 million, ten times the size of what John now hears. Surely the number of the eschatological army would be greater still? The number 144,000 is used for its theological significance rather than its size, developing the symbolism of the number twelve. In Numbers 31, Moses sends a symbolic 12,000 men to fight against Midian, 1,000 from each tribe. Here in Revelation 7, from each of the twelve tribes there is a perfect 12,000 people sealed, so that the total number represents 'Israel squared' times a thousand, a symbolically large number (for an excellent discussion of this, and the whole passage, see Bauckham 1998, 215–29).

Another departure from convention is that the order of names is unusual. Most significantly, John begins the list of tribes not with Reuben, as is usual, but with Judah. This makes sense once we recognise that it creates a connection between this vision and the earlier one, with its announcement of the 'Lion of Judah.' What John hears, then, is unmistakable as a census of the fighting force of the eschatological people of God, like the conquering Lion of chapter 5, whose tribe heads the list. Regardless of how one reads these intriguing details, the overall meaning is the same: what John hears leads him to expect a vision of the fighting men of eschatological Israel, preparing for the messianic war. As with the similar militaristic announcement of the Lion of Judah, however, what he sees next radically reshapes what that means.

The Multitude, vv. 9–17

John hears the earthly census of the eschatological Israelite army, led into battle by the Lion of Judah. What he sees in heaven, however, is a multitude that could not be counted, standing before the Lamb. Rather than seeing them arranged by Israelite tribes, he immediately notices that this is a global gathering, from all nations and tribes and peoples and languages (note the fourfold expression). Their attire does not seem fit for battle, for they wear not armour but white robes and carry not swords but palm branches. Here we see the answer to the question of 6.17 ('who can stand?'), for they are standing before the throne and before the Lamb, to whom they sing a song of praise, again joined by the company of heaven.

This is one of the rare visions in Revelation that is given an interpretation, in verses 13–17. One of the elders explains to John that this white-robed multitude are those who have 'come out of the great ordeal.' How one interprets that phrase will depend in large part on how one reads the whole book of Revelation. If the book is read in some sense as a historical/linear account, this 'tribulation' might be identified with one particular period of history (whether past or future). However, if this is read as a broader description of the time in which the church lives, between the first six seals and the breaking of the seventh, then the 'great ordeal' speaks of that life of the church militant, bearing witness to Christ in the time between his ascension and return, and between the sixth and seventh seals. Some will become martyrs in that time, witnessing to the point of death, but all will be called upon to give faithful testimony. The elder's next words to John explain what that means.

There have been a number of connections already drawn between white robes and the call for God's people to conquer through their witness. White robes were promised to the conquerors in the message to Sardis (3.5) and given to the subaltern martyrs in 6.11. There is a further detail here, which draws this connection out more explicitly, as we are told that the multitude have 'washed their robes and made them white in the blood of the Lamb.' One would expect blood to make clothes red, but that would be to think too literally and to miss the theological point made by this paradoxical imagery. This eschatological war is, in a sense, one that has already been won, not by the cumulative effect of the deaths of martyrs themselves but by one death. The white robes of this army are not simply something of their own doing or even a mark of their own sacrifice, as if they were washed in their own blood, but their participation in the Lamb's sacrifice and therefore his victory. Martyrdom (and indeed all witness, whether resulting in death or not) is nothing in itself. It is only victory inasmuch as it is participation in the victory won at the cross by Christ, *the* faithful witness. This is not a purely passive participation, however, since the elder tells us that 'they have washed their robes,' such that there is still a place for their own agency within this participation in the Lamb's death.

That this is a celebration of a victory already won is further underlined by the song they sing and the palm branches they hold. These are reminiscent of those waved by the Jewish crowd when Simon, leader of the Maccabees, entered the citadel at Jerusalem in triumph (1 Macc 13.51). They were also waved by the people in celebration of the purification of the temple after the desecrations of Antiochus Epiphanes (2 Macc 10.5–7; cf. 1 Macc 4.36–60) and at the celebration of the feast of ingathering/tabernacles (Lev 23.39–43). The waving of palm branches was a feature noted by John the evangelist in his account of Jesus's own triumphal entry (Jn 12.13), where the people shouted the closing words from the *Hallel*, a series of songs of deliverance and victory: 'Hosanna! Blessed is the one who comes in the name of the Lord!' (The *Hallel* is the name given to Psalms 113–118, regularly sung or recited at the major festivals. The crowds' words are from the end of the sequence, Ps 118.25–26. Note also the mention of 'festal branches' in the next verse.) All of these connections, of military victory, temple purification, and the exodus and ingathering of the people of God, are here combined.

Revelation 7 is not a vision of two groups but one: the church, described with great theological effect through the juxtaposition of these two images, one on earth and one in heaven, one heard and one seen. Just as with the Lion-Lamb vision, this juxtaposition must not be resolved in either direction, but we must learn to 'think doubly' in order to allow the imagery to have its appropriate theological effect. It is not, therefore, that this image of an innumerable crowd of martyrs displaces the military imagery of the census. Nor is it the reverse. The two mutually interpret one another, giving us a still deeper image of what it means to 'conquer' according to Revelation. This really is an eschatological army, prepared for holy war. And it really is the true ingathering of Israel. The hearing of the military census must have its place. But what that means has now been radically reshaped by the vision: this eschatological army is an army of martyrs, coming from all nations, who have conquered by their faithful witness to the point of death. Their weapon is their faithful testimony to the deliverance wrought by God through the death and resurrection of Christ, and their armour is their participation in that death and resurrection.

What they have won is described by the elder in beautiful terms: a place before the throne to worship, comforted and protected from hunger, thirst, and heat by God himself. Those who wave the palm branches of the feast of tabernacles will now find a lasting shelter. There is just time for one more wonderful double-vision paradox, too, as we are told that 'the Lamb . . . will be their shepherd.'

We will meet this conquering army of witnesses twice more, as the 144,000 accompanying the Lamb in chapter 14 and the great multitude in heaven of chapter 19, but for now John must leave them behind because the visionary interlude now comes to a close as the seventh seal is finally opened and the sequence rushes to its resolution.

The Seventh Seal and Storm Theophany, 8.1–5

After all of that celestial noise of the gathering crescendo of the six seal judgements and the songs of praise, what comes next is startling and powerful. The seventh seal is opened by the Lamb, but instead of a reading of its contents there is silence in heaven. Certainly this has powerful dramatic effect, but there is much more going on besides aesthetics. In the middle of the vision sequence of Zechariah 1.7–6.8, to which John has been regularly alluding in the seven seals, there is an interlude (Zech 2.6–13). Here, the prophet speaks of the judgement of God, the joy and singing of Zion, and the ingathering of the nations, culminating in a command to silence as the Lord rouses himself from his dwelling to come and dwell in their midst (Zech 2.13; cf. Zeph 1.7). John's seven seals may not be arranged in the same concentric pattern as Zechariah's visions, but both sequences place eschatological silence in the climactic position, as God comes to his people. Silence is an appropriate response to this divine presence. There are other resonances, too. In the Jewish apocalyptic tradition, silence accompanies the eschatological act of new creation, echoing the primeval silence that was in the presence of God before the beginning, such that end-time corresponds to primordial-time (*4 Ezra* 7.30; cf. Barr, *Tales*, 85). The silence at the breaking of the seventh seal, therefore, signals God's coming presence, his imminent final judgement, and his new creative act.

The silence does not last forever. Although it speaks of God's final presence and eschatological judgement, there is more to be said, and as such the silence is cut short by the next cycle of visions. It is a very short time, only about half an hour, before more noise begins, but it is no less significant for that. The theological force of this way of describing time is what matters most, though sadly most commentators move on without reaching firm conclusions. Let us try to pause and say something more.

The image of the 'cut short time' of half an hour is, interpreted theologically, the church's existence between the times of the announcement of God's judgement and his final coming. This is a time contracted and interrupted by the apocalypse of Jesus Christ, a time of affliction but also a time of witness. Paul spoke of this contraction of time when he wrote about how 'the appointed time' had grown short (1 Cor 7.29) and both his own and the church's suffering witness in the 'now time' (*ho nyn kairos*, Rom 3.26; 8.18; 11.5; see Agamben 2005). For his part, John will use similar temporal metaphors to speak of this 'halved time' of the church's suffering witness in subsequent visions (for example in 11.2–3; 12.6l and 13.5 where we find the 42 months or 1,260 days, which is 3.5 years—half of 7). The effect is the same: it is a time contracted and divided for the sake of the elect (cf. Mk 13.20), a catching of the breath before the final coming of God. It is in this halved messianic time that the church fulfils its calling to testify to the revelation of Jesus Christ. It is the silence into which the creative and new-creative Word of God is spoken.

At this point there is a literary 'seam' formed by the end of the seven seals and the next major section of the book, as seven angels are given (presumably by God himself) seven trumpets. Trumpets had a range of purposes in the ancient Near East. They were blown in warfare or to herald the arrival of a king. They were blown at the dedication of the temple and in the worship conducted there. As the seven angels prepare to blow their seven trumpets, some or all of these associations may well have been evoked in the imaginations of the first hearers of Revelation. We have already seen how John often interweaves royal, cultic, and military imagery, and so it is unwise to be too specific in singling out any one of these in our interpretation of the seven trumpets, but rather we should allow for a broader range of meanings to interpenetrate. There is, however, a more specific echo that we should hear. In Joel 2.1, a trumpet is blown to announce the coming Day of the Lord. Descriptions of this day, when God comes to judge and restore the earth, regularly use the whole range of imagery. It is imagined in military terms, as it is here in Joel 2.1–11, with God coming at the head of his army to make war against his enemies. But this is combined with cultic imagery (2.12–17) as the trumpet is blown to gather the congregation (v. 15) for worship.

The New Testament often uses the image of the trumpet in similar ways, when discussing matters of eschatology. In Matthew 24.31, for example, angels are sent out by God with loud trumpets to 'gather his elect from the four winds.' First Thessalonians 4 speaks of the 'sound of God's trumpet' accompanying the descent of the Lord Jesus to gather his people, and a similar image is deployed in 1 Corinthians 15.51–2, where the 'last trumpet' heralds the resurrection of the dead. The blowing of these seven trumpets, then, evokes the coming of God in judgement and deliverance and the summoning of the people of the earth. The royal, military, and cultic resonances of the seven trumpets are, therefore, imbued with eschatological significance.

Before any of them are blown, however, John returns to imagery that he saw much earlier in the throne-room vision. Another angel appears and stands beside the altar, reminding us of the fifth seal and the cries for justice of the subaltern saints (6.9). He takes a golden censer and fills it with the incense and the prayers of the saints (cf. 5.8), which go up like smoke before

God. While the prayers ascend, the censer, like the judgements of the first four seals, is thrown down to earth. The noise of thunder on earth that follows could hardly be a starker contrast with the silence in heaven, but in the biblical tradition both are indicative of divine presence (e.g., Exod 19; Ezek 1). As we noted when we first saw such imagery in 4.5, storm language accompanies theophanies throughout the Scriptures. There has been an increase in John's wording now, however, as an earthquake is added to the thunder, rumblings, and lightning (and a further addition to the storm imagery will be made in 11.19, as the cycle of seven trumpets reaches its climax). In this way the culmination of the seal sequence is the arrival of the presence of God himself, met with silence in heaven and thunder on earth.

We might expect at this point to be whisked at once to the New Jerusalem, to see the new creative act of God, but instead that vision is deferred and a new sequence begins as the seven angels prepare to blow their trumpets. As they do so, John will be given a new series of visions that explore the central themes of the seven seals from a different perspective, deepening and enriching our understanding of the judgements of God and his coming in deliverance.

Seven Trumpets

Revelation 8.6–11.19

Introduction to the Seven Trumpets

As we have just seen, the introduction of the seven trumpets into the final seal vision forms a connection between the two sequences of seven. The nature of this connection has been the occasion for many proposals for the structure of the book of Revelation as a whole. As I argued in the introduction, the most compelling options are those that see this sequence of seven trumpets as essentially (but not merely) recapitulating the seven seals. John's visions do not move in a simple linear fashion through time (whether that is seen as the timeline of the first century or a far-off future) but cycle around in a nonlinear narrative, exploring the coming judgement of God from different temporal and theological perspectives, interwoven or nested within one another. In any case, attempts to arrange the seven trumpet judgements in literal chronological order will run into some continuity problems in these chapters. For example, all the green grass is burned up in 8.7, but the grass is there again and protected in 9.4. The stars, which fell at the breaking of the sixth seal in 6.13, are back again to be struck at the fourth trumpet in 8.12. It is because of these sorts of details, as well as the broader structural and theological matters discussed earlier, that we should read the trumpets as essentially a recapitulation of the seals. That said, we are not here dealing with a bland repetition, albeit in different imagery, of what has just happened, for in this recapitulation there is also a shift of perspective and a deepening of theological insight.

The structural arrangement of the trumpet sequence parallels that of the seals. First there are four judgements (8.7–12), described very briefly and arranged as a set like the four horsemen, and distinct from the other three. In the trumpet judgements this structure is even clearer, owing to the interruption of the narrative at this point by a short vision of an eagle, who indicates the pattern by naming the last three trumpets as three 'woes' (v. 13).

As each of the remaining three trumpets are sounded, the three 'woes' are enumerated (9.12; 11.14). For their part, these three 'woes,' the fifth, sixth, and seventh trumpets (9.1–11; 9.13–21; 11.15–19), are described far more expansively, and thus the sequence of seven is again structured in a four-plus-three arrangement, as it was with the seals. Also like the seal sequence, there is a long visionary 'interlude' placed between the sixth and seventh trumpets (10.1–11.14) that, as we will see, presents us again with a visionary 'diptych' concerning the church in its call to witness in the time before the final consummation. The first four seals were focussed on the lives of humankind, bringing warfare, civil strife, famine, and death, whereas the remaining three had a more 'cosmic' frame of reference. In the trumpets, we find the mirror image of that pattern, such that the first four are images of judgement on the earth itself and the latter three are more focussed on humankind.

There are some terrible things in these trumpet visions, including hail and fire, electrical storms, volcanic eruptions, and meteor strikes. What are we to make of this destructive cosmic imagery? It will be important to notice, as most commentators do, that much of the imagery in these visions is drawn from the ten plagues of Exodus 7–12, though John (as always) is creative in his adaptation, weaving in a variety of other pictures and allusions. As always, the point is not to invite a prosaic decoding of the means of God's judgement but to stimulate theological reflection on its meaning. Exodus imagery is appropriate because the principal theological theme of the seven trumpets is the same as that of the seven seals: the coming of God in judgement and deliverance. There are some differences of emphasis between the two sequences, however. If the four horsemen depicted 'manmade' terrors, the trumpets are more descriptive of 'natural' disasters, now invested with theological significance as signs of God's judgement. As we will see, however, there are important aspects of the imagery in the first four trumpets that suggest God's judgement remains focussed on human injustice and thus on answering the cry of the saints under the altar.

We should not, then, make a clear separation between anthropology and cosmology. The parallel structure of the seal and trumpet sequences invites reflection on the connection between their different concerns. In the breaking of the first four seals, we saw how divine judgement took the form of the removal of restraints, allowing human rebellion to have its way, resulting in war, famine, disease, and death. But these very human actions also affect the whole earth, and it is this global scale that is highlighted by the imagery in the seven trumpets, especially the first four. In Christian thought the human being is not an automaton but is rather a part of the world. There is solidarity and interdependence between humankind and the rest of God's creation, for good and for ill. Humankind was made from the earth and is forever tied to it. Trees are needed for food and for shelter, grass feeds our livestock, rivers provide our water, seas our fish to eat. In Romans 8, we hear about this relationship from the perspective of redemption, as creation groans in expectation of the revelation of the sons of God. But there is also a dark side: creation has become 'subject to futility' (Rom 8.20) and held under bondage to decay because of sin. Here in Revelation 8, there is a visionary presentation of this theological truth, as creation suffers because of the rebellion of humankind. The problem of human sin is not merely one of personal moral failures, or even the collection of all personal moral failures, but concerns our complicity with the power of sin in the cosmos, which has at its heart the idolatry that threatens to undo all of God's world, right down to the grass. It is a structural evil affecting it all. In our world today we have been long accustomed to speaking of 'natural disasters,' but we are becoming increasingly aware that many of these are not 'natural' at all, strictly speaking, but are the results of human injustice and abuse of the earth and its resources. Time and again Revelation will address the essential apocalyptic question, 'To whom does the sovereignty of the world belong?' (Käsemann 1969). In its apocalyptic answer to this question, Revelation reminds us that human beings are not merely 'individuals' but are always caught up in a cosmic battle for the lordship of the world between God and his enemies. God's work of liberation for humankind from its enslavement to sin is, therefore, to be understood as a concrete expression of his deliverance of all creation from bondage.

There are rich scriptural resources that speak of this essential connection between human rebellion and the bondage of the earth. In Genesis 3, for example, the ground is cursed because of Adam's sin. The prophet Isaiah drew a similar logical connection:

> The earth dries up and withers, the world languishes and withers;
> the heavens languish together with the earth.
> The earth lies polluted
> under its inhabitants;
> for they have transgressed laws,
> violated the statutes,
> broken the everlasting covenant.
> Therefore a curse devours the earth,
> and its inhabitants suffer for their guilt;
> therefore the inhabitants of the earth dwindled,
> and few people are left. (Isa 24:4–5, NRSV)

In short, sin is serious, affecting not only humankind but the whole earth. A serious cosmic intervention is needed, answering the cry from under the altar (Rev 6.10), the prayers of the saints (Rev 8.3), and the groaning of creation (Rom 8.22). This wider cosmic frame, with its connection to human sin, is now in view in the imagery of the seven trumpets.

As with the seven seals, there are indications of restraint in God's wrath, as the extent of the destruction is again described in limited terms. But it is not the case that the trumpets are merely a repetition, in different imagery, of the seals. There is also a sense in that in these visions the depiction of divine judgement is both widened, to encompass all creation, and deepened, as these restraints are lessened. This is a spiral rather than a circle, moving forward even as it cycles round. While the judgements thus become more intense, there is also a deeper and clearer indication of their purpose. First, they are intended to bring about repentance, a point that was implicit in the seal judgement but made explicit as the sixth trumpet ended (9.20). As with Joel's vision of the Day of the Lord, God's judgement is oriented toward mercy (Joel 2.12). We will see, however, that the judgements ultimately have no such effect, and the only thing that induces repentance is the witness of the church, the purpose and theme of the visionary interlude in chapters 10 and 11. Second, the purpose of the trumpet judgements is the restoration of God's creation. The target of divine wrath is clearly named as the trumpet sequence ends: the divine judgements here described are not for the destruction of the earth, but 'for destroying the destroyers of the earth' (11.18). Third, there is a liberative purpose in God's judgement against idolatry and oppression, which is signalled by the nature of the imagery used, being drawn from the story of the exodus and from the prophetic tradition, as we will now see.

The First Six Trumpets, 8.6–9.21

Trumpets 1–4: 'Cosmic' Disasters

The seven angels had been given their seven trumpets at the breaking of the last seal, and now they prepare to sound them. After the expansive visionary material of the closing seals and the visionary interlude, the first four trumpets come in arrestingly quick succession. That there are four is not only a function of the structure of the series but is also suggestive of the 'four corners of the earth,' and thus an indication of the global reach of these judgements, especially since we have just seen a vision of four angels in that context (7.1). Four angels sent to the four corners of the earth are also a sign that accompanies the Day of the Lord in the synoptic Gospels (e.g., Mk 13.27). The global scale of the judgements that come with the four trumpets is confirmed by their contents. The earth, the sea, the heavens, and the rivers (a list echoed in 14.7 and reminiscent of the first four days of creation) are all struck in turn. These judgements, then, are terrifying in their global reach.

The images used here strongly echo the plagues of the exodus, though as usual this is not a straightforward copying but rather more of a pastiche (see Fletcher 2017) of different images and tropes. John's adaptations of this tradition are as significant as the similarities, if not more so. There are a number of details that cannot be found in Exodus but are rather drawn from other Old Testament sources, and there is no correspondence in the order of the plagues, either.

The first trumpet brings a terrifying cocktail of 'hail and fire, mixed with blood,' combining the imagery of seventh Egyptian plague (Ex 9.23–24) with that of the first (Ex 7.20). In the Exodus account, the blood killed all of the fish in the river (7.21) and the 'hail with fire' (or 'lightning,' for the Hebrew word is the same) struck everything, humans and animals, all the plants of the field, and every tree (9.25). At the first trumpet in Revelation, by contrast, 'only' a third of the earth and trees are burned up. As we saw with the seals, this quantity (though it is certainly staggering) is a symbolic indication of the restraint in divine judgement. It is not the whole earth that is struck, but a third. This figure of one third is repeated throughout the first four trumpet judgements, indicating a similar proportional destruction of the sea and its creatures (8.9), the rivers (8.10–11), and the heavenly bodies (8.12). This proportion represents an increase on the fourth seal, however, where the limit was set at a quarter (6.8). Despite the terrifying and destructive imagery, the effect is the gradual and controlled loosening of restraints rather than unmitigated divine wrath. This restraint is made clearer when placed in comparison with the language of the Exodus account (though now set on a global scale), and this also has the effect of reminding us of the purpose of this divine judgement: the deliverance of God's people from idolatry and oppression. As Brian Blount succinctly puts it, 'exodus implies liberation' (2013, 166).

Yet the imagery of blood and fire is not simply lifted from the book of Exodus. Once again, as often in these chapters, John is also working with allusions to the prophets. Similar imagery of hail, blood, and fire is used to speak of the judgement of Gog in Ezekiel 38.22 and of the coming Day of the Lord in Joel 2.30–31, a passage that clearly resonated strongly with the apocalyptic sensibilities of early Christian thought, since it is also picked up by the Gospels (Mt 24.29–31; Mk 13.24–25; Lk 21.25–28). In this multiply allusive imagery, then, John weaves together (and not for the last time) the motifs of Exodus deliverance and the eschatological hope of the Day of the Lord.

The second trumpet blows, and something like a volcano is thrown into the sea, turning it to blood and destroying a third of the creatures and the ships. If Revelation is dated in the late first century, this image would no doubt speak powerfully to those who had recent memory of the eruption of Vesuvius in AD 79. It is John's intertextual connections, however, that are more compelling and are most illuminating for his message. Though the blood imagery and the death of aquatic life is another clear echo of the first plague in Exodus, we will search that book in vain to find the 'great mountain, burning with fire.' That feature of this vision is, again, drawn from imagery elsewhere in the prophetic tradition. This time John's combination is not Exodus with Joel but Exodus with Jeremiah. In chapter 51, the weeping prophet issues this oracle of judgement against Babylon:

> I am against you, O destroying mountain, says the LORD,
> that destroys the whole earth (cf. Rev 11.19);
> I will stretch out my hand against you,
> and roll you down from the crags,
> and make you a burned-out mountain. . . .
>
> Raise a standard in the land,
> blow the trumpet among the nations;
> prepare the nations for war against her,
> summon against her the kingdoms . . .
>
> I will dry up her sea
> and make her fountain dry;
> and Babylon shall become a heap of ruins,
> a den of jackals,
> an object of horror and of hissing,
> without inhabitant. (Jer 51:25, 27, 36–37)

There are multiple allusions to the imagery of Jeremiah 51 in this short trumpet judgement, as well as in at least one of those to come. If we allow them to guide our interpretation, the casting down of burning mountain is less a prediction of cosmic destruction, such as a divinely ordered meteorite, and more an imaginative prophetic portrayal of God's overthrow of an idolatrous and oppressive city and the rescue of God's people. This perspective is further strengthened by noting (as those reading Revelation for a second time surely would) how John returns to this same chapter of Jeremiah in the vision of Babylon in chapter 18. In combining it here with the imagery from the plagues of Exodus, John forges a new multivalent image of the Day of the Lord, combining the exodus and the return from exile and emphasising the delivering hand of God in it all.

The third angel blows his trumpet, and another 'cosmic' judgement appears, and again the imagery used, once read alongside the prophets, evokes the theme of divine judgement against oppression. John sees something like a comet or a meteorite, a 'falling star' that hits the rivers of the earth and makes their waters bitter. Throughout the ancient world such astronomical events were often treated as omens, and usually bad ones. As with all the imagery, however, we must be wary of such literalistic interpretations and attend to the way an image like this might work in the literary matrix of the Jewish apocalyptic and prophetic tradition. As in that tradition, John regularly uses astral imagery to refer to angelic beings, as we have already seen (1.20) and as we will see again very soon (9.1). Here, this blazing star comes from heaven, a messenger of divine judgement hurled to earth.

It is given a name, connecting the star to the bitterness of the waters that it causes: Wormwood (*apsinthos* in Greek, from which we get the name of the bitter herbal spirit absinthe). This herb was known throughout the region for its medicinal qualities but also for its extremely bitter flavour, and this bitterness is highlighted here in Revelation 8 and in the prophets from whom John draws the image. Amos deploys it as a description of the perversion of justice (Am 5.7; 6.12), and (perhaps more significantly) Jeremiah uses the image in an oracle of judgement against false prophets: 'I am going to make them eat wormwood (Heb לַעֲנָה, and give them poisoned water to drink' (Jer 23.15). This is poetic justice for those who have tainted the waters of faith with idolatrous impurity (Blount 2013, 170). In the prophetic tradition, then, the image of wormwood relates to divine judgement on false teaching and corrupted justice, which often go hand in hand.

The apocalyptic cosmic signs continue as the fourth trumpet sounds, bringing judgement upon the celestial bodies that were created on the fourth day (Gen 1.14–19). A third of sun, moon, and stars are 'struck' so that they are darkened. The word used here is *eplēgē*, which is etymologically related and acoustically near identical to the word *plēgē*, 'plague.' (See BDAG and Osborne 2002, 355). If it were not already clear enough from the images he is using, John will soon make his intertextual connection to the plagues of Exodus even more explicit. However, it is his allusions to Joel that are clearest in this vision, since in them we find frequent repetition of the darkening of sun, moon, and stars in prophecies of the Day of the Lord (Joel 2.2; 2.10; 3.15). Amos also uses this image (Am 5.18; 8.9), and it is, we recall, picked up and used in similar apocalyptic contexts in the synoptic Gospels (Mt 24.29 and parallels). Darkness is also the ninth Egyptian plague (Ex 10.22), and so here we encounter a many-threaded combination of allusions. Moreover, this judgement also has echoes within the book of Revelation itself, as the fourth trumpet brings the kind of darkness seen in the sixth seal (6.12). There, the stars fell to earth, and the fact that they are now here again to be darkened further confirms that a recapitulative interpretation of the two sequences is to be preferred over a linear/sequential one. In the same manner as we saw in the burning of the earth and trees in the first trumpet judgement, we do not see the complete darkness that came with the Exodus plague but the limited darkening of 'a third of their light.'

Though the cosmic scope of God's judgement shapes the imagery used here, the celestial images of sun, moon, and stars are regularly used in prophetic and visionary contexts to designate sociopolitical upheaval, particularly as regards the casting down of earthly rulers. One thinks immediately of Joseph's dream in Genesis 37, but similar images are found everywhere in the theopolitical imagination of the prophets when describing social upheavals or the denunciation of idolatrous kings. Isaiah speaks this way about the casting down of the king of Babylon, depicted as a falling star (Isa 14.12), Jeremiah uses similar cosmic imagery to describe the exile (Jer 4.23–28), and Ezekiel connects these celestial signs with the judgement of the king of Egypt (Ezek 32.7–8). In this way, the 'earth-shattering' meaning of these political upheavals is described in terms that evoke cosmic collapse, imbuing them with theological significance (see Wright 1992, 282ff.). There are obviously connections here with the more 'sociopolitical' interpretation of the first three trumpets suggested above, especially the second. If this prophetic use of such 'cosmic' signs is allowed to inform our reading of the fourth trumpet, all four can be seen not as prophecies of cosmic destruction but as symbolic depictions, imbued with theological significance, of God's judgement against oppression in the form of idolatrous cities, false teachers, corrupt justice, and human rulers.

Trumpet 5 (and First Woe): The Army of Locusts
Before the fifth trumpet blows, John sees another brief vision, which introduces the three remaining judgements and signals the sevenfold structure. Again, this 'vision' is both visual and acoustic, as John says 'I looked, and I heard,' though this time there is no contrast of two images but simply one. What John sees and hears is an eagle—though the Greek word *aetos* can also be translated 'vulture.' If it is read as 'eagle,' there are possible echoes here of one of the four living creatures in 4.7, and the image evokes the theme of the

swiftness of the coming action (cf. Ezek 17). If it is read as 'vulture,' the associations with death and coming judgement are more dramatic, for vultures gather where there is carrion, an eschatological image found in apocalyptic sayings of Jesus (Mt 24.28; Lk 17.37). Here John does not describe the bird with any details that might help us clarify which of the two species is meant, save to say that it flies in 'midheaven.' However, Revelation 19.17–18 also mentions birds 'in midheaven,' and there the reference is far more obviously to vultures and their like, for they are called to eat carrion, and so it is quite possible that the same is meant here.

The focus, instead, is on what the bird cries out, pronouncing a threefold woe on the inhabitants of the earth corresponding to the remaining three trumpets. In literary terms, this underlines the 'four-plus-three' arrangement of the sequence of seven and indicates that the remaining three are to be given particular attention. It also adds another structural layer to the sequence, such that in addition to counting out the seven trumpets there will also be an enumeration of the three 'woes.' Viewed theologically, the bird's cry also indicates the object of divine judgement: the inhabitants of the earth. As noted above, the seven trumpets are arranged in a pattern that is the mirror image of the seven seals. Seals 1–4 (war, civil strife, famine, death) focussed on people before seals 5–7 came with a wider cosmic frame. Here it is the reverse: the first four trumpets announced judgement on earth and sea, sun and moon, and now the final three 'woes' are directed at the earth's inhabitants.

The fifth trumpet sounds (and therefore the first 'woe' has begun), beginning the fifth vision of the seven. Like the fifth and sixth seals, the descriptions of the next two trumpet judgements are far more expansive and detailed. John sees another falling star, or rather one that has already fallen from heaven to earth, though in this case it quickly becomes clear that John is referring not to a meteorite but to an angelic being of some kind, as was common with this image. There is an ambiguity here in John's description, since the falling of this astral figure may be read either as a forceful 'casting down' or a more neutral 'sending down,' and the implications of each for the figure's identity are very different. If the star has been sent rather than cast down, then it should be read as an angel, sent to carry out divinely mandated duties. However, if it is a more forceful 'casting down,' there may be echoes of the Jewish apocalyptic tradition of depicting Satan and the rebel angels as stars cast out of heaven, fallen to corrupt the earth and its inhabitants (*1 Enoch* 86–88; cf. Lk 10.18). That John describes how this star has 'fallen' and not simply 'descended' suggests that this 'fallen angel' motif is the likelier reading. As we will see, this is a tradition on which Revelation draws in its depiction of cosmic warfare between angelic and Satanic beings (see the longer discussion of Rev 12.7–9 below). In the account found in the apocalypse of *1 Enoch*, the Satanic fallen star is ultimately bound and thrown into an abyss, which is very similar to how Revelation later depicts the fate of Satan (Rev 20). There, an angel holds the keys that lock Satan in the pit. Here, however, the fallen star is not yet bound and thrown into the abyss but is given the keys to open it.

In either reading of the image, what is clear is that this astral figure has authority, since he holds a key, but this remains a delegated authority. Reading the fallen star as Satan (or perhaps one of the lieutenants), this serves as a reminder of the essentially delegated and limited authority given to him by the one who truly rules. Christ, we recall, is the one who possesses such keys (1.18). The fallen star does not own the key to the abyss outright but is given it, the passive voice (*edothē*, 'he was given') indicating divine agency, as it did in the first four seals, and thereby God's ultimate sovereignty over the opening of the pit and what comes out of it.

This is the first mention of the 'bottomless pit' (Greek *abyssos*), an image that will feature a number of times in subsequent chapters (cf. 11.7; 17.8; 20.1–3) in connection with anti-God forces of various kinds. In Revelation, the abyss is not, strictly speaking, the same place as Hades (the realm of the dead) but is a distinct part of the underworld assigned for evil beings, depicted as both the place of their origin and their judgement. Here it is the former, as the fallen star performs his limited duties and opens the shaft of the abyss to release demonic forces (see also Lk 8.31, where the abyss is similarly depicted as the origin and judgement place for the demonic 'Legion').

Out of the pit come billows of smoke that darken the sun, once again echoing the imagery of the Day of the Lord announced by trumpet blast in Joel 2. From Joel's fantastic palette of images another is now borrowed, as a swarm of locusts comes out of the smoke, and John's vision draws heavily on this imagery for a number of its details, as we will see. Locust imagery is used to depict an invading army sent by God (Joel 1.4–7; 2.10–11, 25), an image also picked up by Jeremiah in his oracle against Babylon (Jer 51.14). We can probably assume, then, that John's vision follows this prophetic tradition in using this image to indicate a military invasion, perhaps again playing on the fears of a Parthian cavalry invasion from the east, as he did with the horseman of the first seal (see comments on 6.1–2). But, as with all such imagery in Revelation, this is much more than a simple coded picture of an invading army, as we will see.

An interesting challenge is raised here. Is John using the imagery the same way as Joel did, or the reverse? To answer that we would need to be confident about Joel's usage of the image, but that itself is unclear. Scholars disagree about whether the prophet is depicting a literal locust plague as an invading army (e.g., Seitz 2016, 152) or an invading army as a plague of locusts. If the latter, is it a human army or an apocalyptic/eschatological 'army of the Lord'? The problem is compounded still further once we consider that Joel may be using the imagery one way in chapter 1 and a different way in chapter 2, also a topic of major debate (on which see the helpful discussion in Barton 2001, *ad loc*). This ambiguity can certainly pose a historical puzzle, but from a literary and theological perspective it is a delightfully generative thing. Perhaps Joel is deliberately ambiguous, so that his word about the Day of the Lord might resist being simplistically assigned to a singular historical moment, whether a plague or an invasion, but will, in a sense, stand as a word for all times (see Seitz 2016, 57). Though there may well be single historical moments in view, the surplus of meaning inherent in the ambiguity of the prophetic imagery is an important part of its theological meaning. Likewise, in John's deployment of Joel's ambiguous imagery, a similar double meaning is exploited rather than resolved. Both senses are important: an army is a plague and a plague is an army. And in John, the army in question is unquestionably one with apocalyptic and eschatological significance.

Joel and John are both also echoing the eighth plague of Exodus 10, where a swarm of locusts follows the plague of hail to devour what is left of the Egyptian crops, and every tree. We note in Revelation that the green grass, which was burned up in the first trumpet judgment (8.7), is now present again (another suggestion that simplistic sequential readings of these judgements are not appropriate) and so potentially at risk from the swarm of locusts. In John's vision, however, the swarm is given strict instructions *not* to eat the vegetation (9.4). They have a different objective—after all, this is the first of three 'woes' not on the earth but on its inhabitants.

God in his sovereignty sets limits for this demonic army, in their delegated authority and in the scope and duration of their activities. The scope of their damage is clearly defined. People are to be hurt but not killed, and moreover it is not all who are subject to this judgement but only those 'who do not have the seal of God on their foreheads.' The idea of covenant identity markers affording protection from the devil and his demons was commonplace in Judaism in John's time (see Schreiber 2020). Here this detail also recalls the angelic 'sealing' of the 144,000 in chapter 7 and foreshadows a later vision where we will meet them again and learn that the seal on their foreheads is the name of the Lamb and of his Father (14.1). In the earlier discussion of the sealing of the people in chapter 7, we noted that this is a symbol of protection that alludes to Ezekiel 9.4–6. Those allusions are now strengthened in the recapitulation of this idea here in chapter 9, and it is made clear that this mark protects the people of God not only from divine wrath but also from the powers of evil. The duration of the locusts' torment is, again, cut short by God (cf. Mk 13.19–20 and the discussion of 8.1–5 above) and set at five months (9.5, 10). Certainly this is a long time to endure torture, but in saying that it has been 'allowed' (lit., 'given,' *edothē* again), John indicates once more God's sovereign control in setting limits to these judgements.

John now goes into detail in his description of the locusts, and again he draws from the prophet Joel. John's locust army has the appearance of war horses (Rev 9.7, 9; cf. Joel 2.4) with the teeth of a lion (Rev 9.8, cf. Joel 1.6). Locusts make a perfect metaphor for an army not only because of their tendency to swarm in devastating numbers, evoking feelings of fear in subsistence farmers to this day, but also because of their 'armour-plated' appearance, and John exploits this feature in his depiction of their 'iron breastplates' (Greek *thōrax*) and the thunderous noise of their wings. To this locust imagery, John now adds more entomological imagery. Ordinarily a swarm of locusts, while a danger to crops, is directly harmless to humans. Not so with this swarm, for they are described as possessing the tails and powerful stings of scorpions. And as if this chimeric image of a locust-scorpion were not terrifying enough, John also sees that they have human faces, hair like a woman's hair, and wear golden crowns, indicating their delegated authority to conquer.

In a natural locust swarm, there seems to be order without a single leader (see Prov 30.27). This demonic army, however, has a king to lead it, the 'angel of the bottomless pit' who is now named. His name in Hebrew is *Abaddon*, 'Destruction,' a name found in the Hebrew wisdom literature as an alternative or parallel to *She'ol*, the place of the dead (e.g., Job 31.12; Ps 88.11; Prov 15.11), and that is sometimes personified (e.g., Job 26.6; 28.22). Elsewhere in contemporary Jewish writings, in one text from the Dead Sea Scrolls, Belial (another name for Satan) is liturgically cursed with punishment in an 'eternal pit' and is called the 'angel of the pit' and the 'spirit of Abaddon' (4Q286 Frag. 7, Col. II, vv. 1–7, tr. Wise, Abegg, and Cook; see also Koester 2014, 461). In Greek this name is loosely translated *Apollyon*, 'Destroyer,' the double moniker indicating that the primary character of this figure is the privation of God's creative work. God is praised as the creator of all things (4.11), but this figure is the one who threatens their destruction. He rides into battle at the head of his demonic locust army, bent on the destruction of the earth. In the 'interlude' vision of the seven trumpets we will see another figure ascend from the pit to make war on the saints, the 'beast' (11.7), who then later 'goes to destruction' (*apōleia*, Rev 17.8–11). It is possible that the two figures are the same, but here in chapter 8, the naming of this one and its role as the leader of the demonic locust army makes it more likely that we are to understand it as Satan specifically. As we will see later, however, there is a close relationship between Satan and the beast.

In all of this fantastic imagery we must remember to resist the temptation to engage in a decoding exercise and thereby reduce it to the flat prose of a military invasion. In evoking the imagery of the Day of the Lord from Joel, the oracles of Jeremiah, and the plagues of Exodus, John intends not only to indicate an invading army but to imbue that geopolitical event with profound theological significance. For their part, these invading forces are described in terms that indicate to the readers of Revelation that, though these forces have a 'human face,' a darker power is at work behind the scenes, for they come up from the abode of demons and their commander is the angel of the abyss. But there is also encouragement here, too, for in the phrasing of John's vision he repeatedly emphasises divine sovereignty. Despite the appearance of apparent chaos, there are strict divine limits imposed on this judgement, along with the implicit reminder throughout that, though the Destroyer of the earth has come up from the pit (a fitting origin for the one who is himself 'void'), his end is (equally fittingly) his own destruction (11.18). True victory does not belong to this horde of locusts or to its Satanic king, but to the Lamb and his people. As Jesus's disciples learned in Luke 10, for those whose names are written in heaven there is authority over demons and power to trample scorpions—and their enemy Satan falls like lightning from heaven (Lk 10.17–20).

The sense of divine sovereignty persists with the continued counting of the three woes and the seven trumpets. The first woe has now concluded, and the second begins.

Trumpet 6 (and Second Woe): The Cavalry

The sixth angel blows his trumpet, and John hears a voice coming from the altar that gives instructions to release four angels (we are not told whose voice this is, and it would not be beyond Revelation's imaginative capacity to have the altar itself speak, which is the literal sense here). Are these the same four angels who had been seen at the start of the seal interlude (7.1–3)? If so, it becomes more difficult to sustain a recapitulative reading of the trumpets, since there would be a clear narrative progression in the role of these characters. However, we recall that those four had been sent to the four corners of the earth and given the task of restraining the four destructive winds. In contrast, these four angels are all stationed at the same point, the Euphrates, and are themselves restrained. The sense is that, though there is a literary connection between the two groups, this vision concerns a different team of angels. These are four messengers of judgement, divinely restrained but now released at the appropriate time and sent to the earth to kill. This is not, however, an image of the complete release of divine restraint, for their judgment has been held back for this particular and specific time (indicated by the fourfold designation of hour, day, month, and year) and is given a strict limit of one third of humankind. As we saw with the first four trumpets, this limit of one third represents an increase on the seal sequence but nevertheless indicates divine control and restraint in these otherwise chaotic scenes.

The Euphrates was the largest river in the region, across which the Assyrians and the Babylonians had come to take the people of Israel and Judah into exile. It was thus regularly associated with divine judgement in the prophetic literature (e.g., Isa 7.20; 27.12; Jer 13.4–7; 46.2–10), as the river of Babylon. In the closing visions of the book, John will see a contrasting river in a contrasting city, the new Jerusalem (see Resseguie 2009, 148). The Euphrates was also important in the Roman imagination, marking the eastern frontier of the empire. Beyond here were the Parthians, and thus John invokes the ever-present threat, which particularly gripped the imagination of those who lived in the eastern provinces of the empire, of invasion from the east. It is not the first time he has made this move (see the discussion of the first horseman in 6.1–2), and it will not be the last (see 16.12, where there is an explicit link to 'the kings from the east').

Echoes of the Parthian threat are intensified as the invading army is now described. Again the judgement takes the form of horsemen: suddenly entering the narrative, as if cresting a hill, is a cavalry of two hundred million riders. John does not count them himself but hears their number, just as he did with the military census of the counting of the 144,000. There are other narrative similarities between these two scenes, since here John employs, as in the previous trumpet vision, a combination of 'hearing' and 'seeing.' There are a number of similarities between the descriptions of this cavalry and the locust army of the fifth trumpet. In the previous vision, the locusts were like warhorses with lions' teeth, scorpions' tails, and scales like breastplates (9.7–9). Here the riders wear shining breastplates, and their chimeric horses have lions' heads and snakes' tails. The imaginative connections between the two visions are so many that it is tempting to read them as two interlocking depictions of the same idea. Certainly the overarching theme of a sudden and destructive military invasion is at the heart of both visions. In the fifth trumpet, this threat of invasion is depicted with demonic significance, whereas the sixth trumpet is a more earthly image, albeit a fantastical one that transcends prosaic description. Whether this is the same army viewed from another perspective or a second invasion, the effect is to cast this military threat in dramatic visionary terms that imbue it with theological significance.

The colour of the riders' breastplates is fire and sulphur, and from the mouths of their horses come the same, all recalling the divine judgement on Sodom and Gomorrah (Gen 19.12–29), a judgement evoked in the Gospels' depiction of the coming judgement day (e.g., Lk 17.28–32). These three judgements of fire, smoke, and sulphur are now explicitly called 'plagues' (9.18, 20), again indicating that allusions to Exodus are also woven into this judgement scene. As with the previous trumpet, the target of judgement here is not the earth itself but its inhabitants, and a third of humankind is killed.

As the sixth trumpet vision comes to a close, with the tension building toward the climactic seventh, the narration becomes more explicit about the divine purpose behind these judgements: to bring about the repentance of humankind. The exposure and critique of humanity's sins in 9.20–21 gives the reason for the judgements and goes some way to explaining their form. The principle at work in these last two trumpet judgements seems to be the rule of *lex talionis* (Lev 24.17–21), with the injury suffered corresponding to the injury inflicted. The *Wisdom of Solomon* expresses this idea in terms remarkably similar to the vision John now sees:

> In return for their foolish and wicked thoughts,
> which led them astray to worship irrational serpents and worthless animals,
> you sent upon them a multitude of irrational creatures to punish them,
> so that they might learn that one is punished by the very things by which one sins.
> For your all-powerful hand,
> which created the world out of formless matter,
> did not lack the means to send upon them a multitude of bears, or bold lions,
> or newly created unknown beasts full of rage,
> or such as breathe out fiery breath,
> or belch forth a thick pall of smoke,
> or flash terrible sparks from their eyes;
> not only could the harm they did destroy people,
> but the mere sight of them could kill by fright.
> Even apart from these, people could fall at a single breath
> when pursued by justice
> and scattered by the breath of your power.

But you have arranged all things by measure and number and weight. (Wis 11:15–20)

John would likely agree that 'one is punished by the very things by which one sins.' We are told that the basic sin of humanity is idolatry, and so the punishment fits the crime. For John, the worship of dumb idols of metal and stone is fundamentally coordinate with (possibly even theologically identical with) the worship of demons. And those who unrepentantly worship demons in the form of 'irrational creatures' are handed over to irrational creaturely demonic armies, so that the punishment is appropriate and so that they will see what this sin does and repent. We are also reminded here, however, that idols are essentially inert—they cannot see or hear or walk. The terrors of these demonic forces are, in the end, only given their agency by human sin and divine permission. They are not straightforwardly 'forces' in themselves but are powers of our own making, powers that supervene upon human idolatrous rebellion while also causing and exacerbating it. As the vision of the locusts showed us moments ago, evil may come up from the pit, but it always has a 'human face.' This is why it is appropriate that divine judgement is repeatedly presented as the releasing of seals or the removal of restraint: God is letting their own idols loose upon people so that they might turn from them.

Sadly, repentance is not the result. It seems that retributive justice of this kind, even if administered by angels, does not ultimately produce repentance. As such the judgement scenes tell us as much about the limitations of punishment as they do about human hard-heartedness. In the passage just quoted from the *Wisdom of Solomon*, the writer goes on to say that although God always has the capacity to show his strength in meting out such deserved retributive judgements, in view of his concern for his creation, he chooses instead the way of mercy, desiring repentance not retribution (*Wis* 11.21–26). Though the scenes here in the sixth trumpets are horrifying, there is the same undercurrent of mercy in their measured restraint and the same desire for repentance. Alas, we are told that the remaining two thirds of humankind, left alive through these terrifying ordeals, do not repent but continue in their idolatry and in murder, sorcery, fornication, and theft. This list of sins partially echoes the Ten Commandments and reminds us that it is breach of the first, idolatry, that lies at the heart of the transgression of the other nine, and indeed at the heart of all human sin. The pessimism of the closing words of the sixth trumpet judgement leaves us wondering if anything will be effective in bringing about repentance and life. If the inhabitants of the earth will not turn from their idolatry when faced with a demonic horde, what could possibly induce repentance unto life? We are about to see Revelation's answer to that question.

Interlude, 10.1–11.14

The Angel with a Little Scroll, 10.1–11

As with the seven seals, the narrative has built to a climax, and one now expects to hear the sounding of the seventh and final trumpet, bringing an end to the series of judgements. Instead, there is another narrative interlude, holding the reader in the almost unbearable tension between the inauguration of God's work of judgement and its completion. Again, the primary concern of this visionary interlude is the church in its role of prophetic conquering witness in the time 'between the times.'

Just as in the seal judgements, there are two visionary scenes in this interlude. First, John sees a 'mighty angel.' We first encountered such a 'mighty angel' in 5.2, where his role was to ask about the opening of the scroll. This angel, too, holds a scroll, as we will see shortly. Yet, although there is an obvious literary connection established between them, this seems to be a different angel to the one in chapter 5, as John indicates by calling him *'another* mighty angel.' It is possible that when John says 'another' he means to distinguish this angel not from the angel of 5.2 but from the four angels of 9.14 (thus suggesting we read it as 'another angel, a strong one'; see Mounce 1998, 201). Certainly they are far closer at hand in the narrative of Revelation, and so it makes syntactical sense to read John this way. If that is the case, it is an open question whether this 'mighty angel' is identical with the one in 5.2. Regardless of whether the two appearances of a 'strong angel' (and the third, in 18.21) indicate the same narrative character or not, there are certainly enough similarities in their portrayals for them to be theologically related, as we will see.

John's description of the angel as 'coming down from heaven' implies a shift in his visionary geography. In describing his descent in this way, there is a clear implication that this is a vision with an earthly, rather than heavenly, vantage point. When the seven angels were given their trumpets in 8.2, the location of the vision was in heaven before the throne of God. While this heavenly perspective has continued as the trumpets have sounded, each of the judgements has had a decidedly earthly focus: we have seen hail, a mountain, and stars all thrown down to earth. Now, the narrative action itself has moved to earth, and John has followed it. This is a vision that, though divinely revealed, has an earthly perspective.

There is nothing earthly about this angel, though. His appearance is a complex tapestry of allusions that seems to bring him incredibly close to divine status. First, it echoes aspects of the Son of Man vision in chapter 1: he is wrapped in a cloud (cf. 1.7) with a face shining like the sun (cf. 1.16) and resplendent legs (cf. 1.15). Second, there are also echoes of the throne vision in chapter 4, since the angel is haloed by a rainbow (cf. 4.3). Third, the angel's description evokes the divine presence in the exodus in that it speaks of him being surrounded in cloud and his legs are burnished bronze but 'pillars of fire.' Through pillars of cloud and fire, God was present with his people in the liminal space between Egypt and the promised land. Though what he soon says will distinguish him from God and from Christ, this angel nevertheless reflects the glory of God and represents his presence on earth.

In the angel's hand is a 'little scroll,' which is not sealed but opened. Is this the same scroll as the one with the seven seals, about which the previous 'mighty angel' proclaimed? Or is it a different one? Much has been made of the Greek words used here. In 5.2, John speaks of a *biblion*, a scroll. Here in 10.2, however, he uses the word *biblaridion*, the diminutive form, hence the translation 'little scroll.' For some commentators this is indication enough that we are dealing with a different document. But this, I think, makes too much of a minor shift in vocabulary, and John alternates between both words fairly freely in this passage. The change in visionary geography might be helpful here. In chapter 5, John saw the scroll sealed and from a heavenly perspective, but now he sees it opened and from an earthly one. The scroll is open because the Lamb has opened it, but as yet its contents have not been read. The seven judgements that accompanied the breaking of its seals did not disclose the contents of the scroll. This is now what we expect to see. As we saw in chapter 5, the connections to Zechariah 5 and Ezekiel 2 evoked by this image indicate that the scroll is meant to be read as a symbol of prophetic commission and a divine message of woe. John will soon be asked to take this message from the angel's hand (10.8) and will be commanded to perform his prophetic role (10.11). Even though the judgement cycles are read recapitulatively, there is still a sense of narrative progression, like a spiral rather than a circle.

The angel places one foot on the sea (notice, not 'in' it; see Mangina 2010, 128) and one on land, and as such his actions relate to the whole earth. He shouts in a loud voice, like a Lion, another visionary connection to Christ. This is the sound of the Lion, who is the Lamb, who is worthy to open the scroll and has opened it. The angel's shout looks like it is about to launch us into another sevenfold visionary sequence, as seven thunders sound. Presumably we should expect this sequence to give a further recapitulation and intensification of divine judgement, perhaps growing to half of the earth or more (Bauckham 1993, 82). There would certainly be precedent for this: in Isaiah's heavenly vision, God's judgement continues beyond 90 percent of the earth (Isa 6.13). But instead we are left to speculate, because just as John is about to write the thunders down, a heavenly voice instructs him not to: the content of the seven thunders is to remain sealed. The intensification of divine judgement will not now extend to a third cycle, for as the angel declares, raising his right hand in a solemn oath to the God of heaven, 'there will be no more delay.' (It is now clear that this angel is not a divine figure, for if he were he would swear by himself, and the lesser swears by the greater [cf. Heb 6.13–16]). The seventh trumpet, yet to sound, will fulfil the mystery of God. The time between the sixth and seventh trumpets, as with the seals, is the time of waiting for that fulfilment, as promised to the prophets.

Mention of the prophets takes us to the next phase of this vision (and indeed the subsequent vision in chapter 11), where understanding the prophetic allusions can be very helpful. John is now instructed to take the scroll (*biblion*) from the angel's hand. As he takes the little scroll (*biblaridion*) he is instructed not to read but to eat it (and perhaps this aspect of the vision helps explain why John needs the reduced size!). Expectations that we were about to hear a reading of the scroll's contents are seemingly frustrated, but as we will now see things are not quite so straightforward.

As there were in chapter 5, there are echoes of Ezekiel in this vision, echoes that are now made even more unmistakable. In Ezekiel 2–3, the prophet receives his commission to go to the people of Israel with a rebuke for their rebellion against God. This commission is given in visionary form in 2.9–3.3:

> I looked, and a hand was stretched out to me, and a written scroll was in it. He spread it before me; it had writing on the front and on the back, and written on it were words of lamentation and mourning and woe. He said to me, O mortal, eat what is offered to you; eat this scroll, and go, speak to the house of Israel. So I opened my mouth, and he gave me the scroll to eat. He said to me, Mortal, eat this scroll that I give you and fill your stomach with it. Then I ate it; and in my mouth it was as sweet as honey.

John's vision alludes to this passage in many respects, and so we are led to interpret it as a depiction of his own prophetic commissioning, modelled after that of Ezekiel. There are a number of theological themes to be observed.

First, notice that the divine message is not simply announced by the angel but is given in a text that is handed to a mortal man. Surely it would be simpler for God to give the task of announcing his word to an angel or even to speak to the earth directly himself. Though it would no doubt have been possible for God to do everything through his angels, the visionary prophetic commissioning of both Ezekiel and John reminds us that this is not God's design. God calls human prophets to the vocation of announcing divine truth, and now John joins that long line of witnesses as he takes the scroll from the angel's hand. As we saw at the very start of the book, revelation is passed through a chain of transmission from God to Jesus, to his angel, and then through John to the people of God. Though the Lord could certainly broadcast his word directly from his temple in heaven, he chooses instead to speak from his temple on earth, the people of God, especially in their prophetic witness (see Augustine, *On Christian Teaching*, Preface 6).

Second, the scroll is not merely to be read by the prophets but internalised through the act of ingesting it. The visionary act of reading a text sometimes permits the maintenance of a degree of 'distance' between the reader and what is read. Too often we imagine our relationship to divine revelation in this way—it is something we can hold at arm's length and speak about, even (perhaps especially!) in the act of writing commentary, while assuming an imagined 'critical distance.' This approach to knowledge is a particularly modern myth, and Revelation will have none of it. The imagery of eating allows for no such illusions of detachment: divine revelation is not something to be treated with critical distance but must be internalised, taken into the believer's body in a transformative act of union with the divine Word. Just as divine revelation crosses the boundary between heaven and earth, as John eats the scroll it breaches the boundary between his body and the outside world.

Third, John does not simply swallow the scroll, as if taking his medicine, but *tastes* it. Of the five senses there is perhaps none more intimate, and none more risky, than taste. This is how John, like Ezekiel before him, is to experience divine revelation, not merely in the relatively distant act of reading the scroll but in the intimate, embodied, and experiential act of eating it (see Warren 2017). It is in this way that the contents of the scroll are to be expounded to the earth—not merely through reading what is written but through John's embodied prophetic witness.

Though closely mirroring Ezekiel's visionary commission in all these respects and in its language, John's account in Revelation 10 has a few important differences that stand out in sharp relief. First, John twice tells us that though the scroll is, like Ezekiel's, sweet in his mouth, it is bitter to the stomach. Later in the book, Ezekiel speaks of bitterness in his spirit as the hand of the Lord weighed heavily upon him (3.14), and perhaps John is bringing that bitterness into his depiction. In any case, the meaning is clear:

the calling of a prophet is frequently a bittersweet one, combining the sweetness of tasting the Lord's word with the bitterness that comes from the task of its proclamation to a world that refuses to hear. Second, whereas Ezekiel is sent to Israel and not to the nations (see Ezek 3.4–6), John is explicitly told to 'prophesy again about many peoples and nations and languages and kings' (10.11). The fourfold phrasing of this commission further confirms the global audience of John's prophetic word. As John is now commissioned for his prophetic vocation, it is reasonable to assume, then, that the remainder of the book of Revelation is this prophetic message, hitherto hidden but now revealed to the world.

The Two Witnesses, 11.1–14
In the previous 'interlude,' between the sixth and seventh seals, we saw two related visions of the church militant, portrayed as both the army of 144,000 and the multitude of witnesses. We saw how both images must be allowed to inform our understanding of the church, as a 'double vision.' The same is true here: the first vision in the trumpet interlude must be read together with this second one. In chapter 10, the vision of the angel with the little scroll concerned John's own prophetic commissioning. But this is just one panel of the diptych, and we now see the other in a vision of the church in its own vocation to prophetic witness. On close inspection, chapter 11 is a narrative continuation of chapter 10, for it begins with John continuing to describe his experience of prophetic commissioning.

He tells us first that he was given (the passive voice presumably indicating divine agency) a measuring rod with which to measure the temple of God. The Old Testament allusions are again clear in this scene, directing us once more to the prophet Ezekiel, only this time the later chapters. In Ezekiel 40.3, the prophet has a mountaintop vision of a shining man with a 'measuring reed.' For almost a hundred verses (40.3–42.20), this figure meticulously measures every dimension of the temple and its courts, from the lengths of its walls to the size of the pegs, with Ezekiel observing closely, recording every measurement. Again, there are important differences in John's reworking of this scene. First, we should note that no measuring has been done (yet—John will pick up this image again in the book's closing vision in chapter 21). Second, John himself is instructed to do the measuring, unlike Ezekiel who just watched as the shining figure did the task. Third, his instructions are to 'measure the temple and the altar and those who worship there' (an odd detail!) but not the court outside the temple.

The reason given for this last negative instruction leads to a (divine) descriptive monologue, the principal subject of this chapter. The court outside the temple is not to be measured, we are told, because it is 'given over to the nations' to be trampled for forty-two months. It will likely come as no surprise to learn that the number forty-two here carries symbolic weight. Forty-two months is three and a half years, half of seven. It thus symbolises a cut-short, rather than complete, time—a 'half time,' if you will. We recall that this same combination of ideas and images is found in Jesus's teaching, in relation to apocalyptic signs of the end and especially the fate of the temple: a time of affliction, cut short for the sake of the saints and their witness before the kings and governors of the nations (Mt 24.14, 22; Mk 13.9–11, 20; Lk 21.13). This idea was also indicated in the seal visions (see commentary on 8.1–5). The forty-two months is a time of trampling, but it is not the full seven years, having been cut in half for the sake of the elect and their work of testimony.

This interpretation is confirmed as the passage continues, for the question of prophetic witness now becomes the major theme. The voice (we continue to read it as God's voice) tells John that his authority will be given to 'two witnesses' whose role will be to prophesy in sackcloth. We will discuss their identity shortly, but it is clear from their given task and their attire that they are prophets, and this will be made explicit in verse 10. The duration of their prophetic ministry is measured at 1,260 days. If we take each month to be thirty days (as they were in the ancient calendar) we come to the same figure, and so the connection is clear. The 42 months of trampling and the 1,260 days of witness are two depictions of the same theological truth: a 'cut-short time' of affliction and prophetic witness. It evokes Daniel's 'time, times, and half a time,' which again signals a period of curtailed eschatological affliction before the vindication of God's people and the establishment of his dominion. (See Dan 7.25; 9.27; 12.7. We will see a clearer connection to Daniel when we meet another instance of this same idea in 12.14.)

Why, though, does John not simply repeat the phrase 'forty-two months'? It is not merely stylistic variety for variety's sake but conveys a significant literary and theological effect. The 1,260 days sounds like a very long time to endure affliction and to persist in prophetic witness. But if one calls it forty-two months, or just three and a half years, it perhaps doesn't seem quite as bad, and certainly one gets the sense that it is a strictly limited time. Our experience of time is a fluid thing (and not only our experience but time itself, as Einstein has taught us). Just as 'time flies when you are having fun,' a time of affliction seems to stretch out, and every day is painfully counted. In thus describing this 'cut-short time' in both months and days, John's different depictions of the same time overlay it with theological and experiential significance.

Who, then, are these 'two witnesses'? There is a long and venerable history of interpretative proposals for their identities, and myriad suggestions. Clearly they are prophets, and the long list of proposals certainly reflects that insight. In early and modern interpretations, Enoch and Elijah (who did not die), Elijah and Jeremiah, and Moses and Aaron all appear as Old Testament candidates. From the New Testament, Peter and Paul have been suggested. In some (usually dispensational) circles, there have been attempts to identify them with modern individuals, such as John Wesley and George Whitfield. For some, such attempts to name individuals miss the point of the imagery, which should be read as allegorical symbols of the Old and New Testament witnesses themselves, or of the twofold witness of 'law' and 'gospel' (on the history of these and many other proposals see the thorough discussion of Kovacs and Rowland 2008, 126–30).

Again, attention to John's skilful weaving of Old Testament imagery and allusion is vital for interpretation. For a start, calling them 'two witnesses' calls to mind the Deuteronomistic requirement for two witnesses to confirm the validity of a legal testimony and the conviction of the offender (Dt 17.6; 19.15). The message of these two, then, is established as reliable and convicting (see Woodman 2013, 103). John also tells us that these are the 'two olive trees' and the 'two lampstands.' This is a clear double allusion to one of John's favourite passages, Zechariah, which he echoed in the opening Christological vision as an image of the 'seven spirits' before God's throne (1.4) and also of the churches (1.13, 20). In the throne vision of chapters 4–5, it is an image of the Spirit(s) of God (4.5; cf. 5.6). For John, clearly, there is a close connection between the Spirit and the churches, a connection regularly drawing on Zechariah's vision, and for good reason.

Both of John's symbols, the lamp and the olive trees, are found close together in Zechariah 4. In 4.2–3, the prophet sees a vision of a golden lampstand and, on either side of it, two olive trees. When he asks the angel about the meaning of the vision, he is given the reply 'not by might, nor by power, but by my spirit, says the LORD of hosts' (v. 6). He is then told about the building of the eschatological temple by Zerubbabel (and we recall that Revelation 11 begins with the temple clearly in view) before he asks again about the meaning of the vision of the trees and lamp (v. 11), and specifically two branches of the trees. These branches, he then learns, are two 'anointed ones who stand by the Lord of the whole earth' (v. 14). We should expect, then, that John deploys this image, as he did in the earlier visions, in order to say something about the Spirit of God and his anointed ones.

What is interesting in John's use of the twofold image is that the two witnesses are *both* the olive trees *and* the two lampstands 'that stand before the Lord of the earth' (Rev 11.4, cf. Zech 4.14). There is thus a closer union envisaged between these figures and the Lord himself than Zechariah had imagined. Furthermore, they are not identified as two branches (as in Zech 4.12) but as whole trees. While the image of anointing remains, we should not interpret them as individuals (the branches) so much as the whole (the trees). In short, this is a vision of the whole church in its prophetic ministry. Their testimony is reliable and confirmed (since they are two, cf. Dt 17.6), and they are anointed by the Holy Spirit to bear that prophetic witness in the time between the six trumpet blasts and the consummation of the seventh. The image of the two witnesses is thus a theological recapitulation and intensification of the same theological theme developed in the interval between the sixth and seventh seals: the church as witness in the time 'between the times.'

Though this reading firmly avoids identifying any two individuals as the two witnesses, interpretations that have identified them as Moses and Elijah do have something going for them in terms of the allusions within the text of Revelation 11. In verse 6 we learn that the two witnesses share with those two Old Testament figures power to bring fire and the authority to 'shut the sky' and stop the rain (like Elijah in 1 Kgs 17–18, esp. 17.1; 18.38) and to turn water to blood and bring 'every kind of plague' (like Moses in Ex 7–11). The church's prophetic witness, therefore, is symbolically bound to the witness of the Old Testament, and in particular Moses and Elijah's prophetic witness and judgement against oppression and idolatry. We do well to remember that the image of the people of God in Revelation is a universal one, comprising Jew and Gentile.

As with all the prophets, however, the prophetic witness of the people of God will meet with opposition. Just as with the scroll of John's prophetic commissioning, it is a bittersweet calling. As soon as the witnesses finish their prophetic testimony, John sees a terrible vision. This is our first encounter with the beast, an embodiment of evil who brings to mind the bestial imagery of Daniel and so many other apocalyptic writings. Like the Satanic leader of the locust army (and there are clearly close connections between the two, in their origin and activities), the beast comes up from the abyss to make war against them and to 'conquer them and kill them.' By now a reader who has been paying attention should realise that what it really means to 'conquer' is something Revelation holds up to theological (and especially Christological) scrutiny.

As quickly as it arrived, the beast disappears from the narrative, not to be mentioned again until it receives extensive attention in chapter 13 and beyond (as we discussed in the introduction, John's nonlinear approach to storytelling often does this sort of thing, foreshadowing themes or introducing characters without backstory or explanation, then circling round to them later for a fuller account). The prophets' dead 'body' is left in the street (v. 8). In the majority of Greek manuscripts, *ptōma*, 'body' is in the singular both here and in verse 9 (some English translations 'fix' this to the plural), indicating that, though they are two witnesses, they are a singular corporate people of God. For three and a half days (again, half of seven) they lie unburied in the city. John reminds his readers here, again through the briefest of comments, of a profound theological picture that Revelation has been steadily painting. They lie 'in the great city... where also their Lord was crucified.' The prophetic witness of the people of God, to the point of death, is not merely the martyrdom of a protestor but a sharing in the ministry of Jesus, the faithful witness.

Though this city is identified as the place where Jesus was crucified (and so, prosaically, it is Jerusalem), it carries a twofold prophetic name that extends the significance beyond a simple geographical symbol: it is Sodom, and it is Egypt. The latter city reminds us again that the prophetic ministry of the two witnesses is like that of Moses against Egyptian oppression. The former is the archetypal sinful city. Sodom has a literary afterlife that continues well beyond the narrative account of its sin and destruction in Genesis 19, becoming a byword for human sinfulness. In particular, its name frequently appears in connection with a coming day of judgement in the prophets (e.g., Jer 23.14; 49.18; 50.40), in the synoptic witness to Jesus's eschatological teaching (Mt 10.15; 11.23–24; Lk 10.12; 17.29), and in the New Testament letters (Rom 9.29, quoting Isa 1.9; 2 Pet 2.6; Jude 7).

In one prophetic oracle in particular, many of the images of Revelation 11 are clustered together, and that is Amos chapter 4. There we see a litany of punishments: the withholding of rain on a city (v. 7), a plague of locusts (v. 9), invasion and warfare, and other pestilences like those of Egypt (v. 10). Throughout Amos's oracle, after every image of judgement, there is a repeated refrain: 'yet you did not return to me, says the LORD.' And so the Day of the Lord will come (Amos 5). As we have seen, these are also the contours of God's judgement in Revelation 8–11. The judgements of the six trumpets, containing many of these same terrors, were meant to induce repentance and a return to the Lord, but they did not (9.20–21), and so the Day of the Lord will come. Perhaps, though, this prophetic and sacrificial witness of the people of God will have the desired effect?

The early indications are not good. The prophets lie dead in the street as the people gloat in celebration, glad to be rid of their tormenting witness just as the Egyptians were when Moses led the Israelites out (see Ps 105.38).

Note that we are twice told that these people are the 'inhabitants of the earth' (v. 10) and not just the inhabitants of the city, and as such we are to read this as a picture of global non-repentance to the prophetic witness.

The witness of the people of God, however, is not just union with Christ in his death but also in his resurrection. As Paul puts it, the church is 'always carrying in the body the death of Jesus, so that the life of Jesus may also be made visible in our bodies. For while we live, we are always being given up to death for Jesus's sake, so that the life of Jesus may be made visible in our mortal flesh' (2 Cor 4.10–11). And so, once the 'half time' of three and a half days is up, the two witnesses are raised by the breath (or spirit) of life. Raised to life, they (like John) are then called up to heaven by a divine voice, their earthly witness complete. Only at this point are there indications of repentance by the inhabitants of the earth, who give glory to God, albeit in terror.

Their terror is justified, for a final eschatological judgement now comes as a great earthquake strikes the city. Though this is certainly a terrifying event, the proportion of the destruction, a tenth of the city, is a step backward from the intensification of the seal and trumpet sequences. There are echoes here, once more, of the prophets. A similar eschatological earthquake against a city appears in Isaiah 6.13, where the destruction is assessed at 90 percent (and more). John's proportions, then, are the reverse of Isaiah's: it is a tenth that is destroyed, and nine-tenths left untouched. Again, in 1 Kings 19, as Elijah meets the Lord (not in the earthquake or fire but in the 'sound of sheer silence,' v. 12), he hears of the coming judgement against Israel and those who have killed the prophets (v. 14). Only seven thousand will be preserved, a figure also reversed by John, as seven thousand are killed while the rest survive (see Bauckham 1993, 87). Despite the violence of this imagery, the effect is remarkably restrained and almost salvific, reversing the trajectory of increasing destruction.

And so the second woe (and the twofold vision of the trumpet interval) comes to a close. The witness of the people of God, in the time between the times, has been completed. Only now can the final trumpet blow, bringing in the fulfilment of all these judgements and of God's purposes for the earth.

The Seventh Trumpet and Storm Theophany, 11.15–19

'The third woe is coming very soon,' we are told. But as the seventh angel blows his trumpet, instead of a woe there is praise, as Revelation once again bursts into liturgical song. When the seventh seal was broken, there was silence in heaven. Now, at the sound of the seventh trumpet, we have noise. Loud voices in heaven (their identities are not made clear) declare the arrival of God's kingdom and his eternal reign in words that are familiar to many from their setting in Handel's *Messiah*: 'the kingdom of the world has become the kingdom of our Lord and of his Messiah (Christ), and he will reign forever and ever.' It is interesting that despite the grammatically plural subject of this reign (the Lord and his Christ), the singular is used for the verb (*basileusei*, he will reign). This may be a stylistic or grammatical quirk (Revelation's Greek is known for such oddities) but could well be understood as a deliberate decision, indicating that the Lord and his Messiah rule not as a coalition but as a divine unity. After all, John has already heard Christ say of himself that he 'sat down with [his] Father on his throne' (3.21), and Revelation closes with a vision of this shared throne and shared dominion (22.3).

There is also a shift in tenses that is both literarily arresting and theologically significant. The voices in heaven do not declare the coming kingdom in the future tense ('*will* become') but in the past ('*has* become'). This is a work completed at the sounding of the seventh trumpet. This could be potentially problematic if we were reading the book sequentially, for there is much to come that does not look like the consummation of God's kingdom. Such challenges disappear, however, when this scene is read as a recapitulation, from another perspective, of the consummation depicted at the climax of the seal sequence.

These voices are joined by those of the twenty-four elders, who fall in worship and sing a song of praise to God. It opens by giving thanks to 'the Lord God Almighty, who are and who were' (v. 17). Why do the elders omit the last phrase of the threefold divine title, 'who is to come' (cf. 1.4, 8; 4.8)? It must surely be because it is now obsolete—God and his kingdom have come, and he has taken his power and begun to reign. The coming one has now come. This whole scene, then, is a scene of the consummation of God's kingdom, celebrated in praise and in prophetically political terms. Such political language is commonplace in Jewish and Christian apocalyptic writings, which often deploy visionary material as a critique of oppressive human political systems. Daniel 7, for example, contrasts the kings and kingdoms of Daniel's day, depicted as bestial creatures, with the everlasting kingdom of God. As we will soon see, John will make use of this same apocalyptic tradition in his own bestial depiction of earthly rule.

It is entirely appropriate, then, that John draws upon another very political text for inspiration in the words of this song. The royal and messianic Psalm 2 is echoed in the phrase 'the nations raged' and in the mention of the anointed one (Messiah) who shares God's kingdom reign (v. 15). This Psalm of David, to which John alluded in the message to Thyatira (2.26–27) and to which he will return in a few verses' time (12.5), is a celebration of the sovereignty of God exercised through his anointed king, and a rebuke to the kings of this world who seek to contest or usurp that sovereignty. It was the Psalm the disciples sung when they sought boldness to declare the gospel of Jesus in the face of imprisonment and political/religious oppression (Acts 4.23–30). It is entirely appropriate, then, that its words are woven into the song sung by the elders as the reign of God comes in eschatological fullness. It is not hard to imagine the theopolitical resonances this would have had for the people of God in Asia Minor, whether they were experiencing oppression at the hands of the empire or were profiting from it. Not for the last time, Revelation places the kingdom of God in prophetic contrast to the kingdoms of this world.

If there is woe in this final trumpet, it is for God's enemies. The song describes the consummation of God's purposes in three aspects. There is judgement for the dead, reward for the people of God (especially the prophets), and destruction of 'those who destroy the earth.' There has been a lot of destroying since the first seal was broken at the start of chapter 6. As we have seen throughout, however, all of this has been directed toward this moment, the 'death of death and hell's destruction' (this is a line from the famous hymn 'Guide Me O Thou Great Jehovah' by William Williams [1745], a hymn full of imagery from Revelation). When the kingdom of God comes in its fulness, all that destroys God's earth must itself be destroyed.

But this is not the ultimate end. At the widest frame of God's purposes for his world is not the destruction of evil but something even greater: a new creation with the presence of God himself. Just as in the throne vision (4.5) and then the seal sequence (8.5), here the arrival of divine presence is signalled with a storm theophany scene. The description of the divine storm has acquired further details in each account. In chapter 4, we saw flashes of lightning coming from the throne and heard rumblings and peals of thunder. In chapter 8, as the seven seals ended, there were 'peals of thunder, rumblings, flashes of lightning, *and an earthquake.*' Now there is lightning, rumblings, peals of thunder, an earthquake, '*and heavy hail.*' The increasing layers of description in the three storm theophanies have the effect of a narrative intensification of the divine presence that parallels the intensification of judgment in the cycles of seals and trumpets.

These storm theophanies have also functioned as important structural markers in the shape of Revelation's narrative. Here it marks the end of this second major section of the book. In chapter 4 John saw heaven opened and was summoned from Patmos to the heavenly throne room. Most of the narrative action has been placed there since, with some scenes playing out the consequences of heavenly activity on earth. Now, in 11.19, there is another revelatory opening in heaven, as the 'temple in heaven' is opened, revealing within the ark of the covenant.

The theme of divine presence connects these two visionary features, the storm and the ark. We have already seen how Revelation develops the Jewish tradition of depicting heaven as a temple (and the temple in terms that evoke heaven). Unlike many heavenly ascent accounts in the Jewish apocalyptic tradition, which describe a seer's journey through several heavenly realms, John's ascent to the divine throne room is arresting in its immediacy. Now, however, John describes a further space: the 'temple *in* heaven.' Mention of the ark of the covenant seen within makes identifying this space more straightforward. This is the opening not just of heaven but of the heavenly counterpart to the holy of holies, the inner room of the celestial temple where the ark was kept and where God's presence dwelled.

These final few verses also serve as an introduction to the next major section of the book, functioning like a narrative hinge or seam. John's visionary journey 'inward' to the inner room of the heavenly temple provides a spatial setting that also shapes the temporal framework of the subsequent visions. We recall that Revelation, while having an essentially 'linear' story of God's judgement and victory, tells this story through a nonlinear narrative (on which see the introduction). The first three chapters of Revelation concerned the purposes of God in relation to the earthly time and space of Patmos and Asia Minor. After John's ascent in 4.1, the throne vision and judgement sequences of 4–11 placed that same basic story in its wider heavenly setting. When John entered that scene in heaven, a battle was already raging (though we learn that the Lamb had already won). He has seen visions concerning God's rule and judgement, the present and coming victory of the Lamb over his enemies, and the faithful witness of the saints in the time between. Now he will learn more about the origins and ends of this cosmic conflict, the nature and ultimate source of the 'destroyers of the earth' (v. 18) and how their destruction will come about. The chapters to come will take John 'deeper' into heaven, and 'wider' in time, placing the story of God's triumph over his enemies and the coming of his reign in the widest narrative and theological frame.

Cosmic War

Revelation 12.1–13.18

Introduction to 12:12–20

With the opening of the temple in heaven, the next major section of the book of Revelation now begins. We have reached an important milestone, the halfway point of the book, and the reader would be forgiven for feeling a little lost and confused. It is worth taking a step back to orient ourselves before continuing on, if only to gather strength before we encounter some of Revelation's most grotesque characters and bizarre scenes.

The primary theme of this section is the victory of God and the Lamb, and of his people. This is not a new theme but one that has run through the first two sections of the book, the whole of which is concerned with a central apocalyptic question: 'to whom does the sovereignty of the world belong'? (Käsemann 1969, 135). However, much of the content of these chapters focuses on God's enemies, cosmic and earthly, chiefly the devil himself. Satan's enmity against God and God's people has already been mentioned in relation to his earthly activity in the seven churches of Asia (the 'synagogue of Satan' in 2.9 and 3.9, 'Satan's throne' in 2.13, and the 'deep things of Satan' in 2.24). A repeated refrain throughout has been the call for the churches to 'conquer.' Next, the same grand story was told through a vision of heaven and the judgements of God. Satan's role in leading a demonic horde into war was described in the vision of Apollyon/Abaddon and the locust army (9.11), before the victory of God was announced and a song celebrated his destruction of the destroyers of the earth. In chapter 12, the nonlinear narrative of Revelation (on which see the introduction) now cycles through this story of evil and God's triumph over it from another perspective. As the temple in heaven is opened, John's vision extends to a wider temporal frame to show the ancient origins of this cosmic war. Satan's primordial rebellion against God is first depicted, along with his defeat, before a series of visions shows how this affects the earth, bringing corruption in the political, social, economic, and religious spheres of life.

Though John does not launch into another sequence of seven (at least, not yet), there is still a narrative structure to this section that can help us keep our bearings. There are two basic movements in the narrative, one in heaven and one on earth. First, John sees a vision in heaven concerning the dragon, his war against God, and his defeat (12.1–12). The shape of this basic conflict story is as follows:

1. In Heaven
    A Dragon introduced, enmity against God's people and his Messiah (12.1–6)
        B War in heaven (12.7–9)
    A' Dragon defeated, thrown to earth (12.9–12)

At the end of this first movement, as the dragon is defeated and thrown down, John's attention is directed to earth, where that same story of conflict and victory is told again from an earthly perspective, describing the enemies of God in a series of grotesque visions. First, the dragon pursues and makes war against God's people (12.13–18). He then gives his authority and his voice to two hideous beasts, from sea and land, who deceive the inhabitants of the earth and make war against the saints (ch. 13). Finally, another important figure is introduced, the woman Babylon who rides the beast (ch. 17). Thus the three figures are closely related in the narrative: Babylon rides the beast, and the beast gets its authority from the dragon, who is the head of them all. The sequence then reverses, as each of these interrelated incarnations of evil are judged in turn: first Babylon (ch. 18), then the beasts (ch. 19), and finally the dragon itself (ch. 20). There is thus a grand 'rise and fall' in the narrative that carries us all the way from here to chapter 20 and the beginning of the last section of the book celebrating God's final victory. We can visualise the pattern of this broad narrative like this:

2. On Earth
    A Dragon thrown down, enmity against God's people on earth (12.13–18)
        B Beasts introduced, given authority and voice by the dragon (v. 13)
            C Babylon introduced, riding on the beast (v. 17)
            C' Babylon defeated (v. 18)
        B' Beast(s) defeated (v. 19)
    A' Dragon defeated (v. 20)

Things always look neater when we arrange them in such patterns. The text of Revelation, however, is not quite so neat. This large-scale pattern dealing with the powers of evil and God's victory over them is interrupted, in chapters 14–16, with visions of Christ and the church militant, and the final judgements of God depicted in a series of seven plagues. The overall shape, though, can help us stay oriented. Now that we have a sense of where we are going, let us move forward, beginning with the three scenes of the first story.

The Woman and the Dragon, 12.1–6

John sees a great 'sign' in heaven, a woman, the first of three significant female characters he will encounter in this second half of the book (the others being Babylon the whore and the New Jerusalem bride). She is clothed with the sun, with the moon under her feet and an astral crown (again this is the *stephanos*, the laurel wreath given to a victor rather than the royal crown of a queen). Who might this be? There are a number of candidates, each interpretation drawing on themes and intertextual allusions woven through this passage. Since she is engaged in conflict with a great serpent and is in the pain of childbirth, there are certainly echoes of Eve (cf. Gen 3.15–16). However, her delivery of a Messianic son and her later flight to the wilderness (v. 6a) is perhaps more suggestive of Mary (cf. Mt 2). The contours of Matthew's infancy story deliberately echo the Exodus narrative of Israel's Egyptian slavery and deliverance, and so there are more layers of meaning to uncover even here. Mention of the sun and moon and the twelve stars echoes Joseph's visionary dreams concerning his father, Jacob/Israel, and his brothers, the patriarchs (Gen 37.9). The combination of this imagery with a wilderness sojourn (during which God nourishes her) might therefore suggest that the woman is the people of Israel, from whom Messiah comes. Moreover, the description of her clothing, shining like the sun, reminds us of the same solar brightness of Christ's own appearance in 1.16, reflected in the vision of the mighty angel in 10.1. Perhaps, then, this woman represents the church, those who have 'clothed [themselves] with Christ' (Gal 3.27) or with 'the new self, created according to the likeness of God' (Eph 4.24). The mention of the 1,260 days (v. 6b) also connects this image with the ecclesial visions of the two witnesses (11.2–3), and the fact that she wears a conqueror's crown might also echo the promise to the churches in chapters 2–3.

As usual with Revelation's imagery, we are not required to limit our interpretation to a prosaic decoding of the image to an individual or single referent. As we have said many times, John's images are regularly polyvalent, carrying multiple meaning simultaneously in a way that a prosaic code cannot, exploiting this polyvalence to great theological effect. There is no reason not to expect the same here. The description of the woman simultaneously evokes Eve's primordial conflict with the serpent, the people of Israel in their wilderness wandering, Mary giving birth to Jesus, and the church in its prophetic witness. In the narrative of the Bible, these events occur sequentially in the development of the grand story of God's victory over the forces of evil. In Revelation 12, this earthly historical narrative is seen in its cosmic and theological frame of reference, as a single 'event' that draws all these threads of the story together across all time, a singular moment of cosmic significance, multiply indexed to history. If Revelation were to be read sequentially, we would struggle to see an image of the church here, for the woman gives birth to the Messianic child, and it is he that then establishes the church. But we are not here dealing with such a straightforward linear narrative. As such we can read this woman as a composite image of the people of God, both Israel and the church, and as both Eve and Mary, from whom Christ is born into the world. John is not the only New Testament writer to deploy the apocalyptic image of labour pains to describe the church's eschatological tension. It is imagery found in the Gospels, and in Paul's letters, with similar theological effects (cf. Mk 13.8; Jn 16.21; 1 Thess 5.3, cf. Gaventa 2007).

The woman and her unborn child are under threat, for alongside her John sees another 'sign,' a great red dragon. This character is much more easily identified, since John will be explicit that this 'ancient serpent' is 'called the devil and Satan, the deceiver of the whole world' (v. 9). The dragon is fiery red, like the horseman of war (6.4), and impossibly monstrous, with seven heads and ten horns. A similarly ten-horned beast appears in the apocalyptic visions of Daniel (Dan 7.7). On its seven heads it wears seven crowns, not the victor's *stephanos* but the royal *diadēma*. This is a symbol of the dragon's claim to complete dominion, a claim that (as we will soon see) is blasphemous and void.

The dragon's tail sweeps a third of the stars down to earth, an image that echoes the one-third destruction of the trumpet judgements, though this time the agency is Satanic, not divine. The dragon clearly recognises that its will to power is threatened by the most unlikely character in the scene, the unborn baby. The scene is remarkable in juxtaposing power and weakness, as this terrifying creature stands before the woman, ready to devour the child at his most vulnerable moment. By now we should have learned not to trust the surface appearances of strength and weakness. The dragon's purposes are instantly thwarted as the child is taken away 'to God and to his throne' while the woman escapes to the wilderness. The terrifying beast is left frustrated, pathetic even, in its claims to rule. This is not a vision of a cosmic dualism, a battle of equal and opposite forces, good and evil, in which the fate of the earth hangs in the balance. All the devil's schemes are nothing when compared with the sovereignty of God, who alone rules. While the situation appeared desperate for the woman and her child, God alone was sovereign in acting to bring about his purposes. As Joseph Mangina describes the scene, 'the dramatic tension is resolved almost as soon as it is stated' (2010, 151). Or as Psalm 2 puts it, 'he who sits in heaven laughs . . . saying "I have set my king on Zion"' (Ps 2.4, 6)

Speaking of Psalm 2, another clear allusion to that song makes clear that the child is the Messiah, since he is one 'who is to rule all the nations with a rod of iron' (see Ps 2.7–9), an image also picked up by Isaiah 11.4. And so the woman safely delivers the child, a son. The additional comment that this son (*huios*) is 'a male child' (*arsen*) appears superfluous. Perhaps it is merely poetic parallelism, one of many moments in John's writing where his Greek style echoes that of Hebrew poetry. But there may also be a faint but specific echo of the Immanuel prophecies of Isaiah, especially 7.14, which speaks of a 'sign' of a woman giving birth to a son (*huios*, see also Isa 9.6, where the son is given the throne of David), and 66.7, where the voice of the Lord from his temple compares the deliverance of Zion to a woman giving birth to a 'male' (Heb: *zākār*, Gk: *arsen*). In keeping with the theological timeframe of this vision, the career of the son is depicted in an instant, from birth to ascension and enthronement in the blink of an eye. In earthly history, decades are covered. But from the eternal perspective of heaven the life, death, resurrection, ascension, and heavenly session of Jesus are a single moment of triumph. What this vision expresses, then, is God's eternal decree to become incarnate as Jesus, a decree that determines all of his interactions with creation, including the defeat of its would-be destroyer. God's eternal 'yes' to the son is also his emphatic 'no' to the dragon.

As noted briefly above, the closing verse of this first movement of the vision connects it to earlier visions of the people of God. The woman's time in the wilderness is 1,260 days, the same time that was assigned to the two witnesses in 11.2–3. This is the 'cut-short time' between the enthronement of the son and his final victory over the dragon, the time in which the church lives. It is a time of tribulation, a time of prophetic witness by the people of God in the wilderness, a time of divine nourishment, and a time that is cut short for the sake of the saints. Before this story of the woman and the child is brought to its *dénouement*, however, another scene interrupts the narrative.

War in Heaven, 12.7–12

As the woman flees to the wilderness, in heaven a war breaks out. Here we are in the heart of the book, encountering a narrative of cosmic warfare that stretches back into primeval history. On either side of this scene we see the central conflict echoing outward, to the courts of heaven and to the earth, like ripples on a pond after a stone is dropped. When did/does this war between angels and the dragon happen? As we have said, John's journey 'inward' through heaven has also been a journey 'outward' through time, and here in Revelation 12 the setting seems to be the widest temporal frame. We must not, however, go so far as to set this scene in 'eternity,' since that would elevate the devil to the same eternal status as God and would wrongly make this narrative of combat an eternal cosmic dualism, along the lines of the *Ennuma Elish*. In such accounts we see a chaotic battle between good and evil in eternity past, which generates the created world. That is not the view of Revelation, which follows the witness of the Old Testament in making clear that the world exists simply because of God's will (4.11; 10.6). This, then, is a scene of heavenly rebellion, not a dualistic narrative of creation through warfare.

It is helpful to note, then, that the battle is not between the devil/Satan and God himself, but between the devil and the angelic hosts, led by Michael. There is an ancient tradition in Jewish thought of a primordial angelic rebellion against God, led by Satan, which fails and results in their expulsion from heaven. This story surfaces laconically here and there in the Bible (e.g., Gen 6.2; Isa 14.12–15; Lk 10.17; 2 Pet 2.4) but is more expansively treated in the extra-canonical writings, especially the apocalypses (e.g., *2 Enoch* 29.3–5, where the rebellion is located on the second day of creation, just after the angels are made; see also his subsequent role in the temptation of Eve in *2 Enoch* 31.4–6). Revelation appears to be quite familiar with the basic shape of this primordial warfare narrative, and it's likely John knew at least some of these texts.

God remains enthroned above this primordial battle, and it is the archangel Michael who leads the heavenly host into battle. Michael was one of the more significant angels in Jewish thought, again especially in the apocalyptic tradition (e.g., *1 Enoch* 9.1; 10.11; 20.5; 40.9; 71.3; in 24.6 he is explicitly designated the 'chief' angel). He also appears in the book of Daniel as the angel who joined the fight against the 'prince of the kingdom of Persia' (Dan 10.13, 21) and as the 'great prince' and 'protector of [God's] people' (12.1) who will arise in the last days, which come after 'a time, two times, and half a time' (Dan 12.7, cf. Rev 12.14). The New Testament letter of Jude, which seems to assume knowledge of the angelic rebellion tradition and quotes *1 Enoch* (Jude 14–15, quoting *1 En* 1.9), describes how the archangel Michael 'contended with the devil' (v. 9). While the sense here is more of a judicial rather than military conflict (Michael was well known for both), Jude echoes the Jewish apocalyptic tradition in assigning Michael an important role in primordial and eschatological conflict with the devil and his minions (cf., e.g., *1 Enoch* 54.6 and the Qumran *War Scroll* (1QM) col. xvii:6–7). It is entirely appropriate, then, that it is he who leads the forces of heaven against the dragon here in Revelation 12.

The outcome, unsurprisingly, is resounding victory for the forces of heaven. The dragon and his angels are expelled from heaven and thrown down to earth (see also the earlier discussion of the fifth trumpet in Rev 9). In one of the rare moments in Revelation when an image is explained, we are told in no uncertain terms that the dragon is 'that ancient serpent, who is called the devil and Satan, the deceiver of the whole world' (v. 9). The clarity of this designation, however, belies the murkiness of trying to understand the nature of this figure, whose essence is essentially illogical. To say otherwise would be to bestow upon it the goodness of order, and it possesses no goodness of this or any other sort. As Augustine puts it, 'evil has no positive nature; but the loss of good has received the name "evil"' (*City of God* XI, ch. 9, last line). How does one comment on that which lacks the goodness of logic? Strict theological limits must be applied, therefore, as we explore Revelation's characterisation of Satan in the form of the dragon, lest we give this figure more credit than it is due. First, it is ancient but not eternal. Second, it is the deceiver (*ha-sātān*), a liar and slanderer (*ho diabolos*), and a corrupter of truth not a creator of alternatives. Third, while it clearly possesses agency to make war against angels and saints, it has no independent existence of its own, only a parasitic corrupting existence; any appearance of authority or power it may seem to have is emphatically subordinated to God's sovereign rule. It is a 'theological counter-factual' (Ziegler 2022), the nothingness rejected in God's decision to create the world, and has as much agency and existence as nothingness can have—no more and no less (Barth 2004, *CD* III/3 §50). In the end, if our investigations of the nature of Satan seem to result in incoherent or even absurd proposals, then that is perhaps appropriate as a theological account of the father of lies.

In describing Satan as the 'serpent,' John apparently locates its casting down 'before' the temptation of Eden. We should remain aware, however, that asking such questions of the chronology of these events risks missing the point. The events of this vision in the heart of heaven are indexed to the history of the world in ways that transcend earthly chronology. Just as with the woman and the birth of her son, the casting down of the devil and the rebel angels can be seen as both a primordial event and also one that occurs 'now,' as the church bears faithful witness to Jesus. This casting down, then, is both the first defeat of Satan and the final one, as the victory of the cross ripples back into primordial time and forward into the end (see Ziegler 2022). The church participates in this primordial/eschatological victory whenever it declares the gospel. This is why Jesus can say to the seventy disciples, returning successfully from their mission, that he 'watched Satan fall from heaven like a flash of lightning' (Lk 10.17). Their declaration of the kingdom of God was a participation in an ancient victory, actualised in their present as they bear conquering witness to God's rule. As we will soon see, participation in this witness and this victory remains the calling of the church.

This victory is celebrated, as before, with a loud voice in heaven. It first declares that 'the salvation and the power and the kingdom of our God and the authority of his Messiah' have come *now*. Satan, the accuser, is now defeated, and the kingdom of God has now come. This song of praise also makes explicit what was discussed above, the connection between the victory of Jesus over the enemies of God, won at the cross and in primordial time, and the testimony of the church. Their victory in this cosmic war has not been won by overwhelming force but in the weakness of a Lamb's blood and a word of testimony, a weakness in which God's power is displayed. As they bear faithful witness to Christ, even to the point of death, they participate in his death and his conquest of the one who bears false witness.

Heaven rejoices at the completed victory of God and his Christ. But the earth must wait, for although the deceiver is defeated (and knows it), it has been cast down to the earth to continue exercising its frustrated wrath against the world and its inhabitants. The dragon knows it is beaten, however, and that its earthly activities are doomed to failure. Its time, just like the time of the witness of the saints (for it is the same), is a time cut short. John's narrative follows the dragon from heaven to earth, where we will see the outworking of the war in heaven in the earthly conflict between Satan and the people of God. The song thus provides a narrative and thematic bridge to the last short section of this chapter, and on into the chapters that follow, which contain expansive visions of the nature of the dragon's frustrated earthly warfare against the saints and their patient endurance. It will be a terrifying conflict, to be sure, but this central vision of heavenly victory reminds the saints that this time of faithful suffering witness is a time cut short because the battle is won.

The Dragon on Earth, 12.13–18

The dragon now continues its pursuit of the woman on earth. Here we see a depiction, from the earthly perspective, of the life of God's people, connected to the heavenly vision with a number of shared characters and themes. Though it has 'already' been defeated, the dragon continues to harass God's people and remains an imminent threat to the saints in earthly history. We are reminded that some of these saints, hearing this prophecy read aloud, have not long ago been told that they live 'where Satan has his throne' (2.13) or are beset by the 'synagogue of Satan' (2.9) or false teachers of Satan's 'deep things' (2.24). This is not a conflict contained to the courts of heaven and relegated to the primordial past; it is one that has spilled out and continues to spill out into this present world, as a defeated Satan rages against the people of God. But there are words of comfort here, too, for the saints. As she was in the heavenly vision, the woman is protected by God, flown on eagle's wings—an echo of Exodus 19.4—away from the serpent to the wilderness (once again the image is polyvalent, evoking Eve, Israel, Mary, and the church; see the discussion of 12.1 above). There she is nourished, we are told, for 'a time, and times, and half a time.' As we have seen a few times already, John is clearly alluding to Daniel 7.25 and 12.7 and his sealed-up prophecy of the 'time of the end.' Since this number is half of a complete seven, it has the theological force of a time 'cut short.' It corresponds to the various designations of this time, found throughout Revelation, as three and a half years, 42 months, or 1,260 days. It is the 'interrupted time' of the church's witness to Jesus Christ. In this interrupted time, God has set limits on the activity of Satan in the world, and thus the woman's wilderness sojourn is shortened.

Nevertheless, the serpent continues its attempts to destroy the woman, pouring from its mouth a great torrent to sweep them away. Here there is more Exodus imagery, though instead of the waters of the Red Sea swallowing Pharaoh and his armies, here the flood rushes from the mouth of the enemy toward the people of God. Similar imagery is also found in Psalm 124, which celebrates the deliverance of Israel from its enemies:

> If it had not been the LORD who was on our side
> —let Israel now say—
> if it had not been the LORD who was on our side,
> when our enemies attacked us,
> then they would have swallowed us up alive,
> when their anger was kindled against us;
> then the flood would have swept us away,
> the torrent would have gone over us;

> then over us would have gone
> the raging waters.
> Blessed be the LORD,
> who has not given us
> as prey to their teeth.
> We have escaped like a bird
> from the snare of the fowlers;
> the snare is broken,
> and we have escaped.
> Our help is in the name of the LORD,
> who made heaven and earth.

It is the created earth itself, that comes to the aid of the fleeing woman, opening its own 'mouth' to swallow the dragon's river. In this cosmic battle, not only the angels but even the very ground are on the side of the woman. And no wonder, for their destinies are bound up together. Creation shares with God's children the afflictions of the present time, afflictions described as shared labour pains, and the hope of deliverance from bondage to corruption (Rom 8.18–25, esp. 22; see Gaventa 2007). A groaning Mother Earth, as it were, now rescues a fellow mother.

Despite its many crowns, the dragon has now twice failed to conquer the woman, first in heaven and then on earth. With increasingly frustrated wrath, then, the dragon turns its attention to the seemingly easier target of 'the rest of her children.' In the heavenly depiction of the woman, the focus was on her singular male child, the son. Now we learn that this son has many siblings. It is clear that this, too, is a symbol of the people of God, composed of both Jewish and Gentile believers, since John describes them in double terms as 'those who keep the commandments of God and hold the testimony of Jesus.' The saints will be described in near-identical terms in 14.12. Though there will be terrors in the chapters to come, in this central chapter of the book what has been revealed to John, and with him the church, is the victory of God over their common enemy. The outcome does not hang in the balance—the Lamb has conquered by his blood and testimony. Therefore, as they now confront that enemy in various guises, they know that they participate in that victory in their faithfulness to God's commands and their testimony to Jesus.

As this scene comes to a climax and begins to move to the next, the dragon moves from the wilderness to a new location. He takes his stand on the shore, straddling the chaos of the sea and the order of the earth, in a parody of the great angel's posture in 10.5. From this liminal beachhead, and the unsure footing of the sand, he will launch his attack on the woman's children.

The Sea Beast, 13.1–10

What comes next, however, is not a direct demonic attack on the saints or a torrent of destruction but something more subtly deceptive in its nature. John's visionary depiction of the dragon's conflict with the saints, however, is anything but subtle. A beast rises from the sea. This is not the first mention of such a beast, though it is the fullest description. It was first introduced in 11.7 as 'the beast that comes up from the bottomless pit' to conquer the saints. In this description, it comes up not from the pit but from the sea, though the two realms share a great deal in terms of theological significance.

For those well versed in the Old Testament and other ancient literature, the significance of the beast and its origin come rushing in straight away. The mention of the sea evokes the theme of primordial chaos and the 'formless void and darkness' that covered the waters before creation (Gen 1.2). The sea remained an image of chaos in many writings of the period and was the home of dragons and the untamable beast Leviathan (Job 41; Ps 74.13–14). The arrival of this beast from the sea also establishes a more specific intertextual connection with, once again, the prophet Daniel and his vision of four beasts (Dan 7.1–8). Revelation 13 should thus be read with that chapter of Daniel close to hand. In Daniel's vision four different beasts are described in turn, coming up out of the sea. The first is like a lion with eagle's wings, the second like a bear, the third like a winged leopard, and the fourth a powerful ten-horned beast. Daniel's sequence appears to be working with the same list of animals used to describe the Lord in Hosea 13.7–8 and Jeremiah 5.6 (so Goldingay 2017). Jeremiah's image of a 'lion from the forest' is also echoed in the first century apocalypse of *4 Ezra* (*4 Ez* 11.36–12.3) to describe the Messiah's eschatological judgement of the 'eagle,' revealed as Daniel's fourth beast (*4 Ez* 12.10–11, 32). This connection means that these beasts are not merely terrifying creatures but also blasphemous mockeries of God's own character.

John, in contrast, sees just one beast, but it is a chimeric combination of all four Danielic creatures into one. It looks like a leopard, with bear's feet and a lion's mouth. The dragon, whose nature is not to create but only to deceive and corrupt, summons not a beast of his own creation but a blasphemous corruption of the truth. The beast has ten horns, like Daniel's fourth beast, and seven heads (the combined total of Daniel's four creatures, Koester 2014, 545). But in this respect it is like the dragon itself, who also has ten horns and seven heads, with crowns (13.1, cf. 12.3, though note the difference: the beast has ten crowns, not seven, on the horns and not the heads). This literary connection with the dragon is emphasised in John's account. Rather than attacking them directly, the dragon delegates to this beast his power, throne, and authority (13.2), and it is made, at least partially, in his image. Readers of Revelation are left in no uncertain terms, then, regarding the real Satanic power behind this beast. In keeping that in mind, however, we must also remember that this is a monster who comes up from the void darkness of the pit/sea and is destined to return to that nothingness; it goes to destruction (cf. 17.8, 11) because God's victory is won. Though terrifying in description, and possessing a limited power to make war against God's people, this beast is ultimately no more than nothing, and it stands already judged and defeated.

We pause here to orient ourselves and ask about the meaning of this bestial imagery, again with the help of Daniel 7. After his visions of the beasts ended, Daniel asked for an interpretation (Dan 7.15–28). The four great beasts, he is told, represent four kings and their kingdoms (7.17; cf. the similar interpretation of the statue in Dan 2.31–45). The fourth is given particular attention: it is an earthly kingdom, and its horns are ten kings. Using beasts, especially powerful predators, to speak of kings and kingdoms is a common trope in apocalyptic writings (e.g., *1 Enoch* 85–90; *4 Ezra* 11–12). The political references are sometimes very clear, such that they function as allegories. In the case of Daniel, interpreters vary as to the precise referents of these four historical empires, and indeed on whether such precision should be sought. One option is that they refer to the Babylonian, Medo-Persian, Greek, and Roman empires; another separates the Medo-Persian empire into two and interprets the fourth beast as the Greek/Seleucid empire (an approach that makes sense given the connections between the interpretation of the 'horn' and the career of Antiochus IV Epiphanes). Other readings, while seeing earthly kingdoms represented by these beasts, are more wary of this level of allegorical specificity and find the evidence offered for such identifications thin and often artificial. In any case, a specific answer to this question in interpreting Daniel need not concern us here: it is enough to note that this bestial language, within the Jewish apocalyptic tradition, is a common way of speaking about oppressive imperial regimes and imbuing them with literary and theological significance. Given how deeply John draws on this Danielic/apocalyptic tradition (as well as the allusions already made to kings and kingdoms in Psalm 2), we should expect to read the imagery in a similar way, such that John's beast also speaks of an earthly kingdom, and its heads and horns speak of that kingdom's rulers (see 17.9–14). Indeed, this beast is the *quintessential* earthly kingdom, since it combines all of Daniel's four beasts into one. The obvious candidate for this in first century Asia Minor is the

Roman Empire. This is the route taken by another first century apocalypse, *4 Ezra*, which interprets the fourth beast, an 'eagle' in this account, as Rome (the eagle was, after all, the animal on Roman Imperial standards), though this was not revealed to Daniel (*4 Ezra* 12.10–12, the passage cited above).

However, in recognising that the beast has to do with earthly empires, and in seeking to be specific about who might fit the role, we must not become so obsessed with allegorical specificity that we forget the theological force of the scene: this kingdom is a blasphemous beast, and the dragon stands behind it. John's readers are thus led to read this 'political' image with the knowledge that this imperial power has an appearance of godlikeness but one that is a distortion, for it operates with Satanic power and authority. We should also remember, once again, that the imagery of Revelation does not work like a 'code' with a single identifiable referent. Rather, it addresses specific situations in a way that imbues them with theological meaning that can also surpass those situations. While the first readers of the book would almost certainly recognise this beast as the Roman Empire, we must not allow that insight to limit our reading of the image and restrict its theological force to the first century Mediterranean world. The beast is Rome, to be sure, but it is more than Rome and continues to speak as an image of blasphemous, violent, and satanically influenced political power more generally. There have been other beasts in history, and more will no doubt arise.

There are aspects of the vision, however, that do lead us to give primary interpretative weight to the Roman Empire. For a start, it comes from the sea, which lies west of Asia Minor in the direction of Rome. Moreover, one of the beast's heads, we are told, seems to have been mortally wounded, though it is healed. In this detail, most commentators note a connection to a myth concerning the emperor Nero that circulated in the Roman Empire at that time, usually called *Nero Redivivus*. Nero had died, in AD 68, from a self-inflicted head/neck wound, but there was a rumour that he was not dead, only in exile and preparing to return and reclaim his rule. No doubt the first hearers of Revelation would make these connections in their own world and read the figure of the emperor in the head of the beast. This historical insight must not be allowed to distract us, however, from a more profound idea that the text of Revelation itself expresses. This description of the beast is a parody of the Lamb, a connection that stands out more clearly in the original Greek. The head of the beast is literally described as looking 'as though slain' (*hōs esphagmenēn*), a twisted echo of 5.6, where the Lamb stands 'as though slain' (*hōs esphagmenon*, the same exact phrase, the only changes being in necessary grammatical agreement). In heaven, the Lamb receives worship. On earth, the people respond to the sight of the beast with amazement and allegiance, offering worship to the beast and to the dragon whose authority it possesses. The blasphemous parody continues, as the people's acclaim is expressed in terms reserved in Scripture for God himself: 'who is like the beast?' (the dragon, remember, is but a twister of the truth). The Psalms are full of this rhetorical question of praise (Pss 35.10; 71.19; 113.5), but a special resonance can be heard here with Exodus 15 (a passage John will soon echo again in chapter 15), where Moses sings a song to the Lord, praising him for delivering the people from Egypt. Arriving safely on the far side of the Red Sea, Moses sings of his warrior God, who, when Pharaoh sought to pursue the people of Israel, covered them with the waters. He exclaims in praise:

> Who is like you, O LORD, among the gods?
> Who is like you, majestic in holiness,
> awesome in splendour, doing wonders?
> You stretched out your right hand,
> the earth swallowed them. (Ex 15.11–12)

In Revelation, the dragon has pursued the woman and sought to destroy her, though the earth swallowed his efforts. But instead of acknowledging God's deliverance and giving him praise, the people of the earth now exclaim (apparently without awareness of the dark irony in their words), 'who is like the beast, and who can fight against it?' A stark contrast is set up, therefore, between the saints' worship of the slain Lamb in heaven and the people's worship of the wounded beast on earth. Revelation thus presents its readers with a choice: to which will you give your allegiance? There is no neutral ground here.

The intertextual links with Daniel 7 continue. One of the horns of Daniel's fourth beast spoke words 'against the Most High' and was given power over the saints for 'a time, two times, and half a time' (Dan 7.25). John's beast likewise utters haughty and blasphemous words and is allowed authority for forty-two months, during which he makes war against the saints and conquers them (13.5–6). We have seen this timeframe, in several variations, often enough that the meaning of this temporary authority should by now be clear: this is a divinely curtailed authority, for the 'cut-short time' of three and a half years ('times'), or forty-two months. The propaganda of the Roman Empire (and that of all empires, I would suggest) would have the world believe that theirs was a divinely appointed and eternal kingdom, ushering in a golden age of peace and prosperity. These are false and blasphemous claims. All the kingdoms of this world have their appointed times; none should claim to be everlasting but the kingdom of God. And none but

God should claim to be the bringers of eternal peace. The beast's authority, then, is set at merely forty-two months, a time that has been limited by the one who is truly sovereign and whose peaceable kingdom is everlasting (cf. Dan 7.26–27).

During this time the beast is allowed to 'conquer' the saints. It will be a time of suffering for the people of God, of the 'trampling' spoken of in 11.2, but it is also a time of witness. During this interrupted time of the beast's limited authority, the world is divided in two. On one side are the vast majority of the people of earth, from every tribe, people, language, and nation, who are under the beast's authority and who worship it. On the other side are the people of God, those whose allegiance is to the Lamb who was slain. Their names, we are told, are written in the 'book of life.' Once again John introduces this image suddenly and does not explain it until later in the book (17.8; 20.12–15; 21.27), confusing first-time readers with his nonlinear narrative. Careful listeners will recall, however, that this formed part of the promise to the 'conquerors' in the message to Sardis in 3.5. Here we see those saints, with their names in the book, conquering in their refusal to bow the knee to the beast, even in the face of capture and death. Though the beast may seem to be conquering the saints, Revelation tells a different story of what true victory is. Certainly, this calls for 'endurance and faith' (v. 10), but the saints know that such faithful endurance is not passive quietism but active participation in the Lamb's triumph.

We are told that their names were written in the book of life 'from the foundation of the world' (*apo katabolēs kosmou*), an idea also expressed in 17.8. But perhaps it does not say that here. There is a translation challenge, for the Greek is ambiguous. One might also translate it, following more closely the Greek word order, 'the book of life of the Lamb slaughtered from the foundation of the world.' Something happened in eternity past, but what was it? Was it the writing of the names or the slaughter of the Lamb? The latter option appears to some interpreters as a troubling one, but it need not be so if one reckons with Revelation's complex handling of the relationship between time and eternity, as we have been trying to do, especially in these central chapters of the book. In any case, the ideas encapsulated by both translations will find support elsewhere in the New Testament and are expressed with the exact same phrase. Ephesians 1.4 says that God 'chose us in Christ before the foundation of the world' (*pro katabolēs kosmou*). And 1 Peter 1.20 says of Christ that he is a lamb 'destined before the foundation of the world (*pro katabolēs kosmou*), but revealed at the end of ages.' Which might John have in mind? In the vision of the woman and the child, we saw a picture of God's eternal decision to be incarnate as Jesus (Barth 2004, *CD*

II/1, 622) and his eternal decree to gather the son to his throne. But there is no Jesus who is not the man of Nazareth, crucified at Golgotha; there is no Lamb who is not slain. Thus we see here, in the Lamb slaughtered before the foundation of the world, that aspect of God's eternal decision. We need not choose between the two ideas but can affirm both, as indeed the whole New Testament witness does. What we will see in Revelation 17.8 is simultaneous with what we see here, namely God's eternal decision to choose his people in Christ and write their names in his book. Sometimes the answer 'it's both!' is a cheap way out of a conundrum, but that is not true here, for God's people are united to Christ, sharing in his victory and his destiny. The Lamb's election to death and life, made in the mind of God before the foundation of the world, is also their election to death and life.

The Earth Beast, 13.11–18

After the sea beast comes a second beast, rising up from the earth; after Leviathan comes Behemoth (cf. Job 40.15–24). Again the beast's description combines features of the dragon with parody of the Lamb. It has 'two horns like a lamb,' which (for those unacquainted with lambs) are not fearsome things to behold, and so at first this beast seems quite tame, certainly in comparison to the previous two creatures. But this appearance is deceptive: not only does it speak with the voice of the dragon; it also exercises the sea beast's authority on its behalf. Deception is perhaps the primary characteristic of this second beast, which is fitting given that it speaks with the voice of the dragon, 'the deceiver of the whole world' (12.9).

The first beast depicted blasphemous political and military power; this second beast is an image of deceptive religious and economic power. In the ancient world, a neat division between those spheres of life would not be recognised, however (and I wonder whether they are as neatly separated in our own world as we sometimes think). The main task of this earth beast is to use its delegated Satanic authority to enforce the worship of the first beast from the sea. To this end it engages in all manner of 'religious' activities: in particular it 'performs great signs' like the prophets of old. In a mockery of Elijah on Mount Carmel (1 Kgs 18.36–40) and the two witnesses of chapter 11, this 'false prophet' (which is what it is called in 16.3) calls down fire from heaven. These powerful signs are successful in their deceit, and the inhabitants of the earth turn to the beast in worship. In their worship of the beast, the people of the earth are instructed to craft it an idol, an 'image' (*eikōn*). The earth beast then even has the power to give this image the breath of life, and the ability to police this religious allegiance with violence.

The saints of first century Asia Minor would have had little problem identifying this religious arm of the Roman Imperial system. The so-called 'imperial cult' was widespread in the empire at this time but was embraced with particular fervour at the grass-roots level in the eastern provinces (it 'rose out of the earth'). Through the trappings of organised religion (temples, rituals, and the like), the Roman Empire occupied not just the geopolitical imagination of the people of Asia Minor but also their religious imagination. Indeed this was a conscious and important part of their rule. As we saw in chapters 2–3, the region was full of temples to emperors and to Rome itself, with cities climbing over each other to offer such honour to the powers that be. In Smyrna and in Pergamum ('where Satan has his throne,' 2.13), there were temples to emperor Augustus and to the goddess Roma (the personification of Rome). Among the six temples to Roman emperors in Ephesus, there was a temple to Domitian, built in the 80s, that contained a huge statue in his honour. The system and its ideas are complex, and it's difficult for us, at such historical distance, to make claims about the motivations of those who participated in its rituals. It is quite possible that, for many, this was 'merely' a matter of civic pride without any 'real' religious significance. At the heart of it, however, there was a vital theological claim: the gods have chosen Rome as their agents to bring about a golden age of peace and security, prosperity and fecundity to the world. In short, the manifest destiny of Rome was to bring 'salvation,' with the emperor himself as their prime agent. Moreover, emperors themselves (both dead and alive) received 'divine' titles (such as 'lord' and 'saviour') and were honoured as 'gods' or 'divinised ones' through the practices of the imperial cult. Whether they thought of themselves this way or just permitted the accolades for political expediency, such claims were nonetheless made and were carved in stone and stamped on coins throughout the empire. Revelation names this system for what it is: bestial idolatry.

This *Pax Romana* ('Roman peace') was by no means entirely peaceful. While the religious and political propaganda from the heart of the imperial system declared the gospel of Roman peace, other voices at the fringes of the empire called it as they saw it. Earlier, in the seal judgements, we heard from Roman historian Tacitus quoting the Scottish chieftain Calgacus's assessment of the *Pax Romana*. This voice from the edge of empire is worth hearing again: 'to robbery, slaughter, plunder, they give the lying name of empire; they make a desert and call it peace' (Tacitus, *Agricola*, ch. 30). This 'Roman peace' was nothing of the sort, for its price was the destruction of all who stood in their way. It was the 'peace' of scorched earth.

Once again, however, the recognition of this first-century resonance must not be allowed to exhaust our interpretation of this imagery. Just as there have been many 'sea-beasts,' there have also been many deceptive and idolatrous systems of worship that have supported them. The story of 'civic religion,' of an unholy alliance between 'God and country,' has been repeated time and again in the history of the world, and the line between patriotism and idolatry is always a thin one. Claims that 'God has chosen this nation' or that particular political leaders are divinely endorsed have not been consigned to ancient history. The alliance between political and religious power remains an ever-present threat to the people of God, who are too often deceived by its apparent innocence or tempted by its apparent power, not discerning the delegated authority of bestial and Satanic rule that may lie behind such systems. The church in every age is called to examine its allegiances and to exercise discernment. As John says, this 'calls for wisdom,' and it also calls for an 'apocalypse' (the two are not incompatible) so that the eyes of the church may be opened to the powers at work around us.

In addition to its task of religious deception, the earth beast also has an economic function, though we should again be careful not to separate these spheres of life too neatly (and again this applies to our own world, where economic activity is often described in 'religious' terms). In addition to enforcing idolatry, it also 'causes all . . . to be marked on the right hand or the forehead.' Without this mark, no one can buy or sell. In 7.3 John heard an angelic voice declaring the sealing of the 144,000, marked on the forehead with the seal of the living God. Behind that image, as we saw there, is Ezekiel 9, where a similar mark on the forehead protects the faithful from coming judgement. Here is its Satanic parody, as the earth beast causes a mark to be placed on the foreheads of all other inhabitants of the earth, from across the social spectrum, and those who are marked are not protected but enslaved. It is not hard to imagine how a practice that has the surface appearance of an act of protection can be its twisted distortion, enslavement. As elsewhere, the power of evil is always one of corruption not creation.

The 'mark of the beast' is perhaps one of the most well-known images in the book of Revelation and also one of the most misunderstood. This image has consumed gallons of scholarly ink (and terabytes of less scholarly webpages) in a way that has far exceeded the attention given to the image by John. He does not spend very long on it, and so neither will we, but nevertheless a brief discussion is necessary. To begin with, there are some things about the 'mark of the beast' that are stated quite plainly and that we should keep in mind as we interpret it. Two simple insights alone can help weed out inappropriate interpretations. The first thing we learn is that this mark is required for participation in commerce (v. 17). It is, one might say, a 'trade-mark.' It is the economic aspect of the earth beast's blasphemous call

Cosmic War

for allegiance. Worship and money often go hand in hand, in the ancient world and today.

The second is that we are told it is the beast's name, and the name of a person, expressed in numerical form. Expressing names in the form of numbers is not as strange as it may seem to us, and was fairly widely practised in the ancient world. Greek and Hebrew did not have a separate system of characters for numbers the way English does (having inherited these from Arabic). Instead, it used the letters of the alphabet, much like Roman numerals. These values were fixed for the different alphabets, and thus some fun could be had by counting the value of the letters in a name or word and in other names or words that had the same value. The system is called *gematria*, and these were the values:

Numerical Values of Hebrew Letters		Numerical Values of Greek Letters	
1 = א	60 = ס	A α = 1	N ν = 50
2 = ב	70 = ע	B β = 2	Ξ ξ = 60
3 = ג	80 = פ	Γ γ = 3	O o = 70
4 = ד	90 = צ	Δ δ = 4	Π π = 80
5 = ה	100 = ק	E ϵ = 5	Ϙ ϙ = 90
6 = ו	200 = ר	F ϝ = 6	P ρ = 100
7 = ז	300 = ש	Z ζ = 7	Σ σ = 200
8 = ח	400 = ת	H η = 8	T τ = 300
9 = ט	500 = ך	Θ θ = 9	Υ υ = 400
10 = י	600 = ם	I ι = 10	Φ φ = 500
20 = כ	700 = ן	K κ = 20	X χ = 600
30 = ל	800 = ף	Λ λ = 30	Ψ ψ = 700
40 = מ	900 = ץ	M μ = 40	Ω ω = 800
50 = נ			

That this was a widely known and used system has been established by numerous inscriptions across the Greco-Roman world. Here is one famous example: according to archaeological reports of the excavations of Pompeii (the actual inscription, sadly, is now lost) a well-preserved piece of graffiti on the southern wall of a stone cistern read '*filo hēs arithmos FME* [ΦΜΕ],' 'I love her whose number is 545.' Presumably the girl would see the number and know it was she who was beloved. But perhaps she was mistaken, and the beloved was another whose name also added up to 545? And therein lies the power, and indeed the fun, of this coded riddle system. Names and words that add up to the same total can be played with or even interpreted as signs of deeper associations. The technique is sometimes called *isopsephy*, which literally means 'equal calculation' (note the command in Rev 13.18 for those with wisdom to 'calculate [*psēphisato*] the number'). A less light-hearted example of this use of *gematria* is found in the writings of Suetonius, who records a coded riddle about Nero that fuelled rumours about him committing matricide: 'a new calculation (*neopsēphon*): Nero killed his own mother' (*Nero*, 39). In the Greek form in which it appears here, the name of Nero (*Nerōn*) adds up to 1,005 (N = 50 + ε = 5 + π = 100 + ω = 800 + ν = 50), the 'equal calculation' of 'killed his own mother' (*idian mētera apekteine*). This belief that Nero killed his mother is alluded to in Book VIII of the *Sibylline Oracles*, which is also a good example of the *Nero Redivivus* legend being deployed in an apocalyptic context. The passage foretells a 'matricidal fugitive' (88) coming again to conquer Rome, a dragon breathing fire, a final divine judgement, and the end of the world.

A third, more theologically profound example is found elsewhere in the *Sibylline Oracles*, where the power of *gematria* is exploited to name a different individual:

> Then indeed the son of the great God will come,
> incarnate, likened to mortal men on earth,
> bearing four vowels, and the consonants in him are two.
> I will state explicitly the entire number for you.
> For eight units, and equal number of tens in addition to these,
> and eight hundreds will reveal the name
> to men who are sated with faithlessness . . .

We pause here to calculate the number of this incarnate 'son of the great God.' His number, 888, is the total of the letters in the Greek form of the name of Jesus, *Iēsous* (I = 10 + η = 8 + σ = 200 + o = 70 + υ = 400 + σ = 200). It is an appropriately symbolic number, for the eighth day spoke of the day of circumcision (Gen 17.12; cf. Lk 1.59; 2.21; Phil 3.5) and therefore the day of God's covenant with his people. It was also the day of Jesus's resurrection, the 'eighth day of creation,' the beginning of God's new creative work. Unlike Revelation, the writer of the *Sibylline Oracles* does not leave his readers to follow the trail to this conclusion on their own but is much more explicit in explaining the figure indicated by the *gematria*. The passage continues:

> But you, consider in your heart
> Christ, the son of the most high, immortal God.
> He will fulfil the law of God—he will not destroy it—
> bearing a likeness which corresponds to types, and he will teach everything. (*Sib Or* 1:324–30, tr. Charlesworth)

We need not venture beyond the New Testament itself to see the power of *gematria* at work: the first chapter of Matthew's Gospel uses it, exploiting the numerical values of the letters in the name of David to structure his genealogy of Jesus, arranged in three sets of fourteen generations. In Hebrew, the letters in the name of David, דוד, add up to fourteen (4+6+4).

What, then, of Revelation 13.18 and the number 666? This one takes a little more work, for John is writing with both Hebrew and Greek in mind, but the same system can help us understand this 'number of a person.' Transliterated into Hebrew letters, the Greek word for 'beast,' *thērion*, adds up to 666. That seems straightforward enough—the 'number of the beast' is the number of the word 'beast.' But we are told that it is also the 'number of a person.' How might that be? Applying the same process (transliterating the Greek into Hebrew letters), the name and title of emperor Nero, *Nerōn Kaisar*, also comes to 666. Perhaps this seems a little farfetched, given that it assumes a transliteration between languages to get us to the number we need. Intriguingly, however, if we start with his name in Latin, *Nero Kaisar*, we come up short at 616, which is the same alternative number that is found in a substantial number of manuscripts of Revelation. The chances of exactly this discrepancy in the textual history of this passage matching two reasonable options for the name of Nero are small indeed. We recall, too, that the figure of Nero may already be in the mind of Revelation's first readers from the earlier image of the mortally wounded head (13.3), an image that John has just repeated (13.14), and so wise minds are likely already prepared for this interpretation. For these reasons the majority of modern scholars read this number as a coded reference to Nero, the arch persecutor of the Christians and thus the personification of the beast.

This is the case regularly made for using *gematria* to 'decode' the number of the beast, and it is a compelling one. But we must add a word of caution. We must not isolate this one text from the book of Revelation as a whole and treat this numerical symbol differently to the rest of John's symbolism, especially his other numerical symbols. Though we can see that understanding how *gematria* works can lead us to a clear first-century candidate for this name of the beast, we must avoid treating it as a 'code' that, once cracked, can be dispensed with. We must not simply read '666' and think 'Nero.' If we do this, we turn apocalyptic poetry into flat prose and kill the literary art and theological significance of this way of writing. Furthermore, this misses an important part of how *gematria* worked and why it should be used here (and not, say, another visual image like the beast). The numbers were used to reveal something significant about the person or thing being 'encoded,' especially (as we saw above) when more than one word or idea can have the same 'equal calculation,' or *isopsephism*. The fact that one can arrive at the same number by encoding the word 'beast' means that an association between the two can be forged. One might say that Nero and the beast 'add up to the same thing.' Moreover, the number six carries theological weight of its own, as that which is short of a complete seven and thus an image of imperfection. In its threefold form, such as we find here, it signifies the apotheosis of imperfection. It is, in short, the numerical form of the Satanic trinity, gathered together, personified, and named as the emperor. Whether or not Nero was in power at the time of Revelation was first being read, the message is clear: behind and within the apparently earthly system of imperial rule, summed up in this one man, are the beasts and the dragon.

Before we close this dark chapter, describing the enemies of God with disturbing bestial imagery, there is a final important comment to make. While noting the distinct focus of each bestial image, on political/military power and religious/economic power, it is also important to see the numerous and complex ways in which the two beasts are related to one another and to the dragon who straddles earth and sea. The sea beast has the same number of heads and horns as the dragon (13.1). The dragon gives authority to the sea beast (13.2), who in turn delegates this to the earth beast (13.12). The earth beast speaks with the dragon's voice (13.11) and enforces the worship of the sea beast through signs performed on its behalf and through giving voice to its image (13.14–15). This is a Satanic trinity. The saints are called not only to discern bestial political or religious systems in the world but also to discern the ways in which they are interwoven. Even though it rises up from the earth and is expressed in the mundane tasks of buying and selling, in acts of civic duty and piety, it is revealed to be a deceptive and systemic evil, which is Satanic in origin and therefore destined to destruction. This imagery exposes what we might call 'structural Sin' or 'structural Evil,' the bestial systems through which Satan seeks to exercise his dominion over the world. While not all will be convinced, it seems clear to me that Revelation offers an account of evil that is rightly called 'systemic.' These sinful structures are not simply reducible to the accumulation of human sinful acts but have a form of agency of their own, exercising power over people, influencing or even compelling idolatrous and sinful behaviour. But the recognition of their existence also demands reflection on how our own exercise of agency, through individual human 'sins' or 'evils,' both constructs and is complicit with such structures in our daily lives, through countless individual economic, political, and religious decisions. Thus the beast is both cause and consequence: it compels human sin, and human sin constructs the beast. And, before too long, this bestial systemic evil will come to its own judgement.

Final Battle and Harvest

Revelation 14.1–15.4

The Lamb and the 144,000, 14.1–5

The dragon, the sea beast, and the earth beast have assembled to make war on the saints. Taken together, these bestial visions expose the Satanic influence and idolatrous claims of imperial politics, religion, and economic life. At every point this 'unholy trinity' is a blasphemous mockery and distortion of the true God and the Lamb. Now John sees the Lamb himself, gathering his army for war: an incongruous image if ever there was one, but not for those who have been trained by Revelation's imagery to 'think doubly.'

Though his presence permeates the whole of the book of Revelation, when John last saw the Lamb he was standing in heaven, opening the seven seals. Now he stands on Mount Zion, occupying the high ground and placing the shore-bound dragon at a strategic disadvantage. This location indicates much more than a military advantage. Mount Zion is the appropriate location for the Lamb, for he is the root of David (5.5), the king who established his city here and ruled from this spot. Again we think of Psalm 2, a passage that has been echoed throughout this section of the book, and God's derisive declaration to his would-be opponents: 'I have set my king on Zion, my holy hill' (Ps 2.6). Yet this hill was not only the location of the palace but also of the temple. It is therefore a place of profound cosmological significance, understood in Jewish thought to be the 'navel of the earth' umbilically connecting the heavenly and earthly realms: the holy of holies was where heaven and earth met. As the Lamb stands here, then, he also stands in the heavenly temple. It is, in a sense, the same place. Just as the Lion is also the Lamb, so Zion is both palace and temple.

Mustering with him on Mount Zion are his army of 144,000. In the seal interlude vision of chapter 7, John heard the census of his army: 144,000 sealed from every tribe of Israel. It is not an overwhelming number but one that represents the perfection of Israel's fighting force, as we saw when we met them earlier. Now we see the 144,000 on earth, gathered for battle with their commander. The military imagery is appropriate, since the whole scene has clearly been building to a dramatic conflict between the forces of the dragon and the forces of God. As the forces on both sides take their positions on the field, we are expecting to see the imminent final resolution of the war. But we must remember that the nationalistic and militaristic image of the 144,000 fighting men has already been transformed in our imaginations through its juxtaposition with the universal and uncountable army of martyrs whose weapons are their testimony and the blood of the Lamb. This army is led by the Lamb, not the Lion. It is not a conventional war that is being fought.

The contrast between these people and the rest of the inhabitants of the earth is made clear. Whereas the rest of the people bear the enslaving mark of the beast (13.16–17), the 144,000 are marked on the forehead by the name of the Lamb and his Father. This name indicates their identity and allegiance as those who belong to the Lamb. It also protects them from the idolatrous influence of the beast. As we saw in the 'sealing' of the people of God in 9.4, this idea of covenant identity markers providing protection from the devil and his minions echoes the same theme in Ezekiel 9.4–6, and indeed was common in first century Judaism. Though the world may be deceived by the beasts and the dragon, whose would-be protective 'marks' are in reality the branding of enslavement, those sealed with the name of the Lamb and his father are not so deceived.

The people of earth are inscribed with the name of the beast. The 144,000 are marked by the name of the Lamb. Not for the last time, the clear contrast made between the two divides the world into two camps, bearing two marks of ownership/allegiance, which are the names of their respective lords. There is no middle ground or compromising position in this vision. Perhaps the churches of Asia Minor did not naturally see it in such black-and-white terms. The messages to them in chapters 2 and 3 certainly paint a picture of varied responses to the empire in matters of economics, politics, and imperial religion, including some who sought accommodation with the systems of the world. Through the combined force of this picture and the bestial imagery in chapters 12–13, Revelation permits no such nuanced mediating positions. The dragon and the Lamb are opposing forces, and both demand unequivocal allegiance. You either serve the beast or the Lamb.

We are told that they 'have not defiled themselves with women,' keeping the ritual purity required of Israelite soldiers before battle (e.g., Dt 23.9–10; 1 Sam 21.5). This is not, then, a denigration of women as inherently unclean but an image of an army ritually prepared for a holy war. The passage in 1 Samuel is the very same one to which Jesus appeals in defending his disciples' activities on the Sabbath in Mk 2.23–28, suggesting that they, too, had been enrolled in the eschatological war launched by the arrival of the kingdom of God. The image of sexual purity, however, is far more than an allusion to a soldier's ritual. Throughout Revelation, following a long Old Testament tradition (e.g., Hos 1–2; Jer 3; Ezek 23; cf. Koester 2014, 609), this is an image that refers to purity and fidelity in worship. This helps us explain why this very masculine army is described with the word *parthenoi*, virgins, not usually used to describe men at this time (see Koester 2014, 230f.). Masculine and feminine are thus combined in this image. In the usual manner of John's 'double' images, this is an army of pure worshippers, and the sound that accompanies them is a song of praise. A voice from heaven sings something like 'new song,' which can only be learned or understood by this multitude of the redeemed, sung before those elders and creatures in the court of heaven. We recall that, in 5.9–10, a 'new song' was sung before the throne by the living creatures and the elders, telling of the saints from every tribe and nation, ransomed by the blood of the Lamb and made to reign on the earth. Perhaps they are one and the same song, and what John now sees, his nonlinear narrative cycling around with its different perspectives, is the earthly counterpart to the heavenly worship of chapter 5. Indeed at this point the boundary between the two realms seems to be thin, and the sound of heaven's throne room is heard on earth. The two songs join together in harmony, heaven and earth united in a song of triumph at the very place where those two realms meet. As this army prepares for battle, then, they hear and learn the song of heaven declaring that they will reign because of the already-won victory of the Lamb who leads them.

As usual, the image requires of us a further 'double vision.' The description that follows confirms that this army of 144,000 remains the same universal army of martyrs encountered in 7.9–17, for they are also described in sacrificial language that subverts the militaristic expectations of the scene. As we just saw, Zion was the location of both palace and temple and is therefore already an image 'doubled.' It is the entirely appropriate muster point for the church militant, the people of God who are both a 'kingdom and priests' (5.10).

They are not only priests but also the sacrifice. This army includes those who have been redeemed from the earth as 'first fruits' for God and the Lamb, a metaphor for the people of God that John shares with Jeremiah (Jer 2.2–3) and Paul (1 Cor 15.20–23). It recalls the worship at the start of the festival of weeks (Lev 23.9–21), in which the first sheaf of the harvest was offered, together with an unblemished lamb, as a burnt offering to the Lord. The offering of the first sheaf celebrates the whole harvest, and so there is the suggestion here that this eschatological army is likewise only the 'first fruits' of God's final ingathering to come. Building layers of sacrificial imagery, John tells us that this army, like the sacrificial Lamb it follows, is also 'blameless' and that no lies are found in their mouths, an allusion to the fourth servant song of Isaiah (cf. Isa 53.9). The Lamb now leads them in battle, but this is the same Lamb who was himself led to slaughter (Isa 53.7) and who does no violence (Isa 53.9). The constant juxtaposition between military and sacrificial imagery requires, at every turn, that the reader think doubly, even triply, about the meaning of the scene that lies before us. The army is a sacrifice, and the sacrifice is an army. As the war between the dragon and the Lamb heads toward its climactic earthly battle, it will not be military but sacrificial and agricultural imagery that shapes the narrative. The great harvest is coming, but before that happens, the people of earth are given another chance to repent.

Three Angels, 14.6–13

Once again, Revelation leaves us at a cliffhanger. The armies have taken the field, but the final battle is postponed. John counts out a quick-fire sequence of three angels, each with a proclamation of increasing intensity. The first is seen flying, like the eagle of 8.13, in 'midheaven.' Its message, like the eagle's, is directed at the inhabitants of the earth. There are two aspects of this angel's role. First, it proclaims the gospel, *euangelion*, a word also used by the heralds of the empire to proclaim a new king or a great victory. This gospel, however, is eternal, for it is the proclamation of the Lamb's rule established in heaven before time and now announced, in the fulness of time, to the earth. The proclamation is universal, going out to 'every nation and tribe and language and people,' the people of the world described in the fourfold formula that we have repeatedly seen in contexts dealing with witness and judgment (5.9; 7.9; 11.9; 13.7), though each time the order of its elements has changed. This formula is used here for the fifth and final time, and there is a sense that the task of global witness is reaching completion. Second, there is a call to repentance, for the people of earth, deceived by the bestial powers, to turn from them to God and give him glory and worship as their creator and judge. Again there is a fourfold designation, as God is described as creator of 'heaven and earth, the sea and the springs of water,' the same four realms of creation affected by the first four trumpets (8.7–12) and that also remind us of the first four days of creation. The angel's message repeats the pattern seen throughout Revelation: divine judgement, while depicted in terrifying imagery, has been restrained and controlled and its consummation delayed so that the time of gospel witness might be completed (cf. 6.11) and so the people of the earth might be given chance to repent (cf. 9.20–21). With the first angel's announcement, we see that once again the final judgement of God is held back for this same dual purpose. One gets the sense, however, that this proclamation represents something of a last chance, 'for the hour of his judgement has come.'

A second angel follows behind, and this one has a more specific target for its proclamation. Once again, the order of events in John's narrative confuses the first-time reader, for the angel pronounces judgement on 'Babylon the great,' whom we have yet to meet. Those familiar with the prophets, however, would have recognised the echoes of Isaiah 21.9 and Jeremiah 51 (esp. vv. 7–8), prophetic oracles against the imperial city on the Euphrates that are now redeployed against Rome, the 'new Babylon,' which is enslaving the people of earth. In chapter 17, John will see a vision of this character in detail, along with the nature of her crimes and her punishment. Here the angel proclaims her fall quite suddenly (cf. Jer 51.8), described as an event already completed before the character is even introduced to the narrative; such is the nature of John's nonlinear storytelling. The reason for her judgement is given and is described with a combined image of sexual license and libation: she has made the people of earth 'drink the wine of the wrath of her fornication.' We are not yet told anything about the nature of this crime, but the Old Testament allusions make it clear. In Isaiah 21 and Jeremiah 51, the proclamations of Babylon's fall are linked to idolatry. Moreover, in calling her sin 'fornication' the angel has again brought to mind the imagery of sexual infidelity, so often used in the prophetic witness as a metaphor for idolatry, the corruption of divine union (see above and, again, Hosea 1–2; Jer 3; Ezek 23). This metaphor is combined with another, as the angel speaks of 'the wine of the wrath of her fornication.' The word 'wrath' here immediately suggests divine wrath, which is the sense of the same metaphor in verse 10 below. Here, however, there is a double entendre, for the word translated 'wrath' (*thymos*, also used in 18.3) can also mean 'passion.' What this woman has made the people drink is the passion/wrath of her infidelity.

A third angel follows the first two, and again its role is proclamation. The target of the third announcement is clearer and more specific: those who worship the beast and its image and who receive its mark. These people, the angel proclaims, will also drink 'the wine of God's wrath.' Once again, God's judgement takes the form of allowing evil to receive terrors of its own making—those who drink Babylon's cup of passion (*thymos*) will receive the cup of wrath (*orgē*). The repetition of the cup metaphor establishes a connection between beast and Babylon, a connection that will become clearer in the following chapters. This wine is poured 'unmixed,' that is, undiluted by water (the custom at the time) and therefore full-strength. The images of undiluted divine wrath that follow are possibly the most disturbing in the whole book. Those who continue to worship the beast, having ignored the proclamation of the gospel and the judgement of Babylon, are to be tormented with endless fire and sulphur and denied rest. Fire and sulphur, and rising smoke, were the means of divine judgement on the archetypal impure cities of the plain (Gen 19.24–27), and John joins a long prophetic line (e.g., Isaiah's oracle against Edom in 34.9–10) in echoing it here. It is neither his first nor his last use of the image: fire and sulphur characterised the sixth trumpet judgement (Rev 9.17–18) and will also fill the final place of judgement for Satan and Death itself (Rev 19–20), the final judgement of God's enemies foreshadowed here.

If endless fire and sulphur were not a disturbing enough image of divine judgement, we are also told that this punishment is to be performed in the presence of angels and the Lamb. What are we to make of this? A lot depends on whether this is to be read as a prediction or a threat (though the latter does not get us off the hook, for a threat of such violence is itself violence). Perhaps it is best viewed as a warning to those who worship the beast, and certainly the image shows us the seriousness of idolatry. The beast is not to be trifled with, for its end is destruction and it will take down any who remain in idolatrous union with it. That this happens in the presence of the Lamb by no means indicates his delight in such torments. Where else would it happen? There is no place, not even the most torturous, that is not 'before the Lamb,' for he is Lord of all. Even those who reject his lordship are before him. We must not hastily soften the harshness of this image of eschatological judgement, but perhaps in this there is a crumb of comfort. Whether or not it depicts a real future or just a possible one, in its reading this announcement of judgement for those who persist in beast worship stands as a final warning and a final chance to repent.

Thankfully, the section closes with a hopeful note. The announcement of coming wrath is also a call for 'the endurance of the saints.' Patient endurance (*hypomonē*) may not be the most celebrated of traits in our world (which far prefers heroic action), but it is one of the most often repeated attributes of the church in Revelation. John shared it with the churches of Asia (1.9), and Jesus praised it in Ephesus (2.2–3), Thyatira (2.19), and Philadelphia (3.10). It is the call placed on God's people when faced with the beast (13.10), and now the word is used for the last time. A call to heroic action can sometimes bring out the best in us, but a call to endurance is a much harder one. Revelation does not call the people of God to heroism but to a life of faithful witness and patient endurance. These patiently enduring saints are described as 'those who keep the commandments of God and hold fast to the faith of

Jesus,' echoing the description of the children of the woman targeted by the dragon (cf. 12.17), a connection that reminds us of the Satanic power at work behind Babylon and beast, marshalling these structures to make war on the saints. Here what is to be held is the 'faith' rather than the 'testimony' of Jesus, and both are true. If there is any hope for a world in thrall to the beast and the idolatrous city, it is the steadfast witness of the saints. No wonder this vision of judgement comes with a call to endurance.

The passage closes with a benediction, spoken by a voice from heaven. 'Blessed are the dead' is an odd sort of blessing, but its reason is given by the Spirit, now speaking. Those who die in the Lord during this time of trial and witness are blessed, for (in contrast to the beast worshippers) they will find rest. This rest is not the mere absence of work, for their deeds follow them, but the rest that comes at the completion of the toil of sacrificial witness. Though Revelation regularly reframes such witness as victory, it is under no illusion as to its challenges. Bearing witness to Christ under the conditions of bestial rule in which the saints will find themselves, in the first century and beyond, is a hard calling, and it is a victory won not through effortless glory or deeds of unstoppable power but through patient endurance in holding on to the faith of Christ. This may not seem exciting or heroic, but it is the way of victory according to the Lamb.

Two Harvests, 14.14–20

With the three announcements complete, we now see a vision of the final judgement of God. As with the Lion/Lamb in chapter 5 and the army/multitude in chapter 7, once again what John *hears* is accompanied and explained by what he *sees*. In the first half of this chapter he heard three angels with oracles of judgement and then a voice speaking of the blessedness of those who die in the Lord. What he now sees is a vision that explains and transforms that audition.

Much of the imagery of the last two chapters has been military. The dragon has fought the host of heaven and has made war on the woman's children, the beast has made war on the saints, and an army of 144,000 has mustered on Zion. At this point the imagery shifts from warfare to agriculture, though the theme of eschatological judgement remains. The shift to this harvest imagery is not entirely sudden, however, for there were small anticipations of it in the previous section. The image of a grain harvest echoes with the designation of the 144,000 as 'first fruits' (14.4), and the image of the grape vintage recalls the wine imagery used twice in the judgement against Babylon (14.8, 10). Harvest imagery like this, particularly the gathering and treading of grapes, is regularly used in the prophets to speak of God's final judgment (e.g., Isa 63.1–6). In the closing passages of Joel, for example, the imagery of a coming eschatological battle and the judgement of God is juxtaposed with the following agricultural image:

> Put in the sickle,
> for the harvest is ripe.
> Go in, tread,
> for the winepress is full.
> The vats overflow,
> for their wickedness is great. (Joel 3.13)

Here in Revelation 14, John sees a combined vision of two harvests, one of grain (14.14–16) and one of grapes (14.17–20), which emphasise different theological truths. Let us take each in turn.

First is the grain harvest. John has not seen the Son of Man since the opening Christological vision (Rev 1.13), but now he appears again, seated on a cloud, indicating his heavenly rule (cf. Dan 7.13–14) and crowned with a golden victor's wreath. Yet he holds not a sceptre but a 'sharp sickle.' An angel announces that the earth has now fully ripened and that 'the hour to reap has come.' The Son of Man swings his sickle and reaps the earth. In the popular imagination, the one who bears the sickle is often depicted not as Jesus but as Death himself, the 'Grim Reaper,' and so we are culturally conditioned to view this reaping negatively. This may be especially true in light of the proclamations of fiery judgement that we have just heard. But we must not let this negative image cloud our imagination in interpreting John's first harvest vision, for in the Bible the eschatological grain harvest is almost universally a positive image (Bauckham 1993, 97). It was one of Jesus's favourite images (e.g., Mt 9.37 / Lk 10.2; Mk 4.29; Jn 4.35), usually deployed to depict the joy of the ingathering in God's kingdom. This positive tenor of the vision is further confirmed by recognising that it is the Son of Man, not grim but crowned in glory and everlasting dominion, who does the reaping.

In 14.4 we saw the 'first fruits' of God's people redeemed from humankind; now we see the full harvest gathered. It is interesting to note what is missing in the picture. Normally a grain harvest requires the violence of threshing, to separate wheat and chaff (cf. Mt 3.12), and a reader may well expect to see this process as part of an eschatological vision (e.g., Jer 51.33; Mic 4.12; see Bauckham 1993, 96). It is this specific aspect of the grain harvest, the threshing rather than the ingathering, that carries negative connotations in the prophets. In Jeremiah 51, a text that would already be in the minds of readers from the previous passage, the judgement of Babylon is likened to the process of winnowing (51.2), and the city itself is like a threshing floor (51.33), a place of violent judgement. Yet in John's eschatological grain harvest there is no violence of threshing, only joyful ingathering.

The same cannot be said, however, of the second harvest of grapes. First the clusters of grapes are gathered, and then they are thrown into the winepress to be trodden. The agent of this harvest is not Christ but an angel, one with 'authority over fire.' That the angel harvests the grapes is made clear in verse 19, but this is preceded by a somewhat confusing interchange between the angel and the Son of Man, in which we are led to expect the latter to do this harvesting work. This ambiguity persists into the second phase of the harvest, when the grapes are trodden in the winepress by an unspecified agent. We have good reason to read this as God's action. As with threshing, the prophets regularly likened God's final judgement to the treading of a winepress (e.g., Isa 63.1–6 and Joel 3.11–13, quoted above), no doubt because of the obvious similarities between wine and blood (cf. Gen 49.11). Revelation makes this connection explicit in the closing verse of the vision, as blood is seen flowing from the winepress, six feet deep for two hundred miles. The note that this flow of blood is as deep as a horse's bridle echoes a similar image of eschatological judgement found in the books of *1 Enoch* (100.3) and *4 Ezra* (15.33).

The extent of the flow of blood is symbolically important, a symbolism often hidden when the measurements are converted into modern terms. 'Two hundred miles' is 1,600 stadia, a number that is four squared times one thousand. Four, we recall, is the number of the earth, and a thousand is a symbolically large number. As such, this is an image of global, universal coverage, deep enough to cover every person. But whose blood is it? We might naturally assume that this is the blood of God's enemies, for that is the natural sense of the winepress image elsewhere. Yet when Revelation speaks of blood, as it does often, it is never in this sense. When the blood of a person or people is described (as opposed to blood as a plague judgement), it is either the blood of Christ (1.5; 5.9; 7.14; 12.11) or the blood of the saints (6.10; 16.6; 17.6; 18.24; 19.2). If the blood from the winepress in 14.20 is meant to represent the blood of God's enemies, it is the only place Revelation does this (but cf. the discussion of 19.13 below). The theme of the people of God has been dominant throughout the preceding chapters, and so if this passage now intends to speak of the blood of God's enemies it lacks the clear indications one would expect of such a sudden change in imagery. It makes more sense, then, to read the grapes as another image of the saints, and the blood that flows as their blood. As such, this vision stands as the second half of the diptych accompanying the eschatological army of 14.1–5, and thus the effect of reading both together is similar to the juxtaposition of army and multitude in chapter 7. The conquering army is an army of martyrs, whose blood covers the earth. As the song of 12.11 told us, they have conquered by blood, for they did not cling to life even in the face of death. As throughout Revelation, the witness of the church to the point of death is a participation in the Lamb's witness, death, and victory. They share with Christ a wrath-bearing sacrificial victory, shedding their blood outside the city and sharing in his sanctifying death (cf. Heb 13.12). Thus Revelation Christologically transforms the Isaianic image of the winepress of God's wrath.

This is how Revelation's bifocal imagination works, and we have seen it many times. Two images are juxtaposed and the theological message is found in holding both together simultaneously. But there is a greater level of complexity in this passage, which twice employs this imaginative 'doubling.' Not only does the harvest imagery work with the earlier military imagery to transform our reading of both, but also the two harvests inform each other, such that there is a 'double vision' internal to this passage, too. The positive image of the grain harvest and the negative picture of the vintage mutually inform one another. The saints' joyful ingathering is also their crushing in death. And their crushing in death is also their joyful ingathering.

The Song of Moses and the Song of the Lamb, 15.1–4

The passage that follows both completes this vision sequence and begins the next section. Like the transition between the seals and trumpets in 8.1–5, it is a literary 'seam.' It clearly introduces the next section, for John tells us of 'another portent' (cf. 12.1, 3) of seven angels with seven plagues, setting up expectations of the beginning of another judgement cycle. It will be the last, for with these plagues, we are told, 'the wrath of God is ended,' that is, fulfilled and brought to completion.

However, as we saw when the trumpet angels were similarly introduced in 8.1, these angels do not begin to do their work until a few verses later. And so this passage can also be viewed as the completion of the section. Despite not having the clear enumerated seven judgements of the seals or trumpets, the visions of chapters 12–14 share something of the same broad narrative shape as those earlier sequences. We have seen a series of visions focussed on evil and its judgement (chapters 12–13, and especially the three angels), followed by visions of the church in its witness in the 'in-between' times (chapter 14), and now the purposes of God come to their consummation and are celebrated with a song of praise.

The narrative has returned from earth to heaven, and what John describes recalls many features of his earlier heavenly visions. His attention is drawn primarily to a 'sea of glass mixed with fire.' In chapter 13, the sea was an image of chaos from whence the beast came. But we are not on earth anymore, and the 'sea of glass' in heaven is different. John saw this 'sea' before the throne when he first stepped into heaven in 4.6. There, as we saw, the image speaks not of primordial chaos but of the bronze washing basin that stood in the tabernacle (Ex 30.18) and the more impressive 'sea' that was part of Solomon's temple furniture (1 Kgs 7.23–26; 2 Chr 4.2–6).

As usual, however, the *double entendre* implicit in the word 'sea' is not collapsed in favour of one or the other interpretation but is exploited in John's storytelling, as we will now learn. Beside the sea is a vision of the saints. No longer are they under the altar, slaughtered and asking 'how long?' Now they are seen standing in their victory over the beast and its image (though we do not forget what previous visions have taught us about the manner of that victory and its connection to their slaughter). They are seen in the posture of praise, holding harps and singing.

Not for the first time in this section of the book, John evokes Exodus 15. We have already seen how the language of this passage has been echoed in his account of the dragon in chapter 12 and the beast in chapter 13. The people of earth parodied this passage in exclaiming 'who is like the beast?' (cf. Ex 15.11). It is a passage firmly in the reader's mind, then, when John writes that he saw 'those who had conquered the beast,' the church, beside the sea singing 'the song of Moses, the servant of God' (Rev 15.3, cf. Ex 14.31). Exodus 15 records a song that Moses sang beside the Red Sea, praising God as a warrior who had conquered the Egyptians. The connection is strengthened by the foreshadowing of the seven plagues. The wider context, then, strongly suggests that this 'song of Moses' alludes to the Red Sea song.

These clear allusions are made problematic, however, when the song is heard. There is very little in its content to indicate that John is echoing Exodus 15. Some of the broad themes may be similar (God's triumph over his enemies, the deliverance of his people by mighty deeds, and praise for his holiness and majesty) but the lyrics are very different. There are some possible lyrical connections, though, with a song Moses sang at the end of his life, found in Deuteronomy 32.1–43. For example, these lines have a number of similarities to Revelation 15.3–4:

For I will proclaim the name of the LORD;
ascribe greatness to our God!

> The Rock, his work is perfect,
> and all his ways are just. (Dt 32:3–4)

That song, sung by Moses at another significant water-crossing, as the people were about to cross the Jordan, tells the story of God's justice and covenant faithfulness despite Israel's failings. Here the primary image is not of God as a warrior but God as a judge. Do we have, then, something of an incoherent amalgam, clumsily combining themes? By no means. By now we should be familiar with John's approach to making Old Testament allusions. Rarely is his practice simply a matter of quoting one text or making just one connection. Instead, he weaves complex tapestries with numerous threads connecting across the Old Testament, reframed in a new theological context, and across his own book. The result of this interweaving of allusions is a newly creative combination of theological themes. In this respect his exegetical strategy is similar to his Jewish contemporaries, who often worked in a similar manner. Passages in the Hebrew Scriptures that contained the same words or phrases were brought into dialogue with each other and made to mutually interpret each other. In cases where the passages are separated in time, as well as the first affecting the second, the reverse is also true. There is a dynamic 'dialogue' created by the intertextual connections, and it is this interplay that drives the meaning. In Revelation 15, John works in this way with the two songs of Moses. In the Old Testament narrative, the two songs are like bookends to the wilderness years, the first sung beside the Red Sea celebrating God's deliverance and the second beside the Jordan remembering his faithfulness. John connects the two songs and draws on both in his new composition beside the 'sea' (other texts are drawn upon, too, namely Jer 10.6–7; Pss 86.8–10; 98.1–2. It is a finely worked and complex tapestry. For a fuller discussion of all this see Bauckham 1998, 296–307, and Moyise 2004).

Once we understand this complex exegetical strategy, we can begin to see the theological force of John's interwoven allusions in composing this 'new song' (cf. 5.9; 14.3). In particular, we can now more fully appreciate why this song is also called the 'song of the Lamb.' The new context provides a new theological interpretation of both songs of Moses and therefore of these two defining moments in the life of Israel. It is the song of deliverance in Exodus 15 and the song of covenant faithfulness in Deuteronomy 32, both songs brought together and reworked in the light of the consummation of deliverance and covenant faithfulness found in the Lamb. The Lamb is both the divine warrior and the covenant-keeping, faithful judge. This is not merely a reprise, like the closing medley of a Broadway musical that gathers the themes of many tunes. It is not simply a matter of John's skilful literary craft; it communicates a more profound theological truth. Seen from the perspective of heaven, the song of the Lamb, sung by the conquerors of the beast, is also the song of Moses sung by the people of Israel. Events separated by many hundreds of years in earthly history are, from the perspective of heaven, the singular moment of God's deliverance in Christ. The deliverance and justice of God celebrated by the people beside the heavenly sea is 'simultaneously' his earthly deliverance by the waters of the Red Sea, the Jordan, the Euphrates, and the Mediterranean. If Paul can say that the rock Moses struck in the wilderness was Christ (1 Cor 10.4), then John can say that the song Moses sung by the sea is the song of the Lamb.

Seven Bowls

Revelation 15.5–16.21

Seven Angels Emerge, 15.5–8

After hearing the song, John describes another vision. It begins with another 'opening' in heaven, similar to that of 11.19, and this time what is opened is the 'temple of the tent of witness in heaven.' This is a somewhat awkward phrase. The first 'of' works to clarify the meaning, such that it might more accurately be translated 'the temple, that is, the tent of witness.' The 'tent of witness' is the name given to the wilderness tabernacle, which provides the imagery for this vision rather than the temple in Jerusalem. The exodus imagery thus continues from the previous chapter. The more common Old Testament name for the tabernacle is the 'tent of meeting' or the 'tent of the covenant,' but it is also called the 'tent of witness,' especially in Greek translation (see, e.g., Num 17.22 LXX [= Num 17.7]), for it stood to bear testimony to God's covenant with Israel. Given the importance of the theme of 'witness' in Revelation, it is obvious why John would prefer this designation for the heavenly tabernacle. As we saw in our discussion of chapter 4, in Jewish cosmology heaven itself is understood as being 'temple-' or 'tabernacle-shaped,' since the tabernacle was constructed according to the heavenly pattern revealed to Moses (Ex 25.8–9). Here, however, John describes a temple/tabernacle *in* heaven. Like the earthly tabernacle, John seems to be working with an understanding of heavenly geography involving concentric zones of purity within heaven itself. What is opened, then, is not the curtain between earth and heaven but between heaven's outer court and the inner sanctum, the heavenly equivalent of the most holy place.

Unlike the opening of the temple in heaven in 11.19, here John does not see into the inner heavenly space, or enter it, but instead describes what comes out. The seven angels, which were prefigured in 15.1, now emerge from God's presence in the tabernacle in heaven and prepare to begin a final series of seven judgements on earth. The reader anticipates that this will be the last such series, for we have already been told that the plagues brought by these seven angels will bring God's wrath to an end. The angels are robed in bright linen with golden sashes, like the angelic figures in Daniel's visions (Dan 10.5; 12.6), and evoke the celestial attire of Christ in 1.13.

As with the trumpets in 8.2, these seven angels are first given an object symbolising their commission. One of the four living creatures gives the angels seven offering bowls, perhaps the same ones that the four creatures had back in 5.8. There the bowls contained the prayers of the saints, offered before the throne, but now they are filled with the wrath of God to be poured out on earth. The connection is clear: the same bowls that held the church's cries for justice now contain the answer to those prayers. As this first scene closes, God's own glorious presence fills the temple in the form of liturgical smoke, and we await the consummation of his judgement on the earth. No one can enter the temple until this is complete, for the time for making intercession is over.

Seven Bowls, 16.1–21

The series of seven bowl judgements now begins. It is considerably briefer than the seven seals or seven trumpets but has a similar (though not identical) arrangement. The first three bowls are described more briefly than the last four, the two parts being interrupted by some angelic words. There is an interlude of sorts between the penultimate bowl and the last of the seven, though here it is far briefer than those found in the other cycles, as if John is in a rush to bring things to completion. Not only is the narrative pace quicker, but also the extent of these judgements is more complete in description than the previous cycles, lacking the proportional indications of restraint (one quarter, one third) found in the other sequences, because with these plagues the wrath of God is brought to its completion and fulfilment (cf. 15.1). Continuing the exodus theme, we are told that the bowls contain plagues, and once again the series of judgements contains numerous detailed allusions to the Egyptian plagues, as we will see.

As chapter 16 begins, out of the smoke in the temple comes a loud voice (presumably the voice of God) that instructs the angels to go to the earth, completing their outward journey from the tabernacle in heaven, via the courts of heaven, to the earth. They will not return without fulfilling their duties of judgement. John's narrative follows them, and in a series of rapid-fire scenes, the first three angels pour their bowls on four areas of the earth: land, sea, rivers, and springs.

The first bowl is poured on the earth, bringing a plague of sores, like the sixth Egyptian plague (Ex 9.8–12). As so often in Revelation, there is an 'appropriateness' to divine judgement: those who bear the mark of the beast are marked by sores. We are left to infer that those who bear the name of the lamb (14.1) are protected from this plague. The second angel pours out his bowl, this time into the sea. The water turns to blood, and not only blood (which could symbolise life) but the blood of the dead, killing not only a proportion of the creatures but 'every living thing.' The third bowl has the same effect on the rivers and springs, echoing the first Egyptian plague against the Nile in Exodus 7.17–21.

At this point there is a slight interruption of the sequence, as we hear the words (a song, perhaps?) of an angel, one who seems to have a specific area of responsibility for the waters, like the 'angel who has authority over fire' we saw in 14.18. The angel's words declare the justice of God and focus our attention further on the appropriateness of the form it has taken. The inhabitants of the earth have shed the blood of the saints and prophets, and so it is by blood that they are judged.

Attention now moves away from the earth to different targets. The fourth angel pours out his bowl on the sun, and we expect a plague of darkness (Ex 10.21–29). But rather than the sun being darkened, it is made more intense. Thus the elements of earth, water, and fire have all been implicated in these judgements (air is still to come, in verse 17). John now adds a detail to the narrative that reminds us of the purpose of divine judgement, namely to bring about repentance (cf. 9.20). Once again, however, the people do not repent but curse the name of God for his judgement, and so the sequence of seven bowl plagues continues.

The fifth angel pours out his bowl not on an aspect of the created world but on 'the throne of the beast.' Now we do have a plague of darkness (Ex 10.21–29), though it seems to affect only the kingdom of the beast. Together with the darkness there is pain and boils, reminiscent of the sixth plague (Ex 9.8–12). Again, just as with the hardened heart of Pharaoh, we are explicitly told that there is still no repentance, despite the pain of the sores. Instead of the repentance God desires, the people continue to curse him.

The sixth plague again strikes the rivers, more precisely the Euphrates. This echoes the sixth trumpet, where the angels bound at that river were released, clearing the way for a demonic cavalry breathing fire and smoke and sulphur (which, we recall, were called 'plagues,' 9.18). Here, like the waters of the Red Sea, the river dries up, but with a radically different result. Whereas the drying of the sea brought deliverance for the people of God and watery judgement for the cavalry of Egypt, here the dried-up river allows the 'kings of the east' to cross, bringing judgement to the people. Once again John is perhaps playing on the fear of Parthian invasion from beyond the empire's eastern border (see the discussions of the first seal [6.1–2] and fifth trumpet [9.1–12] above) or on the myth of Nero's return from the east. But whatever the precise historical resonances, what comes next is clearly no mere human cavalry.

As with Revelation's other sequences of seven, the bowls are interrupted at this penultimate moment. But instead of a vision of the church in its eschatological witness (the usual fare of the visionary 'interludes'), John describes visions of the forces of evil. First, coming from the mouth of the dragon, he sees 'three foul spirits like frogs.' The imagery of frogs echoes the second Egyptian plague (Ex 8.1–15), but here the frogs are not described as the direct result of the pouring of a bowl. They do not come from God, but out of the mouths of the 'unholy trinity,' the dragon, the beast, and the false prophet (the designation now given to the earth beast of 13.11–18). We recall that in the plagues of Exodus, Pharaoh's magicians were able to mimic the divine plagues, including producing frogs (Ex 8.7; see Koester 2014, 667). These 'demonic spirits' have a clear task: to deceive the kings of the whole world through the performance of signs and gather them together for a final decisive battle against God and his people on the 'great day' (cf. 6.17).

A sudden and parenthetical remark, apparently spoken by Christ directly to his audience, reminds us that this day cannot be anticipated. That this is Christ speaking is suggested by the numerous echoes of his words to the seven churches, to 'stay awake' (cf. 3.2), for he comes 'like a thief' (cf. 3.3), and to remain 'clothed' in robes (cf. 3.4–5, 18) and not 'naked and exposed' (cf. 3.17). The similarities with similar pronouncements in the synoptic Gospels (esp. in the 'synoptic apocalypse,' Mt 24.43–44 and parallels) and the letters of both Paul (1 Thess 5.2) and Peter (2 Pet 3.10) suggest that this apocalyptic image goes back to the earthly teachings of Jesus himself and profoundly shaped the eschatology of the early church. Like these words, Jesus's coming interrupts the processes of history. His coming is, without contradiction, both an unexpected interruption and the fulfilment of God's purposes.

Although this vision describes demonic activity that appears to signal the coming of the great day of the Lord, it also comes with a warning not to try to calculate the precise timing of that day. The benediction that accompanies this warning tells us that the church's task is to remain ever vigilant, awake and clothed, rather than to engage in speculation and prediction. Like the people of Israel on the night of the exodus, who ate the Passover meal hurriedly and dressed in walking gear (Ex 12.11), the church is always to be ready for the Day of the Lord.

Seven Bowls

Just as suddenly as we left it, we return to the narrative. The kings of the earth, deceived by the frog spirits, gather for the great battle at *Harmagedon*, a place that you will not find on a map. It is a name perhaps derived from Megiddo, which was the site of several battles in the Old Testament and seems to be rather ill-fated, being the location of death for more than one king of Judah due to idolatrous behaviour or a refusal to listen to God. (Ahaziah died there from an arrow wound in 2 Kgs 9.27, and Josiah meets a similar end at the hands of the Egyptian pharaoh Neco in 2 Kgs 23.29–30. The account in 2 Chr 35.20–27 names archers as the cause of Josiah's death.) It is associated, then, with mourning. More significantly, perhaps, Megiddo is also named by the prophet Zechariah in his prophecy of God's eschatological triumph over the nations. He tells of a day coming that will be a day of mourning over another 'pierced one' (Zech 12.10–14), a passage that was echoed right at the start of Revelation, where it was combined with Daniel's imagery of the Day of the Lord (1.7). In Zechariah this day of mourning is also a day on which a fountain of cleansing is opened for the sins of God's people. It will be a day in which the Lord will remove false prophets and unclean spirits (Zech 13.1–4), before a great battle, divine judgement by plagues, and finally the eschatological enthronement of God (Zech 14). Clearly there are a number of points of connection between these chapters of Zechariah and the remaining chapters of Revelation.

The most remarkable thing about 'the battle of Armageddon,' though, is that it simply doesn't happen. There is no need for a battle for sovereignty of the world, for it belongs already to God. The kings have assembled, and the battlefield is chosen, but instead of a battle we get the arrival of the divine presence. The seventh angel pours his bowl into the air, and the voice from the temple (which is already enthroned) speaks again to declare the work done. Then the seven bowls close as the other sequences closed, with a storm theophany. Once more, an element is added. In the throne vision of chapter 4, God's presence is accompanied by 'flashes of lightning, and rumblings and peals of thunder' (4.5). At the close of the seals, we saw the addition of an earthquake to this list (8.5), and at the end of the trumpets hail was added (11.19). Now John describes this storm in even more extreme terms, with 'flashes of lightning, rumblings, peals of thunder, and a violent earthquake . . . and huge hailstones, each weighing about a hundred pounds' (16.18, 21). The intensification of 'the plague of the hail' evokes the seventh plague of Exodus 9.13–35. Like all the other plagues, however, it elicits no repentance from the people of earth, and instead we are told for the third time that they curse God.

With the completion of the seventh bowl, and therefore the fulfilment of God's wrath, we anticipate his final coming. Before we see that glorious consummation, however, John sees further visions of God's judgement. It is not enough for God to bring his judgement against the earth. What is needed is the judgement and destruction of the evil powers (structural and Satanic) that lie behind the earth's abominations. The following series of judgement visions will occupy chapters 17–20 and will deal with God's enemies in the reverse of the order in which they were introduced to the narrative (Koester 2014, 682). This chiastic pattern frames and unites the whole section from chapter 12 to chapter 20, and we are thus reminded of God's purposes, stated just before the section began, to destroy 'those who destroy the earth' (11.18). In addition to this literary insight, the pattern of visions also demonstrates God's controlled dismantling of the idolatrous systems of this world that the dragon has been building since his failed coup in chapter 12. The dragon, the beast, and the city Babylon have been introduced in sequence, and now God's judgement will reverse this, working backward through each in turn. Babylon was introduced most recently, and cryptically, in 14.8, and so she is the first to be judged. 'God remembered great Babylon,' we are told, and gave her (as promised) the wine cup of his fury. The one who 'made all nations drink the wine of the wrath of her fornication' (14.8) will now be made to drink the cup of God's wrath (16.20; cf. 14.10). John will now be shown an extensive vision of this judgement.

Babylon

Revelation 17.1–19.10

Babylon the Great, 17.1–18

Vision of the Whore, 17.1–6a

The passages that follow are clearly of a piece with the bowl sequence, indicated by John's statement that it was one of the angels with the seven bowls who now acts as his guide. The character of Babylon has already been introduced into John's shuffled narrative, at 14.8. There we were told very little about her, save that she made the nations drink 'the wine of the wrath of her fornication.' The next two chapters will deal with this character and her judgment more expansively. As with the Lamb in chapter 5, John first hears an announcement (17.1–2) and then sees a vision (17.3ff.).

Throughout the Scriptures, Babylon looms large as the archetypal oppressive city, the place of exile, and an existential threat to the people of God. Behind Babylon stands Babel, the first human city and symbol of humanity's arrogant will to make a name for itself, perhaps even ascend to God (Gen 11.4). In the brief discussion of Babylon in chapter 14, we saw that John was forging particular connections with the oracles against the historical city in Isaiah 21.9 and Jeremiah 51.7–8. As almost all scholars recognise, these prophetic oracles are reworked by John in these chapters as a prophecy against the 'new Babylon,' the imperial city of Rome. John is not the only New Testament writer to cast Rome in Babylon's role and therefore as having Babylon's character; we see the same metaphor in the first letter of Peter, who signs off with greetings from the 'sister church in Babylon' (1 Pet 5.13). The city is portrayed as a woman, the first of two contrasting figures who are among the key characters in this last section of the book, the second being the bride Jerusalem. Portraying cities as women is commonplace in the prophets, and the specific motif of an unfaithful or promiscuous woman is a regular trope deployed to speak of Samaria or Jerusalem, and therefore the people of God more generally, in their idolatry (Hos 1–2; Jer 3;

Ezek 23). Israel's idolatrous breaking of the covenant was regularly imagined with the metaphor of the breaking of the covenant of marriage. The city-as-woman trope was not restricted to God's people, however. The prophet Nahum deployed this metaphor in his oracle against bloodthirsty Nineveh, who enslaved and deceived the nations (Nah 3.1–7). Again, in Isaiah 23 and Ezekiel 27–28, the same imagery is targeted at the merchant city of Tyre. John's vision of Babylon is a complex combination of all of these oracles, drawing on a rich well of prophetic tradition for his imagery.

Yet the trope of portraying cities as women is not limited to the Hebrew prophets; it was also deeply embedded in the Roman imagination. The city of Rome itself was regularly personified on coins and statues as the goddess *Roma*. This depiction was so common as to be practically formulaic: she is regularly found dressed in military attire, with helmet, spear, and shield, though seated in a serene and virtuous pose. Her seat is either the famous seven hills of the city or a throne made of weapons, the spoils from defeated foes. This image of goddess *Roma* is so immediately identifiable that its presence on the east wall of the *Ara Pacis Augustae* ('Altar of Augustan Peace'), now on display in a dedicated facility in Rome, can be reconstructed from only a fragment. On that monument, *Roma* is placed opposite another female figure, the goddess *Pax* (peace), framed as her mirror image, surrounded by images of fecundity and prosperity. The message of this juxtaposition is clear: the promise of Rome is eternal peace and prosperity, and the means of achieving this promise is the military conquest of all who oppose Rome. *Roma* and *Pax*: together these two goddesses express the heart of the Roman imperial message. As such, what follows is not really a text about a woman but about a city, about human rule and its claims. Moreover, we remind ourselves that, although a first-century reference can clearly be drawn, we must not reduce the imagery to a code to be deciphered. Babylon is Rome, to be sure, but it is more than Rome. She is the personification of all idolatrous human claims to lordship.

However, this observation only partially mitigates the challenge of the misogynist language and the imagery it deploys. Revelation lampoons the image of virtuous *Roma*, satirising Roman propaganda and recasting her in far from virtuous terms. The angel calls her a great *pornē*. How are we to translate this word? One regularly encounters the terms 'whore' or 'prostitute,' but the terms 'courtesan' or 'sex worker' might appear a better, more sensitive choice, avoiding the derogatory tenor of the other words. And yet John's depiction of this character is far from neutral. He intends it to be derogatory, for in this vision he will subvert Rome's claims to be the ruler of the world, reversing its self-depiction as the glorious *dea Roma*. To soften the language would weaken the force of this imaginative satirical critique of the imperial city. As such, here we will maintain the words 'whore' or 'prostitute,' while being aware that these are degrading terms. This makes for hard reading, for language itself can be an act of violence. So, while recognising the power of the imagery for political critique, we must not be ignorant of the pain this metaphor may cause readers today.

The angel first tells John that the whore Babylon sits 'on many waters,' like its historical namesake, which was a city beside many rivers (cf. Ps 137). The Babylon of John's vision has also risen to its position because of its maritime location, which has brought mercantile and naval dominance. In this way, though her name is borrowed from the great imperial city by the Euphrates, Babylon is also like ancient Tyre in Isaiah 23 or Ezekiel 27–28. There are a number of close connections between Revelation 17–18 and these oracles in particular, as we will see.

The 'kings of the earth,' we are told, have become involved with her, an involvement characterised as 'fornication.' We have met these kings a number of times already, first as those who are truly subject to Christ, their ruler (1.5), and then as those who cower in the caves at the coming of God's judgement (6.5). Both of those themes are in mind, then, as we now hear of them again. They are implicated in this vision because they have committed fornication (*porneuō*) with the whore (*pornē*), a common extension of the woman-as-city imagery in prophetic oracles against the people of God caught in idolatrous relationships with neighbouring peoples. Fornication is an act of covenant-breaking, of union without covenant, and prostitution is intimate relationship reduced to financial transaction. Mixing his metaphors, and recalling the imagery from the second and third bowl judgements (14.8, 10), this fornication is also described as a cup of intoxicating wine. As it was in chapter 14, the allusion here is to Jeremiah 51.7 (and indeed that whole chapter), where the prophet describes Babylon making the nations of the earth maddeningly drunk.

This angelic introduction, then, is what John hears; he has yet to see Babylon for himself. That now changes, as he is carried away in the spirit. This is the third time John has mentioned such a spiritual experience, the others being at the opening vision of Christ in 1.10 and the start of the throne vision in 4.2. We are to expect, then, that this marks the start of another major visionary experience. He is carried to 'a wilderness.' It is not clear where this is, though it recalls the setting of chapter 12, where we last saw another female character, the woman clothed with the sun. She was taken to the wilderness to be nourished for the 'cut-short time' of 1,260 days (12.6) or 'a time, and times, and half a time' (12.14). But now we learn that she is not alone in the wilderness, for there we also meet Babylon. These two wilderness women are contrasted. There is the woman nourished by God, there are his faithful people, and there is the whore who makes the people of the earth drunk with infidelity. The time the people of God spend in the wilderness being nourished by God is not an experience of glorious monastic isolation but a time of trial and witness, of conflicting allegiances and a call for fidelity.

The woman is seated, as we expect, but not on 'many waters,' nor (at least on first appearance) on the seven hills of Rome. She rides instead a seven-headed scarlet beast, which has ten horns, like the dragon (12.3), and is 'full of blasphemous names.' Though the description reverses the order of elements, this is obviously the same beast we met in 13.1, which is identical in heads, horns, and names. Its colour is red, like the dragon or the second horseman, but a different shade (the word used is *kokkinos*, 'scarlet', not the fiery-red *pyrros* of the dragon or horse). As we saw in chapter 13, John is working with an established apocalyptic tradition, going back at least to Daniel, of depicting earthly kingdoms as beasts (Dan 7). The implications of the vision are clear: this city owes its mercantile dominance to the military and political power of the beast. It has ridden to its high status on the back of a bestial system.

The woman's attire coordinates with her steed, for she is also robed in purple and scarlet, the most expensive fabrics available. The woman and the beast are, as James Resseguie puts it, 'cut from the same cloth' (2009, 222). Her accessories of gold and jewels and pearls further display ostentatious and gaudy splendour. One might think, then, that this image is more precisely one of a high society courtesan rather than a lower-class prostitute, but that is not what John calls her (Greek has another word, *hetaira*, for such a person; see Koester 2014, 671). His intention is not to celebrate but to mock the splendour of Rome, which, though it gathered the wealth of an empire, liked to portray itself in respectful moderation.

More details are given that create narrative tension with Babylon's apparent wealth. On her forehead is written a mystery, though it is a mystery already revealed in 14.8 and 16.19. She is branded with her name and title, 'Babylon the great, mother of whores and of earth's abominations.' The inscribing of her forehead not only gives us her name and identity but also evokes the ancient practice of the tattooing of slaves, signaling that she is an enslaved prostitute. Once again there is a social dualism implied here, a contrast between two halves of humanity. Those who are the servants of God bear his seal and his name on their foreheads and are thus protected from his judgement (7.3; 9.4; 14.1, echoing Ezek 9). Those who do not receive this seal, Babylon included, are made to bear the mark of the beast who enslaves them (13.16). Babylon is not free but is a slave to the very beast she rides and to the dragon whose authority stands behind them both. The relationship she has with the beast may appear freely entered and mutually beneficial, and indeed she may claim to have become a queen from it (18.7), but in truth she is little more than a slave of God's enemies. As such, she is destined to go with them to destruction.

The last thing John notices about her is that she herself is drunk and so is caught up in the intoxication with which she deceives the kings of the earth (v. 2). It is not wine that has intoxicated her, however, but the blood of the saints and the witnesses to Jesus. The obvious and widespread connection between the images of wine and blood has been made a number of times in the book, most recently in 16.6, and the clear indication here that wine represents the blood of the saints further supports our earlier interpretation of the winepress in 14.19–20. The slaughter of the witnesses to Jesus has made the city drunk on power, consumed by bloodlust. But the attentive reader knows that their slaughter is truly victory (cf. 12.11) and that in drinking this cup of blood great Babylon drinks the wrath of God (cf. 14.4; 16.6). Those kings who drink with her are complicit, therefore, in this systemic brutality and will therefore share in the coming judgement.

In various ways, then, the figure of Babylon is depicted as lacking in freedom. She relies on the beast, and therefore the dragon, for her influence. She is branded as a slave, and she is not acting out of a clear mind but is intoxicated by her bloodlust. We cannot go so far as to exonerate her from guilt, since she is clearly complicit in her evil acts, but nor is she presented as entirely responsible. Babylon is, in a sense, caught up in evil structures not entirely of her own making, carried along by the bestial power summoned by the dragon. The city has become corrupted by its blasphemous participation with the true powers of evil that lie in the background, and that will themselves soon come to judgement.

Interpretation of the Vision, 17.6b–18

The vision is now interpreted. It is a common trope in apocalyptic literature for a guiding angel to explain the meaning of a vision (e.g., Dan 7.15–16). Revelation does not regularly do this, however, preferring to interpret visions with other visions, and so this is a rare moment (we also saw this sort of thing with the elder's explanation of the multitude in 7.13–14). As we will see, however, the angel's 'explanation' is far from totally clarifying, but itself introduces additional visionary language. John has not often drawn attention to his own emotions through his visionary experience (though cf. Rev 5.4), but here he tells the reader that he was greatly amazed and perplexed by what he saw. His angelic guide promises to explain 'the mystery [cf. v. 5] of the woman, and of the beast,' beginning with the latter.

The beast is described as the one John has already seen, confirming that the bestial steed of Babylon is the beast of Revelation 13. It is described, at the beginning and end of verse 8, as the one who 'was, and is not, [and is to come].' There are perhaps here echoes of the *Nero Redivivus* myth discussed earlier in relation to the beast's 'mortal wound' (13.3). More significantly, though, it is a twisted inversion of the thrice-repeated threefold divine title (1.4, 8; 4.8). God is the one 'who is and who was'; the beast is the one who 'was' and '*is not*.' There is a profound truth in this brief description of bestial evil as that which 'is not.' Its nature is non-being, the privation of all that is good. John's imagery of dragons, beasts, and whores should not lead us to view these powers of evil as entities with their own independent natural 'existence,' for that would grant them too much goodness. They do not create but lie, distort, corrupt, and destroy; untruth, distortion, corruption, and destruction are their very nature. What we call evil, and what John depicts in such bestial imagery, is the corruption and absence of goodness, as Augustine argued (see, e.g., *Enchiridion*, ch. 11; *City of God XI*, ch. 9).

God is not only the one who is but the one who 'is to come.' By contrast the beast is the one who ascends from 'the pit,' the place of destruction from which came the destroyer *Apollyon* (9.11, cf. 11.7). Yet it only ascends in order to 'go to destruction,' to the annihilating pit from which it came. This, as with all God's judgements in Revelation, is entirely appropriate. It is, after all, one of the 'destroyers of the earth' (11.18). Destruction itself is destined to be destroyed.

Though its essence is non-being, this bestial figure of corruption does not lack agency. It is deceptively attractive to the inhabitants of the earth whose names are not found in the book of life, who are amazed. The power of the beast looks to the world like divine power, though it is in reality its very opposite. They see that the beast 'was and is not and is to come,' not realising that it is not life but death, and it comes only to be destroyed.

Once again, we are told that this threat of deception calls for 'a mind with wisdom.' John made this appeal in 13.8, after telling of the number of the beast, and it is now repeated as the angel begins to explain the details of the present vision. It is practically a case study in the multivalent power of imagery. The beast's seven heads, the angel tells us, are seven mountains on which the woman sits. Rome was regularly called the city on seven hills, and so the reference to that imperial city is made clearer still. Once again, however, we must not allow this historical insight to kill the force of the metaphor. The city is exalted sevenfold, indicating its hubris and blasphemous claims to be lifted up over the whole earth—this, as we have seen, is the beast's regular claim to global dominion and the cause of its judgement. A simple decoding of the seven heads is further confused by John's statement that the heads are also, confusingly, seven kings. This is not a straightforward allegory but a many-sided image that requires a degree of imaginative 'bifocal vision' from the reader.

At this point we find a long line of commentators who have attempted to name the seven Roman 'kings' whom John has in mind. Much depends on the dating of the book, and the arguments here risk becoming circular. Usually, the seven emperors are counted off in order to arrive at a precise date for the book. But assumptions about dating regularly inform the task of counting emperors, not least the question of with whom one should begin (usually either Julius Caesar or Octavian/Augustus). This historical investigation is not an entirely futile endeavour, for John is clear that anti-God powers are at work in this world through 'real-life' historical systems and rulers. It is reasonable to assume that his first readers would have been able to name these seven emperors, counting back from their present moment, and there are enough details in their description to create a tantalising historical puzzle for us who read it two thousand years later. However, though potentially illuminating for connecting Revelation to its original historical context, the quest for precise identification of the list of kings can all too easily consume the modern interpreter's energies and threatens to pull us once more toward a flat 'decoding' of the narrative imagery, causing us to miss the main theological point being made.

Seven is a symbolic number, speaking of completeness. As with the seven seals or the seven trumpets, the point of these seven kings is to depict the beast's blasphemous claims to lordship of this world in its totality. The beast is not an abstract phenomenon but is manifest in this world through its 'heads,' human political rulers, and through the cities that are carried along by it. Not only that, but the arrangement of the seven kings is significant. Of the seven, five have come and gone, and one is still to come. The present moment is, therefore, the moment of the penultimate 'sixth king,' the time before the end. Hearers of Revelation, whether first century or twenty-first, are therefore to imagine themselves as those who live in this 'penultimate time.' As with the interludes before the seventh seal and the seventh trumpet, this penultimate moment is the time in which the church is called to bear faithful witness to the kingdom of God in the face of the kingdoms of this world, which are passing away. Any earthly claims of an eternal kingdom (whether Rome's or anyone else's) are vanity, for there is only one who has such sovereignty over the world, and he will cut short the reign of any who blasphemously claim an eternal dominion. God will imminently bring to their completion all earthly pretenders to the throne, with the arrival of the seventh king who will not rule eternally but for 'only a little while' (like the dragon, his time is *oligos*, 'short/little,' the same word used in 12.12). The appointed end of blasphemous human rule is inevitable, as is its soon curtailment. As we have seen, the beast rises up only to go to destruction.

If the list of seven kings were not confusing enough, the angel now explains that the beast itself is 'an eighth but it belongs to the seven.' What can this possibly mean? The number eight, as we saw in chapter 13 above, is associated with Christ, who rose on the 'eighth day' (see again *Sib Or* 1:324–30). It is possible, then, that there is a subtle parody of Christ in this 'eighth' who 'was and is not' (the third repetition of this anti-divine name). The angel is quick to point out that this eighth is not an eighth at all but belongs to the seven. The confusing nature of the counting (that number eight can belong to the seven) should give us pause before putting too much confidence in historical counting of kings. That said, it is possible that there is here a further allusion to the myth of *Nero Redivivus*, such that the eighth king is the return of one of the seven who has gone before. This much is certain: since it belongs to the seven, the beast itself is here understood as a king who comes from the list while also gathering all seven together into an eighth. That he is described as being 'out of the seven' may say less about an enumerated list of rulers than it does about the character of bestial rule itself. This rule is symbolically brought to completion in this eighth figure, in a parodic mockery of Christ's completion of and dominion over creation, won through his resurrection on the 'eighth' day. But although it represents the bestial power of empire in its military and political overreach, the image cannot be reduced to an abstract 'idea.' The systemic evil of politically abusive and idolatrous regimes takes physical form in this world, often distilled into one ruler. There is an eighth king, who is the living embodiment of bestial rule. Once again, though, we are immediately assured that this beast-king goes to destruction. Revelation does not leave the reader in suspense about the destiny of these anti-God powers: their end is as assured as the victory of the Lamb.

The angel continues, explaining the various aspects of the vision in turn (though his 'explanations' often raise more questions than they answer). As we listen, we continue our resistance to overly simplistic allegorical 'decoding,' seeking rather to attend to the literary and theological force of the imagery itself. The ten horns, he tells us, are also ten kings. Horns are a regular image for power, especially political/military power, and in the apocalyptic tradition a horn is a stock symbol for a king. This passage closely echoes the similar passage in Daniel 7.15–28, where Daniel's vision of the four beasts is interpreted. There, too, the ten horns are ten kings arising from the fourth bestial kingdom.

Since in John's vision the heads have already been interpreted as kings, how do these relate to the horns? One possibility is that the horns speak of vassal kings, closely related to the beast but not as intrinsically 'connected' as its heads are. We are told that they have not yet received a kingdom of their own and that they yield their power and authority to the beast. In any case, we are told quite plainly that their authority is both delegated and limited: 'they are to receive authority as kings for one hour.' This 'one hour' is another designation of the limited apocalyptic time (cf. Daniel's 'time, times, and half a time') in which the saints are to suffer at the hands of idolatrous earthly powers. They unite with the beast to make war on the Lamb and on the saints (suggesting that these horn-kings are the same as the 'kings of the world' gathered for war in 16.14). But again, the outcome of this would-be battle is already decided, a fact made immediately clear by the angel. The Lamb will have the victory, for he is already King of kings and Lord of lords. Their battle for lordship of this world is futile, for although the kings of the earth come together for battle, the Lord has already installed his conquering king (Ps 2), and those with him (called, chosen, and faithful) share in that victory.

The angel moves on to the rest of the vision. The waters on which the whore sits, he tells John, are 'peoples and multitudes and nations and languages.' Note again the fourfold phrasing: Babylon's influence, which relies heavily on maritime power, is one with a global reach. And yet, as so often with overreaching globalised powers, this universal influence belies an internal structural weakness. The horn-kings and the beast 'hate the whore.' Their relationship is not one of mutual trust and common endeavour, but of pure expediency. The relationships between the beast, the whore, and the kings of the earth are inherently degrading and instrumentalising at every turn. Though their synergy appears to have produced great wealth and global influence, we now have a developed picture of an inherently evil and unstable system built on exploitation rather than the common good. The whore is the slave of the beast whom she rides, and the beast hates the whore. The horn-kings are the vassals of the beast, surrendering their own power and authority to it, becoming its puppets (vv. 13, 17). And, lest we forget, the beast itself only possesses such authority because of the dragon, who stands invisible behind this whole complex of twisted human relations. The whole thing is a complex systemic evil that distorts and degrades God's purposes for human society. A political and economic system founded on violence and built on such terms cannot possibly stand. God's judgement, which is soon to be described in detail, takes the form not of imposing penalties from without but of allowing the inherent self-hatred of this Babylon system to have its way. The beast and the horns, to whom Babylon owes her wealth and global dominance, will soon strip her naked and devour her. The system 'eats itself.' Rome, which was the tangible form of this idolatrous system in John's time, learned this lesson the hard way. The great city who rules over the kings of the earth (though this status really belongs to Christ, 1.5) will fall to those very kings. We recall again, though, that interpretation of this imagery does not involve mere reduction to encoded historical facts but also allowing the imagery to continue to speak in our own world. Other Babylons have and will come and must heed the warning of this passage. The logic of empire, which we can discern in our own politics, economics, and elsewhere, has an inherent tendency to overreach and collapse from the inside, and God will judge human systems that are founded on exploitation and violence and that idolatrously claim the universal dominion belonging only to God. There is a call here for the Christian imagination to be re-formed, discerning Babylon in our world. It may look attractive, and it may promise great things for the world, but the saints must learn to see with new eyes and attend to the marks of the beast in our world.

The Judgement of Babylon, 18.1–19:10

Babylon Is Fallen! 18.1–8

For the next three chapters, the complex systemic evil composed of the dragon and its bestial and blasphemous associates is systematically undone, reversing the order of their introduction to the narrative, beginning with the judgement of Babylon before dealing with the beast and, ultimately, the dragon itself. The judgment promised in 17.1 now begins. Coming down from heaven is another angel, who has been given great authority by God to carry out the coming judgement. When he proclaims in a mighty voice that Babylon is fallen, we are not learning something new; we were told this way back in 14.8. We are reminded, once again, that Revelation's narrative is nonlinear. So now, chapter 18 circles back to Babylon's fall and explores it in more detail.

Practically the whole of chapters 18–19 takes the form of a 'cosmic oratorio,' a series of songs, the first of which has the character of a dirge or a lament for Babylon. Many other songs, short and long, will follow, filling the whole scene and rising to a crescendo with the great hymn of praise in chapter 19, reminding us that the book of Revelation is a distinctively liturgical text. The first song of the sequence is an angelic solo, a poetic oracle of Babylon's destruction, much like the similar oracle in Jeremiah 51. The great city has become desolate, home only to impure things (and therefore the complete opposite of the holy city, which we will see at the close of the book). Demons, foul spirits, birds, and beasts are all imprisoned here (the word *phylakē*, translated 'haunt,' can also mean 'prison'), echoing the description of the day of the Lord's vengeance in Isaiah 34. Once again, this is an image of the twisted and enslaving relationships that characterise the powers of evil right to their core: even demons themselves are not free but imprisoned in this corrupt city. 'Babylon the great' has become an utterly desolate and impure place. The cause of this desolation is made clear again: it is not only she who is judged but also the exploitative relationships she symbolises. The nations (all of them), the kings, and the merchants of the earth have engaged in corrupt relationships with her. We have met the nations and kings a number of times already, and the mention of them drinking 'the wine of the wrath of her fornication' directly quotes 14.8, but this is the first mention of the merchants, who will now play an important role in the judgement of Babylon. These relations between the various categories of people and the whore Babylon are again described as 'fornication,' the reduction of covenant union to mere economic transaction, and it is this commercial aspect of the idolatrous sociopolitical system that receives focussed attention in this chapter. Their involvement with Babylon has been of great profit to them, for they have 'grown rich from the power of her luxury,' but it is a profit that has come through investment in an idolatrous system, now to be judged.

What is the appropriate response of the people of God in the face of such an oracle of judgement? Another solo voice now speaks (or does it sing?) from heaven, the voice of God himself (since the address is to 'my people'), and makes clear what is called for. This divine instruction is a near-quotation of Jeremiah 51.45 and is just as urgent: 'come out of her, my people.' Historically and geographically, the primary audience of Revelation did not live in Rome but in the cities of Asia Minor, and so it is not clear what this command to 'come out' might mean if read in literal terms. But such crude literalism is not what is meant by the command. Just as the kings of the earth are united with Babylon, a union described in sexual terms as 'fornication,' so too the people of God are 'in' Babylon in various ways. The economic and political reality in the seven churches of Asia was, as we saw in chapters 2–3, complex. Some are suffering for their non-compliant faithful witness, while others appear to have reached a relatively comfortable compromised position with their contemporary sociopolitical powers. The obvious example is the church in Laodicea, who described themselves as prosperous and in need of nothing (3.17), a deluded self-description that sounds a lot like Babylon's own self-assessment in 18.7. They are not rich but poor and naked, just as Babylon here is stripped bare. Jesus had strong words for such compromises, and the voice from heaven is just as forceful here. There is no question of entertaining any investment in the Babylon system, for it rides the beast and gets its authority from the dragon. The system is so corrupt that any involvement represents a participation in her sins and thus a share in God's judgements. Like Babel's tower, these sins have piled up to heaven. Perhaps the people of God may have thought, like those in exile in historical Babylon, that their calling was to try to 'seek the welfare of the city' (Jer 29.7). To be sure, there are times when that is the church's proper purpose. But there is also a time to forsake the city, when its corruption has become so complete that it is beyond saving, where the church needs to hear a different word from Jeremiah: 'we have tried to heal Babylon, but she could not be healed. Forsake her, and let each of us go to our own country; for her judgement has reached up to heaven and has been lifted up even to the skies' (Jer 51.9). This connection between Revelation 18 and Jeremiah 51, and the simple urgency of the command to 'come out,' indicate that the people of God are called to the latter response, not the former. At such moments there is no room for a middle way of compromise, being 'in' Babylon but not 'of' it, or of trying to 'work from within' or 'heal the system' or some such thing. No, the simple and hard command to God's people here is to divest, and quickly. How is the church to discern when such a time has come, and how is it to obey this hard command, when Babylon's power covers the world? To paraphrase the psalmist, who sang beside the waters of historical Babylon, how are they to sing the Lord's song in a land ruled by this foreign power? This is a call for wisdom. And it is the calling of the faithful in every generation to recognise idolatrous systems in our world, to discern when a *status confessionis* has been reached, and to withdraw from them as a testimony to the reign of Christ, even if such a witness proves costly, knowing that God's judgement and reward are coming soon.

As he promised, God remembers Babylon (cf. 16.19) and answers the prayers of the slaughtered saints in administering justice. Throughout Revelation, there has regularly been an appropriate proportionality to God's judgement. There is a sense that the powers of evil get what they deserve, often in the form of God allowing sin to 'have its way' rather than administering direct retribution. We might expect, therefore, that the people are to flee from Babylon because the Lord is about to give her (in the words of Jeremiah 51.6) 'what is due.' At this point, however, along with this language of proportionate justice, there appears also to be disproportionality in divine wrath: Babylon is to receive not only 'as she herself has rendered' but also 'double for her deeds,' and a 'double draught . . . in the cup she mixed.' The Greek here is ambiguous. More literally rendered, verse 6 says 'render to her as she herself has rendered; double the doubled things according to her works.' Given the overwhelming preference in Revelation for appropriate proportionality in God's judgement, it is perhaps better to read this not as a disproportionate double punishment for Babylon's acts but a command to 'double' in justice where Babylon herself has 'doubled' her sins. This makes sense of the closing summary in verse 7, commanding a measure of torment and grief corresponding in measure to her self-glorification and ill-gotten luxury.

The nature of this self-glorification is further developed in the words that follow, which express the boasts of the imperial system. In Babylon's imagination, she is a queen whose reign will never see grief. These words, spoken in her heart, echo those attributed to 'mistress Babylon' in Isaiah 47.7–9, a passage John clearly has in mind:

> You said, "I shall be mistress forever,"
> so that you did not lay these things to heart
> or remember their end.
> Now therefore hear this, you lover of pleasures,
> who sit securely,
> who say in your heart,
> "I am, and there is no one besides me;
> I shall not sit as a widow
> or know the loss of children"—
> both these things shall come upon you
> in a moment, in one day:
> the loss of children and widowhood
> shall come upon you in full measure
> in spite of your many sorceries
> and the great power of your enchantments.

The promise of Rome was to build an eternal kingdom of peace and prosperity, and many kings and kingdoms were seduced by that promise. And yet Babylon's declarations of the permanence of her reign, untouched by grief and loss, are now exposed as arrogance and hubris. Such promises of an eternal reign can only be made by God and his anointed king. As such, Babylon's idolatrous boasts of eternal bliss will be exposed as the lies they are, her divine judgement coming 'in a single day.' If the people of God are to obey the command to 'come out,' they had better move fast.

The Lament of Kings and Merchants, 18.9–20

After these arias of lament and judgement, three chorus groups now sing their responses: the kings of the earth (vv. 9–10), the merchants of the earth (vv. 11–17a), and 'all whose trade is on the sea' (vv. 17b–20). As we will see, it is the mercantile aspect of Babylon that receives the most focus. But first we hear the wailing lament of the kings of the earth who, we are reminded, committed 'fornication' with Babylon (cf. 17.2; 18.3) and who came under her rule (17.18). Now, in 'one hour' she has met her end. Her luxury was their luxury, and so her swift demise is also theirs. And yet their relationship may have appeared a close one, but at her moment of destruction, the kings are not to be found in Babylon. They 'stand far off,' afraid to get too close once they see the 'smoke of her burning.' The relationship, however intimate, was always only a matter of expediency rather than solidarity. As Babylon burns, the kings stand at a distance. They weep and wail, to be sure, but there is a sense that their mourning is not so much for Babylon as for their own loss of power.

This self-interested motivation becomes clearer with the second group of mourners, the merchants. They weep and mourn loudly, but not for Babylon herself. They mourn the loss of their principal customer: 'no one buys their cargo anymore.' That was always the arrangement: these merchants never saw Babylon as their bride but always as their whore. Their relationship was a distortion, commercial without being covenantal, and of mutual benefit only inasmuch as it brought mutual satisfaction. It was a dehumanising distortion of good social and economic relationships. Now that her judgement has come, their tears are only for their own loss of profit. Before they sing, John makes sure the point is not missed by giving a list of their commodities. A similar list of wares can be found in the oracle against Tyre in Ezekiel 27, a passage that has clearly informed this whole section of Revelation. Twenty-eight items are listed, which is four times seven, suggesting a global and complete network of trade (Bauckham 1998, 31). Unlike Ezekiel, John does not explicitly name the places of origin in his commodities list. Some historical investigation confirms, however, that it represents trade from across the known world. Gold and silver came from Spain to the west, costly wood and ivory from Africa to the south. East of Rome was the spice route, bringing cinnamon, incense, and myrrh from Asia (for a fuller discussion see Bauckham 1998, 350–71). All of it was brought inward, to Rome, which consumed the commodities of its empire with an insatiable appetite.

The reader of the cargo list is arrested by its final item. At the bottom of the ledger are 'slaves—and human lives.' Ranked alongside cattle and sheep are, as the text literally puts it, 'bodies and souls of people.' John is careful to add 'human souls' (the word *psychē* can mean 'soul' or 'life') as a reminder that their trade was not simply in bodies, mere machines for cheap labour (lit., a 'human resource'), but in human lives, the very image of God commodified for profit (see Mangina 2010, 208, Koester 2014, 706). That a human soul should be listed on an imperial cargo list reveals the depths of corruption in which Babylon and her clients have been engaged. It is a fitting judgement on such abuses, then, that the merchants' song declares the total and permanent loss of all for which Babylon's 'soul' (again, *psychē*) had longed. It was a city built on desire and on the satisfaction of that desire at all costs. And now that city, which had been clothed in wealth and splendour, is laid waste in an hour. Like the kings of the earth before them, the merchants of these wares sing from 'far off, in fear of her torment.'

Along with the kings and merchants of the earth, a third and final party of mourners now joins the singing, though again they stand far off at the sight of 'the smoke of her burning.' Included among the mourners are 'all shipmasters, sailors, and all whose trade is on the sea.' Global trade on such a scale requires not only merchants but a vast network of seafarers, who, no doubt, also benefited greatly from Rome's prosperity and insatiable appetite. But such profit is not value-neutral. Revelation shows that God's judgement on Babylon reverberates through the entire economic system that had grown 'rich by her wealth' (v. 19) through being parasitic on her sin. If we were to ask a randomly selected first-century Mediterranean sailor his views on the moral and religious state of Rome, it is unlikely that we would receive a detailed response. No doubt some would, from time to time, have reflected on the content of their ship's hold, the origin and moral significance of their cargo, but such thoughts were likely fleeting and overshadowed by the need for a successful deal and a safe and profitable journey. Considerations of philosophical matters were for other people, higher up the chain. But that is how such systemic evil has always operated, and it is all too easy to claim deniability while profiting, however indirectly, from economic exploitation. This passage exposes all of that, laying bare God's judgement on the 'great city' and her whole economic network.

The seafarers' assessment of Rome is not, however, something left entirely to our historical imaginations. Their first cry reveals how they feel: 'what city was like the great city?' In words that echo those who earlier praised the beast, their rhetorical question invokes a call for comparison reserved for that which is most highly praised, even for God alone (see 13.4 and cf. Exod 15.11–12). Drunk on Babylon's wine, their desires disordered by her false beauty, they have believed her blasphemous lies and have traded (both figuratively and literally) the city of God for this so-called 'great city.' They are like a client who deceives themselves into thinking that the prostitute's smile means genuine affection, and now that she has fallen, they mourn. What future is there for them? They do not know it yet, but the overthrow of Babylon is their deliverance. For now, they mourn the loss of the 'great city' that made them rich, but by the end of the book another city will be revealed, and there is still time for them to switch allegiances.

The series of choruses closes with a stark contrast. As the kings, merchants, and seafarers mourn, another threefold group of people are told to rejoice. God's judgement on Babylon is cause for mourning by her clients but a cause for joy in heaven and for the 'saints, apostles, and prophets,' whose blood she had shed (cf. v. 24) and who are now vindicated by God. John will soon describe heaven's joyful response to Babylon's demise more expansively.

The Mighty Angel's Proclamation, 18.21–24

Before that joyful song is heard, though, the final section of chapter 18 returns to where it began, with an angelic solo proclaiming Babylon's fall. The three songs of lament are thus sandwiched between two oracles of judgment. A 'mighty angel' (*angelos ischyros*, a designation now appearing for the third and final time, cf. 5.2; 10.1) throws a stone into the sea, an object lesson and prophetic sign of Babylon's coming fall. This fall, which has twice been declared as complete, is now spoken of in the future. By now readers of Revelation should be used to such narrative and chronological nonlinearity. In this prophetic image there are clear echoes, once again, of Jeremiah 51 and the prophet's declaration of God's judgement against historical Babylon. After a poetic oracle of judgment against the city, Jeremiah is instructed to write the coming disasters on a scroll, read it aloud, then tie it to a stone and throw it into the Euphrates as a sign (Jer 51.59–64). Here in Revelation 18, the same 'mighty angel' whom we saw at the breaking of the sealed scroll in 5.2, and holding the little scroll in 10.1, now throws a millstone into the water to declare the judgment of the great city. It will not be a slow sinking, the gradual fading of a commercial empire, but violent and swift and permanent. The sounds of celebration and commercial activity that filled the city will suddenly be silenced (cf. Jer 7.34).

Like the prince-merchants of Tyre in Isaiah 23.8, Babylon's clients were the 'magnates of the earth.' But their greatness was founded on lies and violence, and all of that has now been cast down. The system of trade that made them great was not a neutral phenomenon but a sorcerer's deception propagated through idolatrous propaganda and imperial bloodshed. Babylon is only 'great' because of its reliance on the beast from the earth, who enforces the 'trade-mark' (13.17), and the beast from the sea, on whose back she has ridden (17.3). The two categories of mourners are drawn into this complex systemic evil, and they mirror these two beasts: they are the kings and merchants of the earth and the shipmasters and sailors on the sea. In their accumulation of wealth, they have been intimately involved, whether they knew it or not, in bestial powers summoned and given authority by the dragon. Too easily the church can have its desires disordered by the promise of power and the 'shiny things' of this world and thereby find itself drawn into complicity with this systemic evil. Revelation exposes Babylon for who she is and declares God's judgement, leaving the church with no excuse. No wonder that God's people are called to divest, to 'come out of her,' and no wonder that the end of such a systemic evil is now celebrated by all who were its victims.

The Multitude's Song of Praise, 19.1–10
The scene now begins to crescendo as the songs of mourning turn to a great mass chorus of heavenly praise, as indeed 18.20 had promised. Again it is what John hears that dominates the scene, as he continues to repeat the word *phonē* ('sound' or 'voice') that was found throughout the previous chapter, beginning with the sound/voice of 'a great multitude in heaven.' Perhaps this is the same great multitude John saw in Revelation 7.9. There is little description to tell us either way, but it certainly would make sense that this great crowd of martyrs would be the first to celebrate Babylon's demise. If so, then this song is the song of the church militant. Like the song in chapter 7, it is a celebration of the deliverance of God and his reign. The song launches with a great 'Hallelujah!' For a book that is full of songs of praise, it is remarkable that we have not yet heard this word (Mangina 2010, 217–18). Like a liturgical church at the end of the Lenten season, the word has been reserved and is now joyfully repeated four times in the space of six verses. The focus here, however, is on God's righteous judgement of Babylon, again described as a whore who has 'corrupted the earth.'

The crowd of worshippers, like the mourning kings (18.9) and seafarers (18.17) before them, see the smoke of Babylon's burning, though for them it is a sign of joy. The line that ends their song in verse 3, 'the smoke goes up from her forever and ever,' is a clear echo of Isaiah 34.10, a chapter to which John already alluded in the depiction of Babylon's desolation. It is followed by Isaiah 35, and its vision of the people of God in triumphant singing as they return to Zion, and Revelation 18–19 follows this same narrative progression, moving from the desolation of the corrupt city to the coming triumphant ingathering of the people of God.

As their song comes to an end, the multitude is joined by the rest of the cast from the heavenly throne room scene. The twenty-four elders and the four living creatures have not played a central role in this latter part of the book, but they have been mentioned a few times since the visions of chapters 4–7, and now they enter the narrative again to join the multitude in singing the final 'Amen' and another 'Hallelujah.' As such, the whole of heaven is united in praise. We last saw these characters in chapter 14, where they were present as the 144,000 sang a new song before the throne. We recall that in John's visionary world these two images for the church, as an eschatological army and a great crowd of worshippers, work together. In chapter 14, the sound that John heard was described as 'a voice from heaven like the sound of many waters and like the sound of loud thunder' (14:2), a near-identical description to the sound he now hears in 19.6. Perhaps, then, these are the same voices, and this song is that 'new song' of chapter 14, which only the redeemed army can learn.

The song is interrupted by a voice from the throne, which cannot be God's own voice since it tells the assembled worshippers to 'praise our God.' As such, we should read this as a voice from beside or in front of the throne, rather than that of its occupant. The close connection, however, underscores the ultimate divine approval of what the voice commands. Both 'small and great' (*hoi mikroi kai hoi megaloi*) are instructed to sing, fulfilling the promise of 11.18, where 'small and great' were promised reward when the destroyers of the earth were destroyed. By contrast, in 13.16 the mark of the beast was placed on both 'small and great.' It is a phrase that will be repeated twice more (in 19.18 and, with the order reversed, in 20.12) as the fulfilment of God's purposes are brought about. As we have seen, there is cutting economic critique in this section of the book, and the wealthy kings and merchants have received focussed attention in God's judgements on a corrupt economic system. But we are mistaken if we read this straightforwardly as some kind of economic reversal or financial revolution. Rather, it transcends the established economic classes. The 'small' can be made to wear the mark of the beast just as much as the 'great,' and the 'great' can sing the song of praise at Babylon's burning. After all, her destruction is their deliverance as much as it is the deliverance of the poor. The song now sung is not one only for the underclass, celebrating the demise of the rich, but a song for all people.

Again John tells us that he hears the voice of 'a great multitude,' now named for the third and final time, crying out 'Hallelujah!' This third chorus not only celebrates God's present reign but also points forward to an event that will mark the consummation of the book as a whole. The narrative turn from judgement to hope, like the one from Isaiah 34 to Isaiah 35, is now made. 'The marriage of the Lamb has come,' they declare, 'and his bride has made herself ready.' The reader has yet to meet the Bride of the Lamb (that will come in chapter 21), but she is briefly described in the closing lines of this song. As with the introduction of Babylon, once again Revelation's shuffled narrative places a key character and a decisive event out of narrative order, disorienting the reader and creating anticipation of the scenes to come, which will circle back and describe them in more detail. Her wedding day, we are told, has come.

In stark contrast to the gaudy attire and infidelity of the whore, the bride is clothed in 'fine linen, bright and pure,' suggesting fidelity and moral purity. There is a blink-and-you'll-miss-it narrative aside here, which explains the meaning of this image (a rare thing in Revelation, as we have seen). The clothing of the bride is 'the righteous deeds (*ta dikaiōmata*) of the saints.' Revelation repeatedly expresses the importance of deeds. Babylon's judgement is measured according to her deeds (*ta erga*, 18.6), and, by contrast, those who die in the Lord are blessed, 'for their deeds (*ta erga*) follow them' (14.13). Though the book is repeatedly clear that the saints are not redeemed by such good deeds but by the blood of the Lamb, there yet remains an eschatological importance for righteous works. It is what the church wears on her wedding day. There remains a close theological connection between these two soteriological themes, however, and we should recall that while this passage speaks of the saints' righteous deeds, the saints are also those who have washed their robes in the blood of the Lamb (7.14), and it is only through this that they are white. As such, these righteous deeds with which the bride is enrobed are not logically separate from the redemptive work of Christ but are an expression of the church's union with him in his death. The song of the multitude thus contrasts the two women, Babylon and Bride, and serves as a literary and theological bridge between the judgement of the former and the wedding day of the latter, which is soon to come.

The angel now speaks again to John, and his liturgical blessing brings this great heavenly oratorio to a close. Such benedictions are often skimmed by the reader, but if we do that we will miss another of Revelation's delightful mixed metaphors. 'Blessed are those who are invited to the marriage supper of the Lamb,' the angel says. If the bride is the church, and the Lamb her bridegroom, then who are the wedding guests? The imagery of the book of Revelation resists such overly simplistic correspondences, as we have seen. The people of God are both bride and guests, betrothed to the Lamb and invited to his wedding banquet.

John's response, at the closure of what was no doubt an emotionally draining experience, is to fall at the feet of the angel in worship. For this he is rebuked: only God is to be worshipped. The angel, however glorious, is but another of God's servants, a comrade of those who bear 'the testimony of Jesus' (*tēn martyrian Iēsou*). Once again the ambiguity of a short Greek expression poses us a question, as it did right from the beginning in 1.2, where a near-identical phrase was used to introduce the whole book. In 1.9 John told us that he was on Patmos because of 'the word of God and the testimony of Jesus.' More recently, back at the start of this long visionary section, the children of the woman were those who 'hold the testimony of Jesus' (12.17). What is meant by this phrase? Is it the church's testimony about Jesus, or is it Jesus's own testimony? Theologically speaking, both are true, for the church's primary calling is to bear witness to that which Christ testifies concerning himself (cf. Jn 18.37). Christ is the 'faithful witness' (1.5; 3.14) to whom the church bears witness, and he is both the origin and the content of that testimony. This is why the angel is only a 'fellow servant' with John—the angel is not the revealer but only another witness alongside John, testifying to the one who gave them this commission and who is himself the apocalypse of God. Such testimony, he tells John, is 'the spirit of prophecy.' The self-revelation of God in Christ, as both origin and content of the church's witness (and that of the angels!) is what constitutes and empowers the prophetic ministry. At its heart, the ministry of the prophet is not to engage in abstract prognostication, or even simply rebuke or encouragement, but is fundamentally the act of pointing away from oneself to Jesus, bearing testimony to him (Barth, *CD* IV/3.2, 614). This is why this whole book is the 'apocalypse of Jesus Christ.' As the book cycles one more time toward its glorious conclusion, it is therefore appropriate that what comes next is a vision of Christ himself.

Seven Final Visions

Revelation 19.11–20.15

The combined effect of the great fourfold Hallelujah chorus (19.1–8), the pronouncement of the wedding day (19.7–8), and the angel's liturgical benediction and confirmation of the testimony (19.9) is that it seems as if the book is about to end. But John's apocalypse is not quite finished. Babylon may have fallen, but we have not yet seen the final outworking of God's judgement of his enemies, the beast and the dragon, the true 'destroyers of the earth.' And so John will now be given one final sequence of seven visions that provide a cosmic perspective on divine judgement, the vindication of the saints, and the establishment of God's eschatological kingdom.

Unlike the sequences of seals, trumpets, and bowls, these final seven visions are not explicitly numbered, though by now the reader does not really need such hand-holding. The visions of this final sequence are introduced by a sevenfold repetition of the phrase *kai eidon*, 'and I saw' (19.11; 19.17; 19.19; 20.1; 20.4; 20.11; 20.12). Much of the material in these last two chapters has been aural, but it is the sense of sight that dominates John's final revelatory experience.

The visionary setting is provided in the first scene. There is a sort of return to where we began, with John on earth once again seeing 'heaven opened' (19.11; cf. 4.1). However, this time the opening of heaven is followed not by an invitation to ascend but by a procession of visions emanating from heaven to earth. The end of the previous section, in the first part of chapter 19, has led the reader to expect a wedding day. That day is coming, but before that great nuptial vision we are first transported again to the battlefield.

Vision 1: The Rider on the White Horse, 19.11–16

As heaven is opened, the first thing John sees is a white horse. The reader is reminded of the first of the four horsemen in chapter 6, who rode out to conquer. As John turns his attention to this rider, however, it becomes clear that he is an entirely different figure, to whom the former conquering horseman pales in comparison. This mounted warrior rides to battle, but he does so in righteousness. Once again John is working within a long tradition of depicting God's judgement in terms of a holy war, reaching back to the crossing of the Red Sea in Exodus 14 and echoing as a note of eschatological hope through the prophets (e.g., Isa 63.11–12; Joel 3.11; Zech 14.3–5).

Though this passage introduces a new Christological vision, John's description repeatedly echoes the imagery of the book's opening visions of Jesus. The Rider has eyes of fire, and a sharp sword comes from his mouth, like the Son of Man in the first chapter (1.14, 16; cf. 2.16). His warfare and judgement are based on a searing and penetrating vision and executed by his words of testimony. Though he is clearly a conqueror, he is seen now crowned not with the victor's wreath (as the Son of Man was in 14.14) but with many royal diadems, indicating his true right to rule. The beast and the dragon may have worn diadems (12.3; 13.1), but their would-be reign is soon to end as the one who rides out to meet them is he who truly rules.

The rider himself is given four names in this short passage, the first of which is 'Faithful and True' (*pistos kai alēthinos*), a name that in Revelation can only apply to Jesus Christ. One of the first things said about Jesus is that he is the 'faithful witness' (1.5), and the last of the seven messages to the churches is signed off by him as 'the Amen, the faithful and true (*pistos kai alēthinos*) witness' (3.14). As we will see, this is not the only verbal thread connecting this image to the Christological vision of Revelation's opening chapters. In naming the rider 'Faithful and True,' the image of a warrior is immediately woven with Jesus's role as witness. Already, then, we have indications of what sort of war it is that he wages. The deceiver, and all who stand with him in his lies, will be defeated by the faithful witness of the one who is Truth itself. We should not be surprised to learn that the act of bearing testimony is integral to what it means for this rider to conquer, for Revelation has repeatedly made this connection clear (e.g., 12.11). John further mixes his metaphors in telling us that the Rider not only makes war but also 'judges.' The faithful witness is also the righteous judge.

The second name the Rider is given is one that 'no one knows but himself.' This mystery has generated all sorts of speculation. It could be the same as the other inscribed name, given in verse 16, 'King of kings and Lord of lords.' It could indicate this figure's essentially incomprehensible nature, for to name him completely would reduce him to human understanding. In the light of all the other connections back to the opening Christological vision, however, it is more likely that this is an allusion to the 'new name' promised by Christ to the Philadelphian church in 3.12 (also Pergamum in 2.17), where it is explained as 'the name of my God . . . and my own new name.' That promise was given to those who conquer, and so it is right that it is inscribed on this conquering Rider who, as we will soon see, is accompanied by his people.

His third name is 'the Word of God,' which reminds us of the great prologue of John's Gospel with its echoes of the creation story. Here in Revelation, as we saw when considering the book's opening words, Jesus is not only the one who reveals things to John but is also that which is revealed. He not only speaks but is also the very Word spoken, divine speech enfleshed, God's *apocalypse*.

As he rides out from heaven he is clothed, John tells us, with a bloodied robe. Toward the end of this vision, we are also told that he rides out to 'tread the winepress of the fury of the wrath of God the Almighty,' taking us back to the vision of chapter 14 and the close association between divine judgement and the image of a winepress, and between wine and blood. As we saw in that earlier discussion, this imagery of a grape harvest and winepress as a picture of divine judgment is drawn from Joel 3.11–13 and from Isaiah 63 (a passage that also make connections to the divine warrior motif of Exodus, discussed above). Two insights can be gleaned from reading this passage in the light of this prophetic tradition, Isaiah in particular.

First, there is a simple but profound Christological implication hidden in the statement that it is the Rider who treads the divine winepress. In Isaiah's vision of the winepress, the Lord alone tramples the grapes, and none helps him (63.3). God makes it abundantly clear that his own arm brings him victory (63.5). None other than he has the right to execute his judgement and bring his victory. And yet here it is the Rider who is given that task. The Rider performs an act of judgement reserved for God alone.

Second, there is the more complex question of whose blood it is that stains the Rider's robe. In Isaiah, God is depicted as a warrior returning from battle, dressed in robes spattered red 'like theirs who tread the winepress' (Isa 63.2). There is little doubt that the juice represents the blood of enemies (Isa 63.3). However, when we discussed John's adaptation of the divine winepress imagery in Revelation 14, we saw that it was not so clear whose blood flowed from the press. There is a similar ambiguity in this passage about whose blood it is that stains the Rider's robe. To be sure, it may well indicate the blood of his enemies, and this would be a natural reading of the warfare imagery, tracking with the logic of Isaiah 63. But, as we have seen many times, Revelation's use of Old Testament imagery is rarely so straightforward. What we usually see is a complex tapestry of interconnected allusions and mixed or reinvented metaphors, deployed by John to subvert the normal expectations of his imagery. The expectations raised by the announcement of the Lion of Judah, we recall, were subverted and transformed by the vision of the slain Lamb (5.1–8).

We note that the Rider here is not returning from a battle, as in Isaiah 63, but riding out to one, which will be described in the next passage. How can his robes be stained with blood if the battle has not yet begun? Careful attention to John's use of the image of blood is required. As we saw in our discussion of the winepress in chapter 14, nowhere else does Revelation use the image of blood in relation to God's enemies. It forms part of the imaginative lexicon of eschatological judgment, to be sure, in the images of a blood-red moon or waters turned to blood. But when it is mentioned as belonging to someone it is universally the blood of the Lamb, or of the saints and prophets, that John has in mind (16.6; 17.6; 18.24; 19.2). And so if this is an image of the blood of the Rider's enemies, it is the only such image in the book. This, combined with the fact that the Rider's robe is already stained red before the battle has begun, suggests that the blood is not that of his enemies but is his own. Just as the conquering Lion is the slain Lamb, and vice-versa, so too the Rider conquers by his own blood. And it is also by his blood that he ransomed for God a multitude from every nation, who will share his reign (Rev 5.9). It is to such a vision of his co-regents that John now turns.

The Rider is accompanied by the 'armies of heaven,' who ride out with him on matching horses. Who are these who follow him into battle? It is possible that they are angelic forces, the hosts of heaven. It is more likely, however, that this is an image of the church, since their description closely matches Revelation's accounts of the church elsewhere. They are dressed in pure fine linen, which could make us think of the angels in 15.6 who were similarly enrobed. However, white robes are more often mentioned as the attire of the people of God. They were promised to the conquerors in Sardis (3.5) and Laodicea (3.18) and given to the slain saints under the altar in 6.11 while they awaited eschatological vindication. That those accompanying the Rider are described as an army reminds us of the 144,000-strong force of chapters 7 and 14, who follow the Lamb to eschatological war. We saw in our discussion of chapter 7 that the militaristic imagery was reinterpreted by what John saw next, an innumerable multitude dressed in robes washed white in the blood of the Lamb (7.14, a connection that further supports the reading above). Again, and closer to hand, in 19.8 fine and pure linen was promised to the Bride to wear on her wedding day. All of these different images of the church now come together, as the followers of the Rider are simultaneously an army, a sacrifice, and a bride.

It is the military metaphor that dominates the scene, as Jesus is presented in his power and rule, a Rider who strikes down the nations. His weapon, however, is not the bow carried by the horseman of chapter 6 but the 'sword from his mouth' (cf. 1.16; 2.16). The one who is the Word conquers by his words of testimony, as do his armies (again see 12.11). He is not only the conqueror of the nations but their ruler, a truth John signals with an allusion to Psalm 2, as he did in the cosmic battle with the dragon back in chapter 12. This Rider, then, is the same royal son of 12.5, snatched away from the dragon to God and his throne, destined to return to rule the nations. Just as God declared concerning his anointed in Psalm 2, in vain the nations contest his rule, for it is assured. The Rider is also, however, the same one who promised to share his rule over the nations with his church in Thyatira, promising the iron rod of rulership to those who conquer (2.27). As his army rides out with him, they are assured that the outcome does not hang in the balance, for they share in a victory already won and an authority to rule already gained.

It is entirely appropriate, therefore, that this vision of the Rider closes with his fourth and final name, inscribed on his robe and on his thigh and declaring his right to rule the nations: 'King of kings and Lord of lords.' His rod of rulership, however, is not an image of oppression, swapping one brutal imperial regime for another. Once again John is weaving together multiple Old Testament images in forging his new visions. The image of the rod connects Psalm 2 to Isaiah 11, where it is called the 'rod of his mouth' (Isa 11.4). The Rider's rule, like his conquering, is by his word of testimony, and it is in this way that the church shares in his rule—not through an exercise of worldly political or military power but through the 'testimony of Jesus Christ,' even if that leads to sharing in his sufferings and death. As Revelation repeatedly makes clear, this is the way of the Lamb's victory and the means of his rule.

Vision 2: The 'Supper of God,' 19.17–18

After this opening vision of Christ, the rest of the seven unnumbered visions come thick and fast. The next thing John sees is an angel, standing 'in the sun' and calling out to all the birds in midheaven, gathering them to a great supper. In Revelation 8.13, during the trumpet sequence, John also saw a bird flying 'in midheaven,' either an eagle or a vulture (Greek uses the same word *aetos* for both). Here in chapter 19, it is likely that the birds are vultures or something similar, for instead of the invitation to a wedding supper, the angel calls to the birds to gather to eat carrion from the battlefield. The 'great supper of God' is depicted in horrific terms, for the flesh of God's enemies is on the menu.

As we saw in that earlier discussion in chapter 8, this is an apocalyptic image attested in the sayings of Jesus (Mt 24.28; Lk 17.37), where he is teaching his disciples about the end of the age and the coming of the Son of Man, complete with references to Daniel. Like Jesus, John is not using this image in a literal sense, of the actual eating of the flesh of dead soldiers, but as an apocalyptic sign of the end of the age. It is an image also found in Ezekiel 39, where the Lord God, having defeated the assembled forces of Gog, instructs the prophet in similar terms:

> As for you, mortal, thus says the Lord GOD: Speak to the birds of every kind and to all the wild animals: Assemble and come, gather from all around to the sacrificial feast that I am preparing for you, a great sacrificial feast on the mountains of Israel, and you shall eat flesh and drink blood. You shall eat the flesh of the mighty, and drink the blood of the princes of the earth—of rams, of lambs, and of goats, of bulls, all of them fatlings of Bashan. You shall eat fat until you are filled, and drink blood until you are drunk, at the sacrificial feast that I am preparing for you. And you shall be filled at my table with horses and charioteers, with warriors and all kinds of soldiers, says the Lord GOD. (Ezek 39:17–20)

The larger section of Ezekiel in which this vision is found, chapters 38–48, is alluded to throughout these closing chapters of Revelation, not only for its imagery but also for its narrative arc, as God gives Ezekiel visions of his judgement of his enemies in battle (Ezek 38–39), the return of the glory of the Lord to the eschatological temple (chs. 40–47), and the restoration of the people to the land (47.13–48.35; cf. 39.21–29). John, like many readers of his day, is not restricted to allusions that rely only on echoing vocabulary. He also alludes to and adapts the themes, structures, and narratives of his Old Testament source texts. As John borrows the apocalyptic image of the carrion birds from Ezekiel 39, he also echoes the structure of that section of the book and begins a narrative sequence that will end with the new temple, the new heaven, and the new earth.

But let us not get ahead of ourselves. Once again there is a universal scope to divine judgement. John draws particular attention to the leaders of the armies of the dragon, the kings and captains, the mighty ones and their horses (cf. 16.14). But he also reminds us that 'both free and slave, both small and great' are subject to the coming judgement. Just as both 'small and great' were commanded to praise God and fear him by the heavenly voice (19.5), so there is also a universal scope to this vision of God's judgement.

Vision 3: The Beast Defeated, 19.19–21

As the third vision begins, again with the phrase 'I saw,' the reader is primed for a great final battle scene. The beast gathers his forces, the kings of the earth with their armies, and marches to war against the Rider and the armies of heaven. What follows is remarkably anticlimactic. Before an arrow is fired or a sword unsheathed, the beast is captured. There is no battle, for it has already been won in the heavenly war of chapter 12. What we are seeing here is simply the outworking of that victory. This is inevitable, for (unlike in some other ancient dualistic combat myths) light does not need to battle against darkness, or truth against falsehood, as if they were two equal-and-opposite powers. Darkness has no 'being' as such but is merely the absence of light. And lies are the absence of truth. Likewise, though it fought against the angels in heaven and has exercised a terrifying agency on the earth, the dragon is not a cosmic power locked in eternal struggle against God but only a deceiver and the embodiment of non-being. The presence of Truth dispels the father of lies. And nothingness must capitulate when confronted with the arrival of the one 'who is' (1.8).

And so there is profound theological significance in the way John narrates the outcome of this would-be battle, with an abrupt, almost dismissive quality. The beast from the earth is immediately captured, and with it the false prophet who had deceived the inhabitants of the earth. These two embodiments of structural evil are then thrown into the lake of fire. This is the first mention of the 'lake of fire,' which will be mentioned four more times in the next two chapters. Clearly, this is something different from the shadowy 'abyss,' the abode of evil forces, since it is a place of annihilation and judgement, indicated by the presence of sulphur. The systemic evils embodied by the beast and the false prophet are the first to be thrown into this sulphurous lake. They will soon be joined by their master the devil in 20.10, before Death itself is thrown into this 'second death' (20.14). With the completion of that sequence of judgements, the 'destroyers of the earth' (11.18) will be destroyed.

But what of the kings and their armies? It is significant that they are not thrown into the lake of fire with the two beasts who had deceived them. Instead, they are 'killed by the sword of the rider on the horse.' Have God's purposes to bring about human repentance ultimately failed, then? We should remember John's Christological adaptation of Ezekiel's imagery, that the sword which slays the kings of the earth comes from the Rider's mouth—it is his word that is his weapon. What does it mean for these kings to be 'killed' by a word of testimony? A war against lies is won by the weapon of truth, and as such the sword from the Rider's mouth slays the forces of deception. Those hearing the book for a second time, however, will know that, despite the apparent finality of this image of destruction, this is not the end of these kings. Even though the vision closes with unclean birds eating their fill of the flesh of the kings, they will be seen again among those who enter the New Jerusalem in the book's closing chapters (21.24). Though this image shows the fate of those who refuse to repent of their idolatry and persist in allying themselves with bestial systems, it also shows that this rebellion against God is based on deception and that this judgement it is not God's final word.

Before that final word can be spoken, however, there must be the completion of these seven visions, and above all the consummation of God's judgement of his enemies and the vindication of his people. Babylon has fallen, the beasts have been thrown into the lake of fire, and the deceived kings of the earth lie on the battlefield as food for unclean birds, but all these are merely pawns in this great war. Behind them all stands the true enemy, the dragon, and the time for its judgement has now come.

Vision 4: The Binding of Satan, 20.1–3

The fourth thing that John sees is another angel, descending from heaven. Just like the star of chapter 9 (and perhaps this is the same figure), the angel holds the key to the abyss, reminding us that this realm is not an alternative kingdom but that it, too, is under the authority of heaven. It was in God's authority to release the destroyer and the locust army from that pit, and it is in God's authority to send evil back there. There is no great cosmic showdown; one angel is all it takes to seize the dragon. How small it seems now! We are reminded, as we were when it entered John's narrative in 12.9, of its many names, the dragon, the 'ancient serpent,' the devil (*ho Diabolos*), and the Satan (*ho Satanas*), which means 'deceiver.' Through its bestial minions the dragon may have convinced the nations of the earth of its great power, but that is now revealed for what it is: a paper-thin deception and a mockery of God's true authority.

The angel does not engage the dragon in battle, for there is no need: that primordial battle took place in heaven in chapter 12 and was won there by Michael and his angels. What we see now is the earthly and final outworking of that primordial heavenly victory. We must not forget that the devil has already been defeated and knows it (12.12), and so all that remains is its final judgement. The angel simply seizes the dragon and, just as Michael cast it down in 12.9, throws it into the pit, where it is bound and chained. The deceiver is incarcerated and prevented from deceiving the nations any longer. In such a way—it is almost an anticlimax—God defeats his great enemy.

The prince of falsehood and corruption is defeated by truth. There is a great reversal here: the devil, who threw the saints of Smyrna into jail (2.10), now receives that same judgment. Why, though, is this apparently only an interim judgement so that, after a thousand-year term of imprisonment, the dragon will be released again for 'a little while'? Why is it not now cast into the lake of fire with the beasts and finally judged as they were? The answer to that conundrum lies in the next vision and in John's narrative purposes more generally.

We have seen John's many allusions to Ezekiel through shared imagery and expressions. As noted above, there is also a relationship between the two books on the level of narrative structure. In these last chapters, John's narrative has not only been alluding to Ezekiel's imagery but has been echoing the narrative arc of its closing chapters. God has judged his enemies in battle (Rev 19.11–20.3; cf. Ezek 38–39), and now the story moves to its conclusion with the restoration and vindication of his people before the final return of the glory of the Lord to his temple (Rev 20.4–22.21; cf. Ezek 40–48). A similar narrative trajectory can be traced in another apocalyptic prophecy to whom John is clearly indebted, the book of Daniel. The chapter that has provided much of John's imaginative encyclopaedia, Daniel 7, likewise involves the judgement and destruction of beasts and the establishment of the eternal dominion of the Son of Man and the restoration of the people of God, though the precise ordering of all of Daniel's plot elements is altered by John (on which see Woodman 2013, 226, and Bauckham 1993, 106–107). The plot of Revelation's closing chapters has traced a similar arc. In these final four visions, John interlocks the judgement of Satan with its important narrative corollary: the vindication of the saints. This first vision shows Satan bound; what follows is a vision of the vindication of the saints (20.4–6) before the pattern is repeated in the sixth (20.11) and seventh (20.12–15) visions. This rapidly alternating narrative sequence completes both the 'negative' aspect of God's judgment (the destruction of Satan) and its 'positive' aspect (the vindication of God's people), before the great final consummation of God's purposes can be described. Without the vindication of the saints, the judgement of God remains incomplete.

Vision 5: The Millennial Reign and Satan's Defeat, 20.4–10

In the fifth vision of this sequence, John sees thrones (plural, not singular—that is to come) and describes a scene of the slaughtered saints given authority to sit on them and to reign with Christ for a thousand years. He does not explicitly state where these thrones are, but the connections to Daniel 7.9–14 that are made by this image, and that run through this whole passage, suggest that this is a heavenly vision. It is a remarkable feature of Revelation's history of reception that these three verses have been the cause of so much discussion, not only in modern scholarship but as far back as the church fathers, and that theories about this short paragraph of the book have spawned entire schools of eschatological interpretation. The thousand years of Satan's imprisonment (20.2–3) are also the thousand years of the church's authority, this much is sure. From this insight, and working with the assumption that what is described here is a literal earthly reign of a thousand years, entire systems are constructed around the espousal of either pre-millennial (Jesus's return comes before the thousand-year reign) or post-millennial (Jesus's reign follows the thousand years) interpretations. As with all such apocalyptic expressions in the book of Revelation, however, it is a category error to try to plot these years on a calendar. Pre-millennial and post-millennial readings of whatever sort represent a misreading of Revelation's imagery, treating the book as a code to be cracked and the solutions indexed prosaically to an earthly historical timeline. It is a fundamental misreading of this apocalyptic imagination to ask, in such a way, 'when' this 'thousand years' happens.

The thousand years is, as with all other numerical images in this book, a symbolic number, simply representing a long period of time. This must not be read, however, as a way to defuse the power of this image or explain away the problem of the millennium in vague 'spiritual' terms. Rather our desire is to allow the image to have its full theological and literary force. Therefore, rather than attempting to decode the image into some historical timeline, killing its power, or place the millennium on an eschatological timetable of whatever sort, we are concerned with the more interesting question of what this image means theologically. We ask not the question 'when?' but 'why?' Why is there only a limited period (albeit a very long one) in which the saints rule on thrones while Satan languishes in the pit?

The answer to this question (a far more fruitful and appropriate one) is that God's justice is not merely a matter of restraint and retribution but also of restoration. There is an unhurried progression in God's judgement of the Satan. It was first banished from heaven, then incarcerated in the pit to await its final judgement. But be assured that its end, like that of the beast, is destruction. God is in no rush—Satan's final doom will come, as will the saints' final restoration, but first God rolls back and removes from his world all traces of the destroyer's influence. God's justice and his restoring purposes require that Satan's deceit must not only be punished but also reversed, and so his 'short' (12.12) reign of lies is overturned by this image of a 'thousand years' of truth. Likewise, the slaughtered saints must not only be avenged but also publicly vindicated, and so after being told to wait under the altar for a 'little while' (6.11) they are here described as seated on thrones for a 'thousand years' and given authority to judge. Thus the image of the millennium speaks powerfully of the vindication of the saints and the essentially limited nature of the dragon's power, despite appearances and despite its own claims. Those who had been judged and beheaded because of the word of God and their 'testimony of Jesus' (John repeats this delightfully ambiguous phrase; see the discussion at 1.2 and 19.10) are destined to be raised to life to judge and to reign with Christ.

The dominion that the dragon sought to grasp has been handed to the martyred saints: this is the purpose and core meaning of this image, and we need not push it much further than this (so Bauckham 1993, 106–108). This 'first resurrection,' and the thousand-year reign of the slain people of God, represents the vindication of God's people, whether or not they are literally martyred. John does not imagine a separate class of Christians—all are called to bear witness and to share in the faithful testimony of Jesus. As such, the martyred saints here stand for all witnesses. A greater resurrection is still to come, and a greater restoration of the earth itself, but without this 'first' resurrection the cries for justice from under the altar would not have been appropriately heard. God does not simply meet his enemies with a greater display of force, wiping them from the earth, but instead exposes their lies and restores what they have destroyed. Without such restorative justice there can be no peace for the earth, only the replacement of power with power. This image is the visionary reversal of Satan's purposes and the vindication of those who suffered under his reign of terror.

Though the often-contentious matter of the millennium's timing is now appropriately relegated in our reading, as it is in John's narrative, we are not bound to total silence in response to the 'when?' question. The 'thousand years' is a long but limited period of time during which Satan is bound and the church is rewarded for their faithful witness unto death. As with all attempts to understand this image, we broaden our scope to other New Testament passages that might help us. Interpreters since Augustine (though it even predates him) have made a connection between the binding of Satan in Revelation 20 and Jesus's words in Mark 3.27, where he speaks of 'binding the strong man.' Mark's gospel returns to this image in chapter 5, in the story of the Gerasene demoniac. There Jesus encounters a chained, strong man (Mk 5.4) who is possessed by the demon(s) called *Legion*. Jesus casts them out, sending them down into the watery abyss. The connections are theologically tantalising. Perhaps, then, the binding of Satan and the inauguration of the millennial reign that are described in Revelation, if we are to read that image in relation to human history, happened at the incarnation, with Christ's earthly ministry. To say that, however, is merely to note the intersection, in human history, of the binding of God's enemies that took place in heaven before the foundation of the world. We are thus now only speaking of 'history' in a strictly qualified sense, and without any attempt to index these 'thousand years' to the chronological life of the earth, whether literally or figuratively. The 'thousand years' is the time of the reign of Christ on earth established in his incarnation and at the cross, to which the church bears witness and in which they share by their word of testimony. To bring in another of the Gospels, this is why Jesus can say, following the return of the seventy from their ministry of testimony, that he 'watched Satan fall from heaven like a flash of lightning' and that the disciples had authority over 'all the power of the enemy' (Lk 10.19–20). The millennium is thus another of John's nonlinear narrative recapitulations, another image of the 'time' of the church's witness, variously described throughout the book of Revelation. In saying all this, however, we do not read the 'church age' as some kind of univocal and steady outworking of this millennial reign. We must be careful not to allow this one image of the church's reign to become detached from the truth of Satan's agency in the world, as if this image is the only one that speaks of the church's present situation. We recall that Revelation requires of its readers an apocalyptic 'bifocal vision.' From the earthly perspective, this does not seem to be a golden age at all but rather a time of trial and faithful testimony, with Satan on the move deceiving the nations, and such it is. From this heavenly perspective, however, it is a time of rule and reign, sharing in the victory of Christ, with Satan bound and unable to deceive. Both are true, and an appropriate assessment of the present state of things requires that we 'think doubly' about these things. Such 'double-vision,' however, is only required of those who live within the tensions of human history. Its final consummation will be univocal: the first resurrection is the vindication of the saints in this present time, characterised by such theological tension. The second resurrection, still to come, is the final restoration of God's world. To that glorious vision we will soon turn.

After this symbolic thousand years is ended, the Satan is released from its prison. Its (inevitably doomed) attempts to deceive and corrupt God's world are then described once more, the vision thus returning to the theme of Satan's judgement. John makes his allusions to Ezekiel explicit at this point, naming 'Gog and Magog' as the nations gathered for a would-be final battle. Ezekiel 38–39, however, describes a great battle with the prince Gog *of* Magog, and so John has adapted this image in calling Gog a nation. In the narrative and imagery of Revelation, whom do these nations represent? In chapter 16, in the penultimate sixth bowl judgement, the dragon, beast, and false prophet deceived the 'kings of the whole world' (16.14) and gathered them for the would-be battle of Harmagedon, only to hear the declaration of God's victory already won and the closure of the sequence with the seventh bowl and the storm theophany. Again, in the third vision of this final sequence of seven (19.19–21, which also alluded to Ezek 39), all the kings of the earth and their armies took the field against the Rider and his armies. The world was divided in two: those who bore the mark of the beast and those who bore the name of God. There were no neutral nations left, and the finality of that battle was such that there were no survivors on the side of God's enemies. 'Gog and Magog,' and their innumerable armies, cannot, therefore, stand as a symbol of some remaining human kings. Rather there is a sense of John once again recapitulating the visions of the earlier chapters, describing that same would-be final battle from a new angle.

The forces surround the city where the saints rule, expecting a fight, but there isn't one. As in every other image John deploys to express this final great Day, Satan's forces are immediately consumed by fire from heaven. Now, at last, comes the final judgement of the devil. It is taken again, and this time thrown into the lake of fire to join the beast and the false prophet. And with that, the three powers of evil are consigned to fire, reversing their order of their appearance, as God systematically destroys those who would 'destroy the earth' (11.18). There, we are told, this demonic trinity is 'tormented day and night forever and ever.' What does it mean for the systemic evils represented by the beast and the false prophet to be tormented? And what sort of torment can be given to the devil, the one who is the embodiment of nothingness itself? We cannot speak with certainty about such things. It may help, however, to consider John's use of the well-worn apocalyptic phrase *eis tous aiōnas tōn aiōnōn*, translated 'forever and ever.' The phrase, which can be more literally rendered 'unto the ages of ages,' has more to do with the *quality* of that future 'age' than its *quantity*. And since the quality of that 'age to come' is one saturated with divine life, it is impossible to countenance the enduring existence of sin and nothingness in any meaningful sense. Eternal existence, in the sense of agency and personality 'going on forever and ever,' is simply too good for the devil, even if that existence is one of punishment. When God comes, he comes as a consuming fire that burns away all such corruption so that he may be 'all in all' (1 Cor 15.28).

Vision 6: The Great White Throne, 20.11

The sixth thing John sees is another throne vision, assuring the reader that through all the chaos of what has been seen, God has not left his place of sovereign rule. Unlike the detailed throne room description we saw in chapters 4 and 5, now John now takes only one verse to describe the throne and the one seated on it. The brevity of description is appropriate since, as everywhere else in Revelation, the occupant of the throne is so glorious that he cannot be described. No image, whether verbal or material, can or should be fashioned of him. Here the focus is entirely on the enthroned one. There is no description of the heavenly court, the living beings or elders or angelic attendants—John's vision is entirely filled by the throne and the one seated on it. Even heaven and earth themselves flee from his presence. We recall that heaven has, however, already been rolled up like a scroll, and every mountain and island has been removed twice over (6.14; 16.20). As John's narrative cycles back to this theme for a third time, there is a sense of completeness and finality, which is only underscored by this economical description.

With this return to the throne room, John continues to develop his prophetic allusions, not least to one of his favourite passages, Daniel 7. In that apocalyptic dream-vision, Daniel describes his own throne scene as follows:

> As I watched,
> thrones were set in place,
> and an Ancient One took his throne,
> his clothing was white as snow,
> and the hair of his head like pure wool;
> his throne was fiery flames,
> and its wheels were burning fire.
> A stream of fire issued
> and flowed out from his presence.
> A thousand thousands served him,
> and ten thousand times ten thousand stood attending him.
> The court sat in judgment,
> and the books were opened. (Dan 7.9–10)

John alluded to the details of Daniel's description of the 'Ancient of Days' way back in his opening Christological vision (1.14). As we have already noted, however, it is the arc of Daniel's narrative that John picks up in this vision sequence. In the fifth vision, John, like Daniel in verse 9, sees many thrones. Now in the sixth vision he turns to the great throne of the Ancient One before moving on to describe the opening of books and the final judgement.

John has adapted Daniel's 'timeline' for the vindication of the saints, the judgement of the earth, the destruction of the blasphemous beast, and the handing over of dominion. For one thing, the order of those elements has been shuffled—in John's ordering the destruction of the beast and the devil comes before the dominion of the saints and the final judgement (see Woodman 2013, 226). For another, in John's adaptation of Daniel's sequence, a thousand years separate the establishment of thrones (Dan 7.9a) from the great throne and final judgement (Dan 7.9b–10; see Bauckham 1993, 106). There are good Christological reasons for this adaptation. With the coming of Christ, the power of the evil one has been decisively broken, and his people are vindicated and given authority over him. And yet the final consummation of the Day of the Lord has been held back until now, creating an interlude between the vindication of the saints and the final assize, between (as it were) the 'thrones' and the 'throne.' As we saw in the visions of the church that interrupted the seven seals (ch. 7) and the seven trumpets (10.1–11.14), this moment of penultimate tension is a time when the church is called to bear faithful witness to Christ and when the inhabitants of the earth are called to repentance. That time of witness and repentance, however, is now over. John's cyclical and intensifying vision of the Day of the Lord will now reach its final *dénouement*.

Vision 7: The Dead Judged, 20.12–15

The seventh vision, which completes the sequence, continues to track with the logic of Daniel 7, as it concerns the final judgement and the opening of books (cf. Dan 7.10). Before the throne, John sees the dead, both great and small. At this final judgement earthly status is irrelevant. We are reminded of the other uses of this phrase that have made much the same point: both small and great are promised reward (11.18) but may also bear the mark of the beast (13.16). Both small and great are commanded to fear God and praise him (19.5) but are also to be found slain on the battlefield and as food for birds (19.18). Now the dead, both great and small, presumably including those slain at that battle, stand before the throne. All the dead are brought before this judgement seat, without exception, and there is no partiality given for the 'great ones' of the earth. The sea, too, that place of primordial chaos, gives up its dead. Death and Hades are emptied, presumably by Jesus himself, since, as we heard at the very start of the book, he is the one who holds their keys (1.18).

In Daniel 12.4, we are told that Daniel was instructed to 'keep the words secret' and to seal up the book 'until the time of the end.' In John's vision, however, that time has come, and so books are opened, as in the vision of the final judgement in Daniel 7.10. The books are of two kinds. The first are the ledgers of deeds against which the dead are to be judged (v. 12). In the Protestant tradition, there has been something of an allergy to any sense of works featuring in the final judgement, but Revelation is repeatedly clear about their importance. Jesus's messages to the seven churches bore the repeated refrain, 'I know your works' (2.2, 19; 3.1, 8, 15), as well as the promise that he would give to each as their works deserve (2.23), a promise he will repeat at the very end of Revelation (22.12). While it is the book of life that is decisive, as we shall see shortly, the contents of the books of works are not irrelevant at the final judgement. Nor is it a case, as some commentators have it, that one is judged either by one book or the other, such that sinners are judged by works and saints by the book of life. The text simply does not suggest that interpretation. Both books are opened and both are used in the judgement of all the dead, without exception.

It is important, however, to be precise in how this is understood. In opening the books of deeds, Revelation states that this judgement is 'according to' (*kata*) such works but not 'on the basis of' them, for that is the purpose of the book of life. This is not a vision of a final judgement on the basis of works, as if the point in the end was for people to lift themselves to eternal life by their own moral bootstraps, entering the New Jerusalem on their own merit. Not at all. The only basis for that is the victory won by Christ over death and the share in that victory given to those who are his. But, in concert with the witness of the whole New Testament (not only the voice of James [Jas 2.14–26] but also of Paul [Rom 2.13; 14.12; and, esp., 2 Cor 5.10]), faith must be worked out in the church in word and deed by the power of the Spirit. This is what is meant by Revelation's repeated call to faithful witness. Though the final outcome depends on faith, at the judgement seat of Christ there will be a measure of recompense according to the whole life lived.

This is not a cause for anxiety, however, for those who are in Christ. The second book opened is the 'book of life,' and it is this book that is decisive for the final outcome of judgement. As we saw back in the message to Sardis, where John first used the image (3.5), the 'book of life' is a widespread Old Testament image (e.g., Exod 32.32–33; Dan 12.1; Mal 3.16) that is also found in other second temple literature (e.g., *Jub* 19.9; 30.22). In the only other New Testament use of this image, in Philippians 4.3, Paul mentions it in passing, speaking of such a book as containing the names of his co-workers in the faith. There are also allusions to the idea through having one's name 'written' or 'enrolled' in heaven in Luke 10.20 and Hebrews 12.23, respectively. Revelation uses the image more frequently, prefiguring it three times before this decisive passage. In 3.5, Jesus promised that those who conquer will not be blotted from this book. In 13.8, those whose names have been written in the book of life from the foundation of the world are protected from the beast's deceptions, a theme repeated in 17.8, though from the other side of that great divide. Here, and again in 21.27, the book of life is more fully described, and its purpose is revealed as the basis for the final judgement.

With the devil finally thrown into the fire, one might think John's account of the destruction of the 'destroyers of the earth' (11.18) was complete, but the sequence of seven visions has one last note of divine judgement. Death itself, along with the now-empty Hades, are thrown into the lake of fire, which John calls 'the second death.' This is a phrase John first used, tantalisingly, in the message to Smyrna in 2.11: 'whoever conquers,' Jesus promised, 'will not be harmed by the second death.' This image is now explained as the lake of fire, the place of final judgment. The evil systems of the beast and the false prophet have already been thrown in (19.20), followed by the dragon itself (20.10). Now Death and Hades, the final threats to God's world, must join them. As Paul puts it, 'the last enemy to be destroyed is death' (1 Cor 15.26). Death itself must die, the great destroyer destroyed.

We must not ignore, however, the note of warning that continues to sound for the people of earth: those whose names are not found in the decisive 'book of life' will meet the same end as the beasts, the dragon, Death, and Hades. For one's name to be absent from this book or removed from it means, somewhat obviously, death (Ps 69.28), and in John's terms it means the 'second death,' which is the lake of fire. It is better to read this as more of a warning than a prediction, just as with Jesus's suggestion, in 3.5, that names might be 'blotted out' from the book. Certainly, it is unwise for any of us to speculate on who might be counted in this number. That is a matter for God alone, who inscribes names in his book as he chooses. What Revelation does tell us, however, is that the lake of fire is the destiny of any who are not counted with Christ. Those who are in the book of life are protected from this 'second death.' It holds no power over them, for they share in the resurrection of Jesus and are thus united to the living one, the conqueror of death (20.6). We note, as this section closes, that there is no 'book of death' corresponding to the 'book of life' (Barth, *CD* II/2, 16). This would suggest a dualistic cosmology of two opposing realms, of death and life, each with its own 'being' (Mangina 2010, 236). No, there is no 'book of death' in which one's name might be written, but only the absence of the name from the 'book of life.' Death may well be the last enemy, but, like evil itself, it is an enemy constituted as non-being, not a force in itself but 'merely' the negation and absence of life, which is the gift of God. No wonder the apostle Paul joins the prophets in mocking it: 'Death has been swallowed up in victory. Where, O death, is your victory? Where, O death, is your sting?' (1 Cor 15.54–55, quoting Isa 25.8 and Hos 13.14). Just as darkness is nothing but the absence of light, and is dispelled at light's arrival, so too Death is but the absence of God's gift of life and will in the end be destroyed by 'the living one' (1.18).

The New Jerusalem

Revelation 21.1–22.21

In the previous section of the book, a sequence of seven visions was introduced with the phrase 'and I saw' (*kai eidon*). As John's final visions begin, the phrase is used for an eighth and final time. As we saw in our discussion of *gematria* in chapter 13, and also in relation to the heads of the beast in 17.11, the number eight is associated with the covenant (since Hebrew boys were circumcised on the eighth day) and also with Christ, who rose from the dead on the 'eighth day' to launch the new creative purposes of God (see again *Sib Or* 1:324–30). This eighth vision, then, indicates the fulfilment of God's covenant promises and the beginning of his work of new creation.

The vision of the new creation that John now sees will fill the remainder of the book and will bring his entire visionary journey to its conclusion, as each cycle converges at this point of fulfilment. It will be no surprise to learn that John's description of the new heaven and new earth, and the New Jerusalem, is full of allusions to the prophets, and indeed barely a verse goes by in these closing chapters that does not echo them. In particular, John draws on the closing visions of new creation found in Isaiah 65–66 and Ezekiel 40–48. Here, perhaps more than anywhere, Revelation is consciously narrated as the fulfilment of Israel's prophetic hopes. The first thing John says is a clear allusion to Isaiah 65.17: 'a new heaven and a new earth.'

The language of 'newness' requires that we think about the theological question of continuity and discontinuity. It is not enough to see what follows as a mere rejuvenation of the heavens and the earth, as if all that is needed is a clean-up operation: John tells us that 'the first heaven and the first earth had passed away.' The new does not grow up out of the old (as if the new Jerusalem could be built by human hands) but comes *down* out of heaven from God as a gift, as we will soon see. However, John does not say that the first heaven and earth were destroyed but rather that they 'passed away.' The destroying fire is reserved for the destroyers of the earth, not for the earth itself. Moreover, to construe the new creation as a destruction and replacement does not do justice to the covenant faithfulness of God, who promised Noah never again to do such a thing to his creation (Gen 9.9–17; cf. Isa 54.9). As with the vision of Isaiah 65, there is a strong note of continuity in the description of the new creation, in its fabric and its people. The God who is now doing a 'new thing' (Isa 43.19) is the same God who created the heavens and the earth and entered into an eternal covenant with it.

The New Jerusalem: Prologue, 21.1–8

What John sees is a city coming down out of heaven from God. He describes it twice, giving first a brief comment (21.1–2) as part of an introductory section before the bulk of the vision describes the city in more detail (21.9–22.5). In both places, the city is described as a bride, an image first mentioned in 19.7 to speak of the people of God, who are to be dressed in the pure linen of their righteous deeds. The marriage of the Lamb announced in 19.7 has now come, and the bride is prepared and adorned for her husband. It is also an image regularly invoked by the Old Testament to speak of the covenant relationship between God and his people, not least in the great 'new covenant' vision of Jeremiah, where God himself is described as the husband of Israel (Jer 31.31–32). The image of the bride stands in clear juxtaposition to the whore of Babylon. The two women-cities are starkly contrasted in their description, character, and destiny, and this contrast invites readers to reflect on their own ethical position. Are they joined to Babylon, or are they part of the bride? John's vision speaks, then, of the New Jerusalem as a people. But, as with all of John's images, it is simultaneously more than this. Since the bride is a city, it is also a place, and no less than the dwelling place of God. This is why John is clear to name it as not just any city but 'the new Jerusalem,' the place where God chose to be present in the temple. And as such, it is an image that speaks powerfully of divine presence: 'God himself will be with them.'

John hears a voice from the throne, Revelation's regular way of indicating the voice of God, declaring this threefold reality of the new Jerusalem as people, place, and presence (Bauckham 1993, 126–43). Three times in this one verse John uses the preposition 'with' (*meta*), driving home the point of this vision of divine presence with his people (Resseguie 2009, 252). There are strong allusions here to Zechariah 2.10 ('Sing and rejoice, O daughter Zion! For lo, I will come and dwell in your midst, says the LORD') and especially to Ezekiel 37.27–28: 'My dwelling place shall be with them; and I will be their God, and they shall be my people. Then the nations shall know that I the LORD sanctify Israel, when my sanctuary is among them forevermore.' The closing chapters of Ezekiel, to which John will regularly allude in what follows, are filled with visions of this promised restoration of Israel and the establishment of the new temple as a permanent dwelling for God. In light of this, it is interesting to note that John's voice from the throne describes this divine presence not by evoking the eschatological temple, but in wilderness tabernacle language (regrettably obscured in some translations): 'the home (*skēnē*, lit. 'tabernacle') of God is among mortals. He will dwell (*skēnōsei*, lit. 'he will tabernacle') with them as their God.' In the famous prologue of the Gospel of John, the same language is used to describe the divine presence in the incarnation of Jesus: 'the Word became flesh and lived (*eskēnōsen*, lit. 'he tabernacled') among us' (Jn 1.14). Now it is used to speak of the final dwelling of God with humans in the new creation. The New Jerusalem is the fulfilment of God's liberating and guiding presence with a wilderness people. The voice echoes the regular Old Testament affirmation of the covenant, repeatedly spoken in the new covenant promises of Jeremiah 30–31: 'I will be their God, and they will be my people.' But note what Revelation says: not just *a* people, singular, but 'peoples,' plural. The multitude delivered from Egypt were a 'mixed crowd' (Ex 12.38), and as such there were peoples of other nations present with Israel from the very beginning of that wilderness journey toward the promised land. And so as the voice now speaks of the final consummation of God's purposes, he declares that God will tabernacle among all humankind and that the peoples of the earth, plural, will belong to him. As we have seen throughout Revelation, expectations of an 'eschatological Israel' are readily transformed by John into visions of a multitude from every nation, tribe, people, and language (e.g., ch. 7). This echoes the most universal eschatological hopes of the prophets, hopes expressed in the new covenant prophecy of Jeremiah 30–31, the promise of divine presence in Zechariah 2.10–11, and the eschatological feast of Isaiah 25.6–8.

The 'newness' of the new creation is particularly signalled by what is absent from it. First, John tells us that there is no more sea. In the first creation, God set limits to the sea, the image of primordial chaos and of separation of peoples. In his creation of the world he said 'No' to that chaos; now, in the consummation of his creative purposes, it is finally no more. This is not an image of the destruction of a part of God's creation but the final absence of that which represents all that is antithetical to it. Second, and as an extension of this logic, there is no more death. In the eschatological vision of Isaiah 65, the glorious hope of God's new creation included the promise of longevity. The inhabitants of the renewed Jerusalem would not die young but would live out long and happy lives. Isaiah did not, however, promise the end of death. Those who died at a hundred would be considered to have died young (Isa 65.20), but they would still have died. In John's vision of the new creation, however, death is utterly absent. This stands to reason, since we have just heard that Death itself, the negation of life, has been thrown into the lake of fire. This last enemy of God has no place in the new creation. Third, with the swallowing up of Death comes the end of mourning and crying (cf. Isa 25.8; 65.19). These belong to the first order of things, which has now passed away. The things that negate being (chaos, death, and corruption) have no place in God's new creation any more than the devil, who is their personification. In short, what is absent from the new creation are all the things to which God said 'No' when he said 'Yes' to creation. What John has seen in this vision is then confirmed by the divine voice from the throne saying 'see, I am making all things new.' The 'new thing' promised to Isaiah (in Isa 43.19) was the deliverance from historical Babylon and the restoration of the people and the land. Here we see that imagery projected on a universal scale, as people from all nations are delivered from Babylon and the deceptive power behind her, and gathered at the renewal of all things. All that is left is God's 'Yes.'

The voice speaks again, repeating the words spoken when the seventh angel poured his bowl (16.17), declaring the completion of the work of God with the announcement 'it is done!' The voice also commands John to write, as it did at the start of the book (1.11, 19), and the speaker identifies himself with the same name we heard back in Revelation 1.8: 'I am the Alpha and the Omega.' To this is added 'beginning and the end' and the combination of this self-identification, the promises and warnings of the verses that follow, and the command for John to write make this whole speech very reminiscent of John's opening encounter with Christ (cf. 1.17–19). Not for the last time, the identity of Jesus and the identity of God are closely interwoven (cf. 22.13). This connection only strengthens as the divine voice then makes a promise to 'those who conquer.' Is this voice from the throne the voice of Jesus, then? There are certainly many reasons to think so. It was Jesus who instructed John to write at the start of the book, and he now repeats that command as the book draws to a conclusion. It was Jesus who identified himself as Alpha and Omega, as the voice does again here, and it was he who made promises to the conquerors in the seven messages. And it is Jesus who is the one through whom God created, and so the voice now declares his agency in the new creation.

A promise to 'those who conquer' was the regular refrain of the seven messages (2.7, 11, 17, 26, 28; 3.12, 21) and a common feature of descriptions of the saints elsewhere in Revelation (e.g., 12.11; 15.2). Through various images, Revelation has defined such victory as bearing faithful witness to Christ, even unto death, and sharing in the victory of the Lamb. Here the conquerors will be called the children of God, and thus John here mixes his bridal metaphor with one of adoption. These children are promised an inheritance of 'these things,' presumably referring to the whole of what has just been promised, rather than just the immediately preceding detail of the springs of water. The wilderness imagery persists with the metaphor of thirst and water, though the metaphor extends to speak of a longing for God more generally (e.g., Ps 42). The God who provided water from the rock in the wilderness (Ex 17) promises his children the gift of water from the spring of life. These waters will be described in more detail at the start of chapter 22. Although we are just one chapter short of the end of the book, John still has space for a final piece of narrative foreshadowing.

This promise is sharply contrasted with a warning to those who rebel, and a rapid-fire 'vice list' of seven kinds of such people follows. It is not simply a list of transgressors of commandments (there are obvious omissions such as thieves and the covetous) but a sevenfold depiction of human sin united by a common theological theme. As with all vices, all of those listed here do not have an independent reality of their own but are corruptions of virtue and the negation of the positive traits Revelation encourages (see Webster 2012, ch. 10, 'Curiosity'). In the place of conquering there is cowardice, its absence. In the place of faithful witness, faithlessness. The 'polluted' speaks of the corruption of the good, and the murderers (the fourth and central item in the list of seven) the denial of life. Fornication is the twisted version of covenant union (and thus the image is regularly extended to speak of Israel's infidelity to God); sorcery and idolatry are the distortion of true worship. The list of seven is concluded, and indeed summarised, by an eighth: 'all liars.' This is an appropriate summary term, for these seven are all forms of the negation of the truth. The list reminds us that we cannot restrict our view of 'sin' to an abstract, systemic phenomenon, an anti-God power. Certainly, this is an important part of Revelation's vision of evil and one that received a great deal of attention in the visions of the dragon, the beasts, and the whore. But in all of this attention to the power and judgement of structural evil, Revelation does not forget that sin is also something done by people. And so this list sums up human complicity with the power of sin in our actions. Those listed here are those who, following the father of lies, persist in twisting or negating the good things of God's world. There is no place for such distortion in the new Jerusalem, and such negations are themselves negated by God's judgment. Those who participate in the destruction of the earth will themselves be destroyed (cf. 11.18), and their destiny is to join the Satan, the deceiver, in the lake of fire. This is the 'second death,' from which the people of God are protected (Rev 2.11; 20.6).

The New Jerusalem: Vision, 21.9–22.5

Description of the City, 21.9–21

At this point, one of the seven angels from the bowl sequence enters the scene, indicating that these closing chapters are the culmination of a large narrative arc that stretches back at least to chapter 15. The terrifying visions of God's judgement must not be the final word in this story. The scene that follows echoes the one in 17.1, where one of the bowl-angels acted as guide for John's vision of Babylon. Perhaps, then, it is the same angel who guides John here. Certainly the scenes are designed to mirror one another, thus creating a contrast between the two women/cities. The opening phrases of both passages are identical, as are the angel's first few words, 'come, I will show you . . . .' This time, instead of the judgement of the whore there is the 'bride, the wife of the Lamb.' John has already seen the bride as he saw the holy city descend in verse 2. His account of that vision was interrupted, however, by the voice from heaven. Now he returns to it, guided by the angel, and offers a detailed description. Once again, there is audio and there is video.

Another parallel with chapter 17 follows, as John is carried away 'in the Spirit' to a symbolic geographical location. In 17.3, he was taken to the wilderness. Now he is transported to 'a great, high mountain.' It does not matter that the mountain is not named, for that is beside the point. The mountain is the place, throughout the Bible, where heaven and earth touch. It is a place of theophany, and of revelation, in both testaments. Most significant for John at this point is the mountaintop encounter of Ezekiel, described in chapters 40–48, in which he sees a vision of a city and the eschatological temple, guided at each step by an angel. John picks up Ezekiel's story where he left it after the great battle with Gog (Ezek 38–39) to which he alluded in Revelation 20.8. John will make many more allusions to Ezekiel's descriptive details, and we will note some of them as we go, but we must also remember that he is echoing the narrative shape of that passage, too. Moreover, we are just as interested in John's departures from and adaptations of Ezekiel's vision as we are the echoes.

We see his first major adaptation when John arrives on the mountaintop. Instead of seeing a city on the summit (Ezek 40.2), the 'holy city Jerusalem' descends from heaven. Three things should be noted for their theological significance. First, it is a city. This is not a vision of Eden regained, a return to a time of primordial innocence in the garden before humanity's city-building exploits destroyed God's world. Revelation closes with a vision not of the garden but of a garden-city. There is a place in the new creation for the endeavour of humankind, suitably purified (see 21.24, 26). Second, however, this city of God is not built from the ground up. While human endeavour will have a part to play in the New Jerusalem, it is fundamentally a gift of God, not made by human hands but spoken into existence by the divine new-creative word. The city descends 'out of heaven from God.' Third, this is not a vision of a 'generic' city. Unlike the unnamed mountain, which one will not locate on a map, the city is named as Jerusalem. This is not to limit the image to a mere geographical location, since this is a city descending from heaven. But the name is far more than geography—the city is Jerusalem because that is 'the holy city.'

Jerusalem was not holy because of anything it possessed in and of itself. Jerusalem was holy because God chose to dwell there. This is no less true of the eschatological Jerusalem of Ezekiel's vision, which, in the book's closing words, is called 'The LORD is There' (Ezek 48.35). The radiance of this new heavenly Jerusalem, which John now describes, is likewise not its own but because of the 'glory of God.' As he did in the throne vision of chapter 4, John stretches language to its breaking point in his description of the glory before him, drawing on the most radiant metaphors he can find. The city even looks like God's glory, reflected in the radiance of jasper like the one seated on the throne (4.3). The contrast between the faithful purity of the Bride and the unfaithful impurities of the whore could not be starker. Both women are described as displaying great wealth and splendour, but where Babylon's attire was gaudy and full of impurities (17.4), the Bride is adorned in radiance and holiness. The clarity of the gemstones and the purity of the precious metals that John repeatedly describes in this vision reflect the purity of the Bride's attire, reminding us of the promise in 19.8.

Continuing to track with the shape of Ezekiel's temple vision, John's attention is first drawn to the outside of the city, its walls and gates (cf. Ezek 40.5–16). The gates are described first. There are twelve, three on each side of the square city, and each is guarded by an angel. In case the number twelve alone did not immediately evoke the patriarchs of Israel, John makes that connection explicit in telling us that each gate bears the name of one of the twelve tribes. This was also a feature of Ezekiel's vision, in the closing passage of the book (Ezek 48.30–35). For their part, the walls are also twelvefold, in that they have twelve foundations. On these are the names of the apostles, and in this imagery John and Paul are similar:

> So then you are no longer strangers and aliens, but you are citizens with the saints and also members of the household of God, built upon the foundation of the apostles and prophets, with Christ Jesus himself as the

cornerstone. In him the whole structure is joined together and grows into a holy temple in the Lord; in whom you also are built together spiritually into a dwelling place for God. (Eph 2.19–22)

The outer frame of the New Jerusalem, then, in its foundations and gates, has brought together the whole people of God, Israel and church, into one structure. It is a vision of a combined people: not an amalgam or an erasure of difference, for the distinction between Israel and the nations remains, but nevertheless one people and one city. Once again we see that the New Jerusalem is described as place (it is a city), as presence (God's glory dwells there), and as people (its foundations and gates; again see Bauckham 1993, 126–43).

In chapter 11, in the interlude between the sixth and seventh trumpets, John was given a measuring rod and told to measure the temple of God. We recall that this never happened, for that vision was subsequently filled with the account of the two witnesses. This, as we saw, was a vision of the church in its faithful testimony to Jesus. Now it is the angel who holds a measuring rod, and we do have the measuring of the city, another clear allusion to Ezekiel 40–48. There, every inch of the temple is measured by the angel and recorded by Ezekiel, from the smallest peg to the length of the walls. By contrast, John's account of the measuring is much less detailed. The dimensions he does give, however, test the limits of our imaginations. The city is square and measures 1,500 miles in each direction, a thousand times larger than Ezekiel's city and large enough to cover the Mediterranean from Jerusalem to Rome, or the equivalent of the landmass of the whole Roman empire (Kraybill 2010, 177, 212). These insights are suggestive, and it is powerful to reflect on what this city might look like on a map of the world as John knew it, and on the imaginative challenge that presents to the claims of Roman global dominion. However, again numerical symbolism is not to be interpreted in flatly prosaic terms. The translation to modern units of distance obscures the theological significance of the figures: twelve thousand *stadia* in length, width, and height. The footprint of this square city, then, is 12,000 times 12,000, a figure that clearly echoes the counting of the 144,000 of Israel in the seal interlude of chapter 7. In case this symbolism is missed, the walls are also measured at 144 cubits (presumably this is their thickness, for if it were their height it would be a laughably small wall for such a large city). The point of these multiples of twelve is clear: the New Jerusalem is not just a vision of a place but also a people, the eschatological perfection of the universal people of God, reflecting his glory and enjoying his presence. God's people are not only called to live in the holy city; they *are* the holy city (see Augustine's reading of this passage in *City of God* 20.17; see also Gundry 1987).

The walls, John says again, are like jasper, echoing the vision of God in chapter 4, and the city itself is of 'pure gold.' In verses 19–21, John turns again to the gates and foundations first mentioned in verses 12–14, taking them in the reverse order this time. This creates a neat narrative pattern to the passage while also reminding us that neither group is more important than the other in the universal people of God. The image of a bejewelled city weaves the prophecies of Ezekiel with those of Isaiah, where we read this promise of restoration from God to his holy city:

> For the mountains may depart
> and the hills be removed,
> but my steadfast love shall not depart from you,
> and my covenant of peace shall not be removed,
> says the LORD, who has compassion on you.
> O afflicted one, storm-tossed, and not comforted
> I am about to set your stones in antimony,
> and lay your foundations with sapphires.
> I will make your pinnacles of rubies,
> your gates of jewels,
> and all your wall of precious stones. (Isa 54:10–12)

The foundations of the walls of the New Jerusalem, which bear the names of the apostles, are like twelve precious stones. Many have seen here an echo of the twelve gemstones that adorned the priestly breastplate, which was also square in shape, with four rows of three stones (Ex 28.15–21; 39.8–21). It is hard to rule on this definitively, for the precise identification of gemstones in ancient languages is a tricky business, and it is certainly the case the John is not following the Exodus gem list exactly or in the same order. In any case, slavish repetition is certainly not John's normal practice when it comes to his use of the Old Testament: he is usually far more creative than that. Looking more widely, another possible allusion might be found in Ezekiel 28 and the description of Eden in jewelled splendour. This passage, like the present one, also mentions the mountain of God and angelic guards, and the oracle against Tyre was also important in John's shaping of the Babylon vision. These are all details that increase the likelihood that this text is in his mind. It is entirely possible that John is here weaving together both the Exodus and Ezekiel passages, connected through their shared imagery of precious stones. If this is so, what we have is a combined image of the people, represented by the priesthood and the creation imagery of Eden. Both are symbolic of divine presence. Moreover, if there is an allusion to the priestly breastplate it is remarkable for another reason, since it is not the twelve tribes whose names are on the gemstone foundations (as one might expect) but the twelve apostles. It is the gates that bear the names of the tribes (v. 12), shaped from huge pearls.

Hidden among all of these glorious gems is a tantalising 'blink-and-you'll-miss-it' detail. The dimensions of the city, he tells us, are equal in length and width (v. 16). This seems a superfluous comment, since he already told us it was 'foursquare.' At the end of the verse, however, he says 'its length and width *and height* are equal.' What he sees, then, is not only a square but a cube. In Ezekiel 42.15–20 the temple is measured as a square, and the same is true of the city itself in 48.30–35. To find the source of John's cubic dimensions we need to turn to another set of temple measurements, that of Solomon's temple, described in 1 Kings 6. There we learn that it is the innermost sanctuary, which is cubic in shape and overlaid with pure gold (1 Kg 6.20). The point is of profound theological significance: the city that John sees, in its shape and its fabric, looks like the holy of holies, the place where the presence of God dwelled.

The Temple and the Nations, 21.22–27
Seven times, and then an eighth, John has told us what he saw. Now, as he moves from the outside to the inside of the city, he tells us something he does not see: he sees no temple. Although Ezekiel's vision gives detailed attention to the walls and gates, the climax to which it builds is the measurement of the eschatological temple, the return of the divine glory, and the restoration of the people of God. John's theological concerns are the same, but there is an important and radical departure from the pattern of Ezekiel. In John's vision of the New Jerusalem, there is no temple. Since the city itself is shaped like the holy of holies, and since it is filled with the glory of God, there is no need for a sanctuary. As the writer of Hebrews might put it, there is no need for the 'sketch and shadow' (Heb 8.5) when perfection has come. The unmediated presence and glory of God and of the Lamb fills the enormous city, covering the earth 'as the waters cover the sea' (Isa 11.9; cf. Hab 2.14). We recall that this is an image not only of holy presence and of a holy place but also of a holy people. The people of God, those who are in faithful marriage union with the Lamb, are the locus of God's presence. If the Lamb is the temple, then, in him, so are his people.

The Lamb's inclusion here, twice in two verses, speaks a profound Christological truth. The glorious eschatological hope expressed by the prophet Isaiah includes this vision of perpetual light in the city of God:

> The sun shall no longer be your light by day,
> nor for brightness shall the moon give light to you by night;
> but the LORD will be your everlasting light, and your God will be your glory.
> Your sun shall no more go down, or your moon withdraw itself;
> for the LORD will be your everlasting light, and your days of mourning shall be ended. (Isa 60.19–20)

John takes up this hope and reworks it around the person of Christ. The temple of God, the place of his presence, is 'the Lord God the Almighty *and the Lamb.*' And the city is illumined by the glory of God himself and by its lamp, which 'is the Lamb.' Jesus is both the locus of God's presence and the radiance of his glory (here once again Revelation's theology sounds very much like Hebrews [Heb 1.3] and the Johannine prologue; cf. Jn 1.9, 14). When John finally beholds the presence of God's glory in this climactic vision of the holy city, what he sees—and indeed the very light by which he is able to see—is God and the Lamb. It is God who reveals God's self by his own light, and Jesus is both revealer and the one revealed.

Of all the Christological images in this book, John closes not with the glorious Son of Man, or the Lion of Judah, or the Rider on the white horse, but with the slain Lamb who stands with God in the new Jerusalem. As John's visions culminate in the final victory of God, the Lamb is not replaced with a more (apparently) powerful image, for the manner of Christ's victory is through sacrifice. Moreover, we can now see that this was not just a means to an end, such that Christ's sacrificial witness was a necessary stage leading to domination in the end, but his very nature. He remains the victorious Lion, but the image of the exalted Christ in the New Jerusalem is that of the Lamb.

What comes next is a surprising feature. That the nations walk by the light of the city is not a surprise, given the universal tenor of the vision so far. This aspect of the vision continues to echo the universal hope of Isaiah 60, especially verse 3: 'Nations shall come to your light, and kings to the brightness of your dawn.' What is remarkable, though, is what John does with this imagery. Not just kings, but the 'kings of the earth' enter into the New Jerusalem, bringing their glory. These are the same kings who hid in the rocks at the judgement of God and refused to repent (6.15), who committed fornication with Babylon (17.2; 18.3, 9) and subjected themselves to her rule (17.18), and who gathered with the beast to make war against Christ and his people (19.19). The last time we saw them they lay dead on the battlefield, food for birds. How is it, then, that these same kings, the enemies of the people of God, now enter the New Jerusalem? All the dead have been raised and judged. At that point, anyone whose name was not found in the book of life was thrown into the lake of fire (20.15). If any have demonstrated through their works that they are not in that book, it is surely these kings of the earth. And yet, here they are, recognising the rightful rule of Christ over them, which was announced in the book's opening paragraph (1.5).

They enter through gates that are perpetually open. There is no need to shut them, for any enemies who might threaten this city have been thrown into the lake of fire. Moreover, the city dwells in the perpetual light of God and the Lamb, and so there is no threat of night. In the presence of the true light, darkness (which is, after all, only the absence of light) is utterly and finally dispelled.

What they bring in tribute to their rightful king is 'their glory.' This, too, is remarkable. The city has been depicted, in stark contrast to Babylon, as not only glorious but pure. Nothing impure can enter it, as we are now told (cf. 21.8). If the kings of the earth now enter in, bringing their glory, it can only be because they and their works have now been purified. These kings were once practitioners of abominations and falsehoods, sharers in the sins of Babylon. But now they enter the city. One might be minded to read this act of supplication as an unwilling bending of the knee before final judgement, but that is not how the text runs. If no impure thing, and none but those written in the book of life, can enter the city, we must conclude that the names of these kings are now written in that book and their glory purified. Moreover, it is not enough to read the presentation of their glory as merely an act of tribute, a compulsion of conquered kings. That kind of forced compliance is what Babylon extracted from its vassals, and the New Jerusalem is its polar opposite. Moreover, throughout Revelation, to 'give glory' means not mere obeisance but willing worship (4.9, 11; 5.12–13; 7.12; 11.13; 14.7; 19.1, 7; see Koester 2014, 833). The redemptive truth of this scene is remarkable: the onetime enemies of God now offer him praise.

Isaiah 60 goes on to describe the eschatological hope of the conversion of the nations, whose glory is brought to Jerusalem, and John also develops this image. The kings of the earth are joined in this act of worship by people bringing the glory of the nations, who are also regular enemies of God in Revelation. These 'nations' share the career of the 'kings of the earth': they trampled the holy city (11.2), raged against the Lord (11.18), drank Babylon's wine (14.8; 18.3), and were deceived and gathered for war (20.8) but ultimately defeated by the sword of the Rider's mouth (19.15). And yet here they are, bringing in their glory and recognising the true reign of God and his Son over them (15.3-4; cf. 12.5). The most universalistic hopes of the whole book are encapsulated in this vision. Even the most trenchant enemies of God may enter the New Jerusalem, whose gates remain open forever, if they recognise the Lamb's true lordship.

This universalistic hope sounds a note of apparent discord with the terrible image of fiery judgement in the first brief description of the New Jerusalem, which insisted that idolaters such as these kings and nations will end in the lake of fire (21.8). What are we to make of this apparent contradiction? The two images reflect a tension that runs, in truth, through the whole book of Revelation, a tension between two visions of salvation, one limited and one universal. We saw a similar tension in the two harvests of chapter 14, for example. In interpreting this tension, we are faced with essentially three options. The first is to read the universal images as primary and controlling for the more limited ones, interpreting them accordingly. The second is the reverse, reading images of universal hope in the light of the vision of limited salvation. A third option, which is the route we shall take here, is not to see this as a logical conundrum to be resolved but as a deliberate act of the imagination, another instance of John's 'bifocal vision.' If we read John's imagery as not straightforwardly predictive but rather as a prophetic act of imagination, we have no need to resolve apparent logical inconsistencies (cf. Blount 2013, 383, Bauckham 1993, 102–103). Like a Picasso portrait, it appears to be a distorted or confused picture, but in these apparent contradictions, it is able to speak a deeper truth (and perhaps even challenge all attempts at 'precision' as untruths), since it can provide more than one perspective at the same time. John presents the reader simultaneously with two visions of the end, one universal and one limited, and invites us to hold both images in our minds and to reflect on what that means. Images of judgement stand as prophetic warnings of the destiny that awaits those who persist in rebellion against God, the destruction that is the end of those who ally themselves with the Destroyer. The purpose of such visions is not to predict an outcome but to elicit repentance. Images of universal hope, however, offer an invitation and a promise that even the most hardened enemy of God may enter the holy city, the people and place of God's presence. As we have seen in many of John's apparently contradictory images, the dialectical tension created by this 'double vision' is a large part of how the book of Revelation works both as literature and as theology.

The River of Life, 22.1–5

John has now followed his angelic guide to the very centre of the city, and here his celestial journey ends. He sees a river, the 'water of life' promised in 7.17 and 21.6. Again there is a contrast with Babylon and an implied choice to make: to drink the wine of wrath (14.8, 10) or the water of life. John's imagery is drawn once more from the closing chapters of Ezekiel, this time from 47.1–12, and once again it is the adaptations of the vision that are particularly revealing. In Ezekiel's vision, there is water flowing from the temple. But there is no temple in the New Jerusalem, and so John's river flows from the throne itself. The throne is the 'throne of God and of the Lamb,' a singular seat of rulership occupied by both, a depiction with profound theological consequences. The throne is no longer in heaven, accessible to humankind only by a seer's ascent or a priest's entrance into the sanctuary, but has descended with the New Jerusalem, as heaven and earth are united at last and the home of God is among his people (21.3).

Again echoing Ezekiel, John sees trees beside this river (cf. Ezek 47.7). Or, to be more precise, he sees a singular tree, the 'tree of life,' and as such his allusions reach back before Ezekiel to Eden, where God first planted that tree (Gen 2.9; 3.22). The New Jerusalem is thus a garden city. This tree, the fruit of which was denied to Adam and Eve but promised to the church in Ephesus in 2.7, produces twelve kinds of fruit, such that each month of the year there is produce. The city thus has not only perpetual light but perpetual food, and this fruit brings eternal life. The tree's leaves, John tells us, are for healing, an image that again alludes clearly to Ezekiel 47.12, though John subtly adapts it in the light of his most universalistic hope, adding to Ezekiel's vision of healing leaves the detail that it is for 'the nations.' Just as the nations brought their glory in, so healing flows out from the throne to them. It is not enough that they come grovelling into the New Jerusalem, like vassal nations bringing unwilling tribute. From the throne of God flows their healing, their restoration. The tree of life whose fruit was promised to one church at the start of the book is the source of healing and life not only for the Ephesian believers but for all the nations. Generations of commentators have also seen in this tree a figure of the cross, the 'tree' on which Christ was crucified to end the curse of sin (Gal 3.13; 1 Pet 2.24). In history, that tree stood outside the city of Jerusalem. In John's vision of the New Jerusalem, it stands in its very centre, geographically and theologically, and brings healing to the nations.

As we noted in those early chapters, there are numerous connections between this climactic vision and the promises Christ makes to the conquerors in the messages to the seven churches. The message to Sardis promised the preservation of their names in the book of life (3.5; cf. 21.27), and the message to Smyrna promised protection from the 'second death' (2.11; cf. 21.8). Now, in addition to the Ephesian promise of the tree of life, we can add the promise of a new name given to Pergamum and Philadelphia

(2.17; 3.12; cf. 22.4) and the promise of a universal reign, shared with Christ, given to Smyrna, Thyatira, and Laodicea (2.10–11; 2.26–27; 3.21; cf. 22.5). As such John anchors the present realities of the churches in Asia Minor to this heavenly and eschatological vision of the whole people of God.

As this vision of the New Jerusalem begins to come to a close, John offers something of a summary of the hope it expresses, and in doing so he gathers up the main theological themes of the book as a whole, and its central theological question: 'to whom does the sovereignty of the world belong?' (Käsemann 1969). Nothing accursed is found in the city of God, for the curse of sin and all the corruption that comes with it has been destroyed. Instead, the city is the place of God's rightful reign, which he shares with the Lamb. And the Lamb in turn shares this reign with the saints, those who bore faithful witness to Jesus even unto death now made to be a kingdom and priests forever, as he promised (1.6; 5.10). It is a place with no night, since the true light of God has banished the non-being of darkness. It is a place, and a people, of perpetual worship, as those who are the servants of God and who are marked with his name (cf. 7.3; 14.1) behold his face, just as Moses, the servant of God, beheld the face of God in the tabernacle.

Though this vision expresses the future hope of the church, it is also, in a sense, a present theological reality. John's vision of the New Jerusalem expresses not simply a distant hope, a dream of heavenly utopia to opiate the church or to motivate its earthly witness. It is a vision inaugurated in the present reality of the people of God and thus able to effect a transformation of their theological imagination. Those who bear faithful witness to Christ are not merely promised a future reward but are shown a revelation of their reign with Christ, a reign in which they share through their victorious faithful witness, which may seem to the world like failure, but when seen from the perspective of heaven, is a share in the Lamb's glorious rule.

The Angel's Closing Words, 22.6–7

John's vision of the New Jerusalem closes with words from his angelic guide, repeating what was heard from the throne at the start of the vision in 21.5, with the repeated phrase forming a pair of bookends to the whole New Jerusalem vision: 'these words are trustworthy and true.' This angelic pronouncement confirms the authority of the witness that John has recorded. Written words have permanence, and the angelic seal of approval also gives them moral authority. This will be a theme carried through into the book's epilogue.

In Revelation 1.1–2, the book began with this phrase: 'the revelation of Jesus Christ, which God gave him to show his servants what must soon take place; he made it known by sending his angel to his servant John, who testified to the word of God and to the testimony of Jesus Christ, even to all that he saw.' Thus a great chain of revelation established the divine authority of the book, handed to Christ and from him via an angel to John and the churches. Here, as this revelation draws to a close, the angel repeats those opening words, but with an important twist: 'the Lord, the God of the spirits of the prophets, has sent his angel to show his servants what must soon take place.' The role assigned to Christ in 1.2 is the transmission of the revelation to John and his servants. In 22.6 that role is performed by the Lord God himself. Not for the first time, John assigns divine roles to Christ, and vice-versa. What God does, Christ does.

Another repetition of Revelation's opening phrases comes in the next verse, as the angel pronounces a closing benediction on 'the one who keeps the words of the prophecy of this book' (cf. 1.3). There is a clear sense, then, that verse 7 is something of an ending. Even here, however, John does not merely quote himself but introduces an important adaptation. There is an addition to the wording with the phrase, abruptly interrupting the flow: 'See, I am coming soon!' Who is it that speaks now? Is it the guiding angel? That would certainly be odd, for nowhere is the coming of an angel promised. Rather, the one who is repeatedly described as the one 'who is to come' (1.4, 8; 4.8) is the Lord God himself. There is a confusion in the way John's narrative runs at this point, making it hard to separate the voices of God, Jesus, and the guiding angel. This lack of clarity persists until verse 16, where we hear the second of three uses of this same phrase, the speaker identifying himself more clearly. But perhaps this is not merely a case of unclear writing, but rather a deliberate interplay between voices, reminding us of the 'chain of revelation' that connects John to the angel, to Christ, and to God himself. Whose word is this which has been spoken? Regardless of whose line it is in the script, the words are from God, and so they are a trustworthy and true testimony.

Final Warnings and Benedictions, 22.8–21

And with that, John's heavenly visions come to an end. We are returned with him to the island of Patmos, where John first heard the voice like a trumpet instructing him to write this book. As he did at the book's opening (1.9), John offers his own authorial imprimatur, speaking in his own voice to confirm that he 'saw and heard' these things, reminding us once more that the sounds of Revelation are as important as its visions. He then narrates his response to his spiritual experience. On hearing and seeing these things, he tells us, he fell down before the guiding angel, not in exhaustion or in fear, but in worship. But the angel rebukes John, just as he did in the similar scene in 19.10, for worship must be reserved for God alone. This repeated insistence on monolatry, that worship be reserved for God, makes the scene we have just witnessed even more remarkable, for there we saw God share not only his throne but also his worship with the Lamb (22.3).

Angels, even those given power to reveal such mysteries, are but fellow servants with John and his 'comrades' (lit., 'brothers') the prophets. John's status among the prophets is thus indirectly confirmed by this angelic rebuke. His book, in which he has woven hundreds of threads of allusion to his brothers Isaiah, Jeremiah, Ezekiel, Daniel, and others, is not a mere work of 'fan-fiction.' John is not just a tribute act but a member of the company of the prophets, and indeed his book is the climax of Israel's prophetic tradition, bringing all of their visions of God's purposes together in this final 'revelation of Jesus Christ.' What is to be done with this book of prophecy? How are its readers to be numbered with 'those who keep the words of this book,' as the angel has twice indicated? John's epilogue answers such questions with a number of instructions, appeals, blessings, and warnings.

The first instruction is that the book is not to be sealed up. In this respect, it is unlike the prophecy of Daniel, who was instructed to 'keep the words secret and the book sealed until the time of the end' (Dan 12.4). John's vision is not to be sealed, for the 'time is near' (cf. 1.3). At this, readers ancient and modern have joined the subaltern saints in asking 'how long will it be?' (Rev 6.10). The only answer we are given is the same as theirs: 'a little longer,' 'soon,' 'the time is near.' It is a fool's errand to try to calculate what 'near' means. As we have seen, the nature of time in the book of Revelation, and the relationship between time and eternity, is a complex one that resists such human linear chronologies. We can no more locate this eschatological 'soon' on a calendar than we can measure the courts of heaven with a ruler. In any case, 'soon' in God's purposes is rarely 'soon' in ours. As Peter said, alluding to the Psalms, 'with the Lord one day is like a thousand years, and a thousand years are like one day' (2 Pet 3.8; cf. Ps 90.4). That does not mean, however, that the phrase is theologically useless. What matters in this 'near time' is that the people of God place their trust in God, who will not delay in bringing about his judgement, their vindication, and the establishment of his kingdom. He is 'the coming one' and is coming soon. As we have seen in numerous ways, the book of Revelation presents visions of the church as those who live in the 'interrupted' time, the time just before the end, between penultimate and ultimate things. It is a time for the church to awake and bear witness to the already-won and soon-coming triumph of Jesus Christ. The Lamb's victory, and the saints' faithful and enduring testimony to it, has been the dominant theme of the whole book. As such, this book is not to be sealed but read and kept by all God's people as the word of testimony for this time of apocalyptic imminence, the time when the Lord stands at the door and knocks. The apostle Paul makes a similar eschatological point, and with similarly apocalyptic metaphors, in his letter to the church in Rome: 'you know what time it is, how it is now the moment for you to wake from sleep. For salvation is nearer to us now than when we became believers; the night is far gone, the day is near. Let us then lay aside the works of darkness and put on the armour of light' (Rom 13:11–12).

This eschatological 'nearness' establishes the theological framework for the instruction that follows: 'let the evildoer still do evil, and the filthy still be filthy, and the righteous still do right, and the holy still be holy.' Revelation has revealed that the power of evil and the uncleanness of corruption are time-limited and destined for destruction. But during this penultimate time, the world will be characterised by these coexisting realities. Through the church and its faithful witness, Christ has established his reign; his enemies have been cast down and are defeated. And yet until the final consummation of that reign there is still evil and impurity on the earth, existing side by side with righteousness and holiness. In his own apocalyptic teachings, Jesus described this situation in agricultural terms. The weeds and the crops grow up together until the 'end of the age,' and only then will come their separation and judgement (Mt 13.36–43). The sheep and the goats will graze together until the Son of Man comes in glory with his angels, and only then will they be separated (Mt 25.32). Until that day, the church is called to submit to this deferred judgement, not seeking to preempt God's final word but to bear witness and endure patiently in this 'in-between time.'

Jesus knows that this patient endurance will not be easy. He assures them again that this time will not stretch on forever. As we have seen, it is a 'cut-short' time, with set limits by the providence of God. And so he says again, for the second of three times, 'I am coming soon' (and so we now know who it was who spoke in verse 7) and promises rewards to those who conquer through the work of patient endurance. This promise to come is not just a statement about his future actions in the economy of history, however, but a declaration of his nature. Revelation presents a vision not only of Jesus doing what God does but of Jesus being included in God's very identity. As such, in this closing address to his people, Jesus gathers together all of the various divine titles found on God's own lips in the opening and closing sections of the book and assigns them to himself (see Bauckham 1993, 25–26; 54–58). He is the 'coming one' (1.8). He is the 'Alpha and the Omega' (1.8; 21.6), the 'first and the last' (1.17), and the 'beginning and the end' (21.6). The church can be assured of his promise and their reward since

Christ, the faithful witness, is himself the beginning and end of history. The one through whom creation and its history came to be is the one in whom these things will be brought to their consummation.

Another ethical appeal comes in the form of a combined benediction and warning, which draws upon the imagery of what has come before. The blessing is for those who 'wash their robes,' to whom is promised entrance to the city through the gates (the ones bearing the names of the tribes of Israel; 22.12) and access to the tree of life (22.2). White robes, we recall, are promised to those who conquer through their witness (3.5) but are nevertheless a gift to the saints, not something earned (6.11). The washing of the robes is in the blood of the Lamb, as the saints share in his sufferings through their faithful witness (7.14).

With this benediction and promise comes a warning: not all will enter the city. Those who practice sorcery, fornication, murder, and idolatry will be excluded. The language here echoes that in 21.27 and closely follows the sevenfold vice list of 21.8. As with that list, what unites these categories is their distortion and denial of good things, whether it is human relations, human life, or the worship of God. Again, these are all summed up as 'falsehood,' which is not something that has an identity of its own but is the corruption of the truth (see the discussion of 'all liars' in 21.8). There is no place in the city of God for such corruption. Another item is added to the list here: the 'dogs.' This is a broad-spectrum insult in the Scriptures, developing through metaphor the ritual impurity of dogs, which eat unclean things (including their own vomit, 2 Pet 2.22, citing Prov 26.11). Like pigs, dogs represented the antithesis of holy things (Mt 7.6). In one famous instance the word was used as a slur against the Gentiles, those who were not God's children (Mt 15.26–27; Mk 7.27–28), though this is instantly challenged in that narrative, reminding us that judgements about what is pure and impure belong to God (Act 10.15, 28). This did not stop Paul from deploying it as an epithet for his opponents, however, as those who worked evil and corrupted the gospel (Phil 3.2). It is fitting, then, that dogs are excluded from the city, for nothing unclean can enter in.

Jesus identifies himself and confirms this testimony, which is for the churches, as his own, adding to the earlier confirmations spoken by the angel (22.6) and by John (22.8). After all, Jesus himself is 'the faithful witness' (1.5), and it is only because of his testimony that the testimonies of angels and prophets have any authority. Moreover, the testimony recorded in this book is not only a revelation from him but his own self-revelation. Jesus himself is the divine apocalypse.

Here he names himself as the 'root and descendent of David.' The epithet 'root of David' was discussed in 5.5 and is an allusion to the messianic hope of Isaiah 11, a title for the one who brings in the peaceable kingdom described there (as we saw earlier, there are also echoes of Jer 23.5; 33.15; and Zech 3.8; 6.12). That he is also the 'descendent' of David is not merely a matter of human genealogy but also invokes God's promise of an everlasting kingdom from David's line (2 Sam 7.12–16). Jesus can be both root and descendent since he is divine and human, descended from David (and so qualified to rule) while also being the one through whom David, and all humankind, came to be. Christ also names himself as the 'bright morning star,' another messianic title that alludes to the prophecy of Balaam (Num 24.15–19) and is found throughout the writings of the second-temple period. Jesus mentioned Balaam in relation to false teaching and idolatrous worship in his message to Pergamum (2.14), but here he evokes his prophecy with its proper referent and names himself as the 'morning star' rising from Jacob to rule.

There is time for a final liturgical element, and here it is not hard to imagine a first-century reader of the book inviting their hearers to join in something like a call-and-response. To the coming one, the Spirit and the bride join together in saying 'come!' The bride, the people of God, do not utter this cry alone but join with the voice of the Holy Spirit as they cry out for the coming of Christ. All who hear the words of this book are invited to join them in this response, and Christ in turn says 'come' to all who are thirsty. The invitation remains open, during this 'in-between time,' to hear the testimony of this book and respond. To join the throng of those who bear witness to the Lamb will mean separation from Babylon and a life lived in the 'in-between time' awaking another city and another citizenship. It will mean enduring opposition from the beasts of land and sea, systemic evils that have corrupted the governance and worship of this world, the true power behind which is that of the dragon, the great deceiver. It may even mean imprisonment or death. But Revelation has revealed that those who bear such faithful witness are the true conquerors, and they are promised the water of life as a gift, joining the saints in the New Jerusalem whose gates remain ever open.

Once again, however, this glorious invitation is paired with a warning. Those who add to the words of this testimony will receive the plagues found here. And those who take words away will have their share in the tree and the city removed. Once again we must read this as a prophetic, not predictive, word. Christ does not here predict the loss of salvation but makes a prophetic pronouncement to underscore the sanctity of his own testimony, which Revelation records: a divine word that must not be altered by human words. Since this revelation, this apocalypse, is both of Christ and from him (see the discussion of 1.1), and since it has been confirmed as trustworthy and true by witnesses angelic, human, and divine, any addition or subtraction will be a corruption.

And so at last we come to Jesus's final words, the third promise of his near-arrival confirmed now with emphasis: 'surely (*nai*, lit. 'yes') I am coming soon' (cf. 22.7, 12). God's 'No' to corruption and falsehood, and to the devil, the personification of that non-being, is not the final word spoken in this book, but the divine 'Yes.' It is this 'Yes' that confirms the promise of Jesus's soon coming, and indeed 'in him every one of God's promises is a "Yes"' (2 Cor 1.20). The church, and indeed all of creation, can say nothing else in response to this divine 'Yes' and to Christ's thrice-repeated promise except to utter the cry, 'Amen. Come, Lord Jesus!' And for his part, John of Patmos can add nothing to this 'Yes' except to sign off his letter to the churches (and to the Church) with a benediction invoking the grace of the Lord Jesus with all the saints, in their ongoing witness to his lordship, finally joining them with his own 'Amen.' In the end, that is what there will be, echoing into all eternity: God's 'Yes' and his people's 'Amen.'

Works Cited

Agamben, Giorgio. 2005. *The Time That Remains: A Commentary on the Letter to the Romans*. Stanford: Stanford University Press.

Allen, Garrick. 2017. *The Book of Revelation and Early Jewish Textual Culture (SNTSMS 168)*. Cambridge: Cambridge University Press.

Augustine of Hippo, *On Christian Teaching*.

———, *The City of God*.

———, *Enchiridion*.

Aune, David. 2017. *Revelation (Word Biblical Commentary)*. 2 volumes. Grand Rapids: Zondervan Academic.

Barr, David L. 1986. 'The Apocalypse of John as Oral Enactment.' *Interpretation* 40/3: 243–56.

———. 1998. *Tales of the End: A Narrative Commentary on the Book of Revelation*. Salem: Polebridge.

Barth, Karl. 2004. *Church Dogmatics*. 4 volumes. Translated by G. W. Bromiley and T. F. Torrance. London: T&T Clark.

Barton, John. 2001. *Joel and Obadiah: A Commentary*. Old Testament Library. Louisville: Westminster John Knox.

Bauckham, Richard. 1993. *The Theology of the Book of Revelation*. Cambridge: Cambridge University Press.

———. 1998. *Climax of Prophecy: Studies on the Book of Revelation*. London: Bloomsbury.

Beale, Gregory K. 1999. *The Book of Revelation*. New International Greek Testament Commentary. Grand Rapids: Eerdmans.

Best, Garrett. 2021. '*Imitatio Ezechielis*: The Irregular Grammar of Revelation Reconsidered.' PhD dissertation, Asbury Theological Seminary.

Block, Daniel. July 1988. 'Text and Emotion: A Study in the 'Corruptions' in Ezekiel's Inaugural Vision (Ezekiel 1:4–28).' *CBQ* 50/3: 418–42.

Blount, Brian K. 2013. *Revelation: A Commentary*. New Testament Library. Louisville: Westminster John Knox Press.

Caird, George B. 1984. *The Revelation of Saint John the Divine*. Black's New Testament Commentaries. London: A & C Black.

Charlesworth, J. H. 1986. 'The Jewish Roots of Christology: The Discovery of the Hypostatic Voice.' *Scottish Journal of Theology* 39: 19–41.

———, editor. 1983. *The Old Testament Pseudepigrapha, Volume One: Apocalyptic Literature and Testaments*. Peabody: Hendrickson.

Collins, John J. 1979. 'Towards the Morphology of a Genre.' *Semeia* 14: 1–20.

Crossley, James G. 2003. '*Halakah* and Mark 7.4: ". . . and beds".' *JSNT* 25/4: 433–447.

Fletcher, Michelle. 2017. *Reading Revelation as Pastiche: Imitating the Past*. London: Bloomsbury.

Fowler, Alastair. 1982. *Kinds of Literature: An Introduction to the Theory of Genres and Modes*. Cambridge: Harvard University Press.

Friesen, Steven J. 2001. *Imperial Cults and the Apocalypse of John: Reading Revelation in the Ruins* Oxford: Oxford University Press.

Gaventa, Beverly Roberts. 2007. *Our Mother Saint Paul*. Louisville: Westminster John Knox.

Goldingay, John. 2017. *Daniel*. Word Biblical Commentary. Grand Rapids: Zondervan Academic.

Gorman, Michael J. 2011. *Reading Revelation Responsibly: Uncivil Worship and Witness: Following the Lamb into the New Creation*. Eugene: Wipf and Stock.

Gundry, Robert H. 1987. 'The New Jerusalem: People as Place, Not Place for People.' *NovT* 29/3: 254–264.

Hemer, Colin J. 1986. *The Letters to the Seven Churches of Asia in Their Local Setting*. London: A&C Black.

Himmelfarb, Martha. 1993. *Ascent to Heaven in Jewish and Christian Apocalypses*. Oxford: Oxford University Press.

Käsemann, Ernst. 1969. *New Testament Questions of Today*. London: SCM.

Koester, Craig R. 2003. 'The Message to Laodicea and the Problem of Its Local Context.' *NTS* 49: 407–424.

———. 2014. *Revelation: A New Translation with Introduction and Commentary*. New Haven: Yale University Press.

Kovacs, Judith, and Christopher Rowland. 2008. *Revelation: The Apocalypse of Jesus Christ*. Oxford: Blackwell.

Kraybill, J. Nelson. 2010. *Apocalypse and Allegiance: Worship, Politics, and Devotion in the Book of Revelation*. Grand Rapids: Brazos.

Longenecker, Richard. 1999. *Biblical Exegesis in the Apostolic Period*. 2nd edition. Grand Rapids: Eerdmans.

Mangina, Joseph L. 2010. *Revelation*. Brazos Theological Commentary on the Bible. Grand Rapids: Baker.

Mathewson, David L. 2020. *A Companion to the Book of Revelation*. Eugene: Cascade.

Mounce, Robert H. 1998. *The Book of Revelation*. New International Commentary on the New Testament. Grand Rapids: Eerdmans.

Moyise, Steve. 1995. *The Old Testament in the Book of Revelation*. London: T & T Clark.

———. 2004. 'Singing the Song of Moses and the Lamb: John's Dialogical Use of Scripture.' *Andrews University Seminary Studies* 42/2: 347–360.

Osborne, Grant R. 2002. *Revelation*. Baker Exegetical Commentary on the New Testament. Grand Rapids: Baker Academic.

Paul, Ian. 2018. *Revelation: An Introduction and Commentary*. Grand Rapids: InterVarsity Press.

Portier-Young, A. 2011. *Apocalypse Against Empire: Theologies of Resistance in Early Judaism*. Grand Rapids: Eerdmans.

Price, S. R. F. 1984. *Rituals and Power: The Roman Imperial Cult in Asia Minor*. Cambridge: Cambridge University Press.

Resseguie, James L. 2009. *The Revelation of John: A Narrative Commentary*. Grand Rapids: Baker Academic.

Reynolds, Benjamin. 2020. 'Son of Man.' In D. Gurtner and L. Stuckenbruck, editors, *T & T Clark Encyclopedia of Second Temple Judaism*. London: T & T Clark. 749–751.

Schreiber, Stefan. 2020. 'Satan and Related Figures.' In Gurtner and Stuckenbruck, eds., *T & T Clark Encyclopedia of Second Temple Judaism*. London: T & T Clark. 710-11.

Seitz, Christopher R. 2016. *Joel*. International Theological Commentary. London: T & T Clark.

Smalley, Stephen S. 2015. *The Revelation to John: A Commentary on the Greek Text of the Apocalypse*. Grand Rapids: InterVarsity.

Sonderegger, Katherine. 2020. *The Doctrine of the Holy Trinity: Processions and Persons*. Volume 2 of Systematic Theology. Minneapolis: Fortress.

Sweet, J. P. M. 1979. *Revelation*. New Testament Commentaries. Philadelphia: Westminster.

Thomas, John Christopher, and Frank D. Macchia. 2016. *Revelation. The Two Horizons New Testament Commentary*. Grand Rapids: Eerdmans.

Victorinus of Petovium. 2011. 'Commentary on the Apocalypse.' In William C. Weinrich, editor, *Ancient Christian Texts: Latin Commentaries on Revelation*. Grand Rapids: InterVarsity Press.

Warren, Meredith. 2017. 'Tasting the Little Scroll: A Sensory Analysis of Divine Interaction in Revelation 10.8-101.' *JSNT* 40/1: 101–119.

Webster, John. 2012. *The Domain of the Word: Scripture and Theological Reason*. London: T & T Clark.

Weima, Jeffrey. 2021. *The Sermons to the Seven Churches of Revelation: A Commentary and Guide*. Grand Rapids: Baker Academic.

Wink, Walter. 1993. *Unmasking the Powers: The Invisible Forces that Determine Human Existence*. Minneapolis: Fortress.

Woodman, Simon. 2013. *SCM Core Text: The Book of Revelation*. London: SCM.

Wright, N. T. 1992. *The New Testament and The People of God*. London: SPCK.

Yong, Amos. 2021. *Revelation: Belief: A Theological Commentary on the Bible*. Louisville: Westminster John Knox.

Ziegler, Philip G. 2022. 'The First and Final "No"—The Finality of the Gospel and the Old Enemy.' In K. Dugan and P. G. Ziegler, editors, *The Finality of the Gospel: Karl Barth and the Tasks of Eschatology*. Leiden: Brill. 193–213.

www.ingramcontent.com/pod-product-compliance
Lightning Source LLC
Chambersburg PA
CBHW051113230426
43667CB00014B/2555